ROUTLEDGE ENGLISH TEXTS
GENERAL EDITOR JOHN DRAKAKIS

JOHN MILTON

Selected Longer Poems and Prose

ROUTLEDGE · ENGLISH · TEXTS

GENERAL EDITOR · JOHN DRAKAKIS

WILLIAM BLAKE: *Selected Poetry and Prose* ed. David Punter
EMILY BRONTË: *Wuthering Heights* ed. Heather Glen
ROBERT BROWNING: *Selected Poetry* ed. Aidan Day
JOHN CLARE: *Selected Poetry and Prose* ed. Merryn and Raymond Williams
JOSEPH CONRAD: *Selected Literary Criticism and The Shadow-Line* ed. Allan Ingram
CHARLES DICKENS: *Hard Times* ed. Terry Eagleton
JOHN DONNE: *Selected Poetry and Prose* ed. T. W. and R. J. Craik
GEORGE ELIOT: *The Mill on The Floss* ed. Sally Shuttleworth
HENRY FIELDING: *Joseph Andrews* ed. Stephen Copley
BEN JONSON: *The Alchemist* ed. Peter Bement
D. H. LAWRENCE: *Selected Poetry and Non-fictional Prose* ed. John Lucas
ANDREW MARVELL: *Selected Poetry and Prose* ed. Robert Wilcher
JOHN MILTON: *Selected Shorter Poems and Prose* ed. Tony Davies
WILFRED OWEN: *Selected Poetry and Prose* ed. Jennifer Breen
ALEXANDER POPE: *Selected Poetry and Prose* ed. Robin Sowerby
PERCY BYSSHE SHELLEY: *Selected Poetry and Prose* ed. Alasdair Macrae
WILLIAM WORDSWORTH: *Selected Poetry* ed. Philip Hobsbaum

JOHN MILTON

Selected Longer Poems and Prose

Edited by Tony Davies

ROUTLEDGE

LONDON AND NEW YORK

First published 1992
by Routledge
11 New Fetter Lane,
London EC4P 4EE

Simultaneously published in the
USA and Canada
by Routledge
a division of Routledge,
Chapman and Hall, Inc.
29 West 35th Street,
New York, NY 10001

Phototypeset by Intype, London
Printed in Great Britain by Clays Ltd,
St Ives plc

British Library Cataloguing in Publication Data
Milton, John 1608–1674
Selected longer poems and prose. – (Routledge English texts)
1. English poetry
I. Title II. Davies, Tony
821.4

Library of Congress Cataloging in Publication Data
Milton, John, 1608–1674.
[Selections. 1992]
Selected longer poems and prose/John Milton: edited by Tony Davies.
p. cm. — (Routledge English texts)
Includes bibliographical references and index.
I. Davies, Tony. II. Title.
III. Series.
PR3553.D38 1992
821'.4—dc20 91–10675

ISBN 0–415–04946–6

Contents

Acknowledgements

Among the many colleagues, students and friends who have helped me to understand Milton a little better, I owe a special gratitude to Robert Wilcher, Richard David and, for his advice and encouragement with this edition and its predecessor, John Drakakis. My greatest debt, in this and everything, is to Teresa Davies: partner, lover, friend.

Introduction

On Tuesday 29 May 1660, his thirtieth birthday, in the company of his brothers James and Henry, with six hundred gentlemen in doublets of velvet and cloth of silver, the aldermen and members of the City companies in scarlet and gold, a troop of lackeys in purple velvet and a guard of twenty thousand soldiers in uniforms trimmed with silver lace, to the continuous firing of guns and ringing of church bells, Charles Stuart rode across London Bridge and through the city to the Palace of Whitehall and, on the spot where, just over eleven years before and after seven years of bitter and bloody civil war, his father had been executed as a traitor and murderer, listened politely as the Speakers of both Houses of Parliament welcomed him home with effusive protestations of imperishable loyalty and gratitude. The crowds cheered; the streets were strewn with herbs and flowers; wine flowed from the public taps and conduits; and the writer John Evelyn, who in 1649 had refused to attend the execution of Charles I and who had ever since observed the anniversary of that 'execrable wickedness' as a fast, 'stood in the Strand and beheld it, and blessed God. And all this was done without one drop of blood shed, and by that very army which rebelled against him; but it was the Lord's doing, for such a restoration was never mentioned in any history ancient or modern, since the return of the Jews from the Babylonish captivity; nor so joyful a day and so bright ever seen in this nation, this happening when to expect or effect it was past all human policy' (Evelyn 1890: 265). So ended the 'great rebellion', the revolutionary constitutional experiment of government without a monarch: ended, it must have seemed, to those who had supported it as well as to those, like Evelyn, who abominated it, in humiliating failure and defeat.

There was an element of stage management, to be sure; public demonstrations of joy are rarely as spontaneous as they seem to the casual or partisan spectator. Twenty thousand soldiers make a good show, but they also serve as a reminder of the realities of power behind the ritual and display of a royal occasion; and the militias that lined the route from Dover to Whitehall no doubt helped ensure that the enthusiasm of the crowds had a respectably royalist character. Charles himself asked with ironic mock-naivety where all his father's enemies had gone, since he had met no-one all day 'who does not protest that he had ever wished for my return'. But the celebrations that lasted for the rest of the week did undoubtedly express a genuine pleasure and relief, however temporary. For the revolution of 1649–60 had never managed to strike roots in popular sentiment, never made the vital transition from seizure of power to secure government, and so never escaped the grim logic of Marvell's warning to the triumphant Cromwell, returning from the conquest of Ireland in 1650: 'The same arts that did gain/A power must it maintain'.[1] As Evelyn observed, the New Model Army that defeated the first Charles Stuart restored the second one; and if the absolutist ambitions of Charles I represented one sort of tyranny, the desperate constitutional improvisations of an increasingly authoritarian Protector and the factional squabbles of a junta of army officers represented another, no less dependent in the last resort on the naked weapon of military force. For a few months, at least, the sense that a world which had been turned upside down was on its feet again, that the embittered, saturnine and sardonic king was a 'merry monarch', that the reappearance of bishops and maypoles really did mean the restoration of traditional Englishry, found expression in a holiday mood of festive ebullience.

Festive, but also vengeful. To Charles's question about his father's enemies, they might have replied: in hiding or on the run. And with good reason. Less than five months after his entry into London, the crowds were out in Whitehall again, and once more Evelyn was there: 'Scot, Scroope, Cook and Jones suffered for reward of their iniquities at Charing Cross, in sight of the place where they put to death their natural Prince, and in the presence of the King his son, whom they also sought to kill. I saw not their execution, but met their quarters mangled and cut and reeking as they were brought from the gallows in baskets on the hurdle. Oh the miraculous providence of God!' (Evelyn 1890: 268). The four regicides so savagely and humiliatingly punished (their bodies, first hanged and the entrails drawn, then decapitated, quartered, and boiled to prevent putrefaction, were finally nailed to the city gates, with the severed heads impaled alongside on poles) had been members of the tribunal that had tried and sentenced Charles I. Six of their colleagues had been butchered in the same way a few days earlier. All had been specifically excluded from the Act of Oblivion that Charles II had offered as a condition of his restoration. Others, escaping overseas, were sentenced to death in their absence. And even those forever beyond the reach of judge and hangman did not escape the humiliation of a ritual revenge. On the morning of 30 January 1661, the twelfth anniversary of the death of the king, the remains of Cromwell and two of his closest associates were dug up from their graves in Westminster Abbey, displayed all day on the public gallows at Tyburn, then buried in a pit beneath the gibbet. 'Oh the stupendous and inscrutable judgments of God!', exclaimed the pious Evelyn, and drew the proper moral: 'Fear God and honour the King; but meddle not with them who are given to change!' (Evelyn 1890: 271)

Prominent among those 'given to change', someone whom many would have been happy to see alongside the regicides at Charing Cross and whose name was canvassed by the parliamentary committee compiling a list of people too active in promoting or supporting the revolution to enjoy immunity under the Act of Oblivion, was John Milton. Better known in 1660 as a pamphleteer than as a poet, Milton had consistently given public support to the radical cause and its adherents in Church, Parliament and army. In the early forties he had written passionately against ecclesiastical and, by implication, royal prerogative. By the end of the decade, with Charles on trial, he was openly defending the people's right to execute a tyrannical monarch as 'the highest top of their civil glory and emulation'. In the fifties, as an employee of the revolutionary Council of State, he championed its actions in a fierce attack on the cult of the 'royal martyr' and in two massive *Defences of the English People* (written in Latin for European circulation). As late as April 1660, with Charles II making preparations for his return, he was still pleading with his compatriots not 'to put our necks again under kingship' (*SSPP* 146). And if anybody had bothered to glance again at the little book of poems he had brought out in 1645, they would have noticed the proud claim that one of them, first published in 1638, 'by occasion foretells the ruin of our corrupted clergy, then in their height' – the same high-Anglican and royalist clergy, many of them, who were at that very moment easing themselves back into the beneficed livings, Oxford fellowships and remunerative sinecures from which they had been ejected in the 1640s (*SSPP* 200). Long after the appearance of *Paradise Lost* and the other late poems had established his reputation as a major poet, Evelyn remembered him only as 'that Milton who wrote for the regicides'; and a century later, with rebellion once again stirring at home and abroad, the tory Samuel Johnson reminded readers of his *Life of Milton* that the author of *Paradise Lost* had also been 'an acrimonious and surly republican' (Johnson 1906: I, 112).

In the end Milton escaped serious punishment, though after some months lying low with friends the blind fifty-one-year-old poet was arrested, spent some time in gaol and had to pay the expenses of the sergeant-at-arms who arrested him. Influential friends, including the poet Marvell, now an MP, spoke up for him, and his name never appeared on the committee's list. But punishment he endured nonetheless; not so much the loss of his savings, put by for his three daughters and his own old age, which disappeared when the bank crashed at the restoration; not even his blindness, total for getting on for ten years now, though his enemies liked to vaunt it as evidence of divine displeasure; but the defeat of what he and other radicals called the 'Good Old Cause': the cause of republican government, of uncensored freedom of opinion and expression and of unconstrained liberty of conscience and practice, in religion and in secular life alike. And behind that defeat, which after all could always be explained away as the fruit of human weakness, cowardice or stupidity, loomed a harder question still: if the Good Old Cause was also, as Milton had always believed, God's cause, then how was it possible for it to fail? 'God is decreeing', he had written in 1644, 'to begin some new and great period in his Church, even to the reforming of reformation itself. What does he then but reveal himself to his servants, and as his manner is, first to his Englishmen?' (*SSPP* 100). But what of God's Englishmen now, fawning on the tyrant's son; within sight of the Canaan of liberty, and enthusiastically 'choosing them a captain back for Egypt' (*SSPP* 147)? And what of the God who had turned to them in the 1640s, only to avert his face now when his help was needed most?

These are the questions that animate all Milton's writings from the restoration of Charles II until his own death fourteen years later. Of course they are not new. Milton is hardly the first writer to record the painful experience of disillusion with a world 'to good malignant, to bad men benign' (*PL* XII, 538), and the search for rationality and moral consistency in a universe that seems both capricious and unjust is the deep theme of *Lycidas* in 1638 as it is of *Paradise Lost* and *Samson Agonistes* thirty years later. But 1660 gave them a special urgency and focus precisely because for a few years in between it really had seemed that English history was being guided by a more than human hand towards some great providential denouement, perhaps even (and this was widely believed) towards that ultimate apocalyptic confrontation of light and darkness that Milton himself had looked forward to in 1641 'when thou, the eternal and shortly-expected King, shalt open the clouds to judge the several kingdoms of the world, and distributing national honours and rewards to religious and just commonwealths, shalt put an end to all earthly tyrannies, proclaiming thy universal and mild monarchy through Heaven and Earth' (*SSPP* 84). They are questions about psychology, about people's fear of freedom, their resistance to change, their deep hunger for the familiar. They are certainly questions about politics, about the exercise of power, the collective organisation of human means and energies, the possibility of a just and rational society. Above all they are questions about history, about its hidden logic and structure, its meaning for present and future.

Of course they are also, as so many of Milton's later critics have insisted, questions about theology; or, as I'd rather put it, theology is the mother-discourse from which in the seventeenth century psychological, political and historical questions still draw most of their key terms and central references. 'Religious and theological debate', remarks Fredric Jameson, paraphrasing Marx, 'is the form, in pre-capitalist societies, in which groups become aware of their political differences and fight them out' (Barker 1986: 38–9). Late-renaissance England is moving rapidly towards a more sceptical and secularised – a more 'modern' – culture, one in which the ideological authority of the Church will be greatly weakened, in which the prestige of experimental science, and perhaps a certain weariness with the embattled doctrinal confrontations of the mid-century, will accommodate the uncompromising pronouncements of a bloodthirsty near-eastern deity and the irresistible urgings of sovereign conscience to the pragmatic priorities of lawyers, businessmen and civil servants. Religious belief, suggested the philosopher Thomas Hobbes, is nothing but 'fear of power invisible, feigned by the mind, or imagined from tales publicly allowed' (*Leviathan*, ch.6); but although he was denounced by some as an atheist and shared with Milton the distinction of having his books burned by the hangman, he was otherwise unmolested. Milton too is a modern, sympathetic to the enquiring and sceptical temper of the period; but he remained to the end a theist and a Christian, of his own singular kind. Radical in so many respects, he continued to the end to probe 'the unsearchable dispose/Of highest wisdom' (*SA* 1746–7), to insist that poetry was the divinely-inspired sister and mouthpiece of that wisdom and that the poet's ultimate task was to 'justify the ways of God to men' (*PL* I, 26).

But Milton's theology is no mere conventional pietism. On the contrary, it is as argumentative and anti-traditional as the politics from which it is inextricable. To 'justify the ways of

God to men' is to assume not only that the ways of God to men can be justified but that they need to be justified – that is, that their apparently gross injustice and incoherence can be shown to be rationally and morally tolerable. Some traditions of salvationist Christianity, foregrounding the loving or suffering Jesus at the expense of the fulminating Jehovah, emphasise the individual experience of guilt and reconciliation (the quietist Anglicanism of George Herbert would be an example). Others (Fifth Monarchists and similar millenarian sects, for instance) cancel the injustice and brutality of experience at a stroke by appealing to the expectation, vengeful or triumphant, of judgement and ultimate victory. For others, the ways of God will always be mysterious, a matter of faith rather than understanding; for some, indeed, the mystery may be the reason for belief: Sir Thomas Browne quotes approvingly Tertullian's 'certum quia impossibile' – I believe *because* it is impossible.[2] Milton belongs with none of these. Largely bypassing the traditional icons of Christian piety, the infant Jesus and the crucified Christ (the poem on the Nativity completely ignores the domestic and sentimental associations of the scene, and for a Christian poet he is curiously uninterested in the crucifixion), his writings are drawn compulsively to the bitter heart of the dilemma, searching out those narratives and figures (the Fall, Samson) in which the contradictions are most starkly and unmitigatedly represented, those parts of scripture (the brutal folktales of *Genesis*, the sanguinary tribal warfare of *Judges*) most troubling to the decent liberal Christian conscience. In the rich tissue of scriptural allusion that runs through his later writings, the part of the Bible that features least is the gospels; and when he does at last deal directly, in *Paradise Regained*, with the founder of Christianity, his Jesus is neither charismatic miracle-worker nor afflicted saviour but a severe, ascetic, argumentative young man, his mind since childhood 'set/Serious to learn and know' (*PR* I, 202–3), struggling in solitude to understand his own terrible sense of responsibility for the world around him. For Milton the way to regeneration lies pre-eminently neither through faith nor works (the orthodox dyad), but through knowledge; and knowledge, like virtue, comes 'by what is contrary' (*SSPP* 88): by debate, argument and incessant questioning in the hard school of experience and failure.

The nature of Milton's theology has itself been the subject of much debate and argument. Blake's devil claimed him for 'the Devil's party without knowing it', suggesting a turbulently dissident imagination only partially restrained by theocratic orthodoxy (Blake 1959: 44). For C.S. Lewis or Douglas Bush the orthodoxy is the key, and A.N. Wilson will even have him a pious Anglican, despite his hatred for the established Church and the striking fact that though he married three times and fathered six children there is no evidence that he ever entered a church or observed any recognised form of worship after leaving university. For Denis Saurat he is deep in the mysteries of the Cabbala, his Christianity richly coloured by rabbinical and esoteric wisdom; while for Christopher Hill he is a radical heretic, mortalist and antinomian like the Ranters, Quakers and his communist contemporary Gerard Winstanley. None of this would have much bothered his seventeenth-century readers (worries about his anti-trinitarianism date from the doctrinally jittery eighteenth century). When the ecclesiastical censor Thomas Tomkins combed *Paradise Lost* for anything that would give him an excuse to ban it, it was the politics of the text he was interested in, not its theology, as we can see from what he found (see I, 597n); and when the same dutiful functionary insisted on the removal of some passages of the *History of Britain* that he found 'too sharp against the clergy', it was not the spiritual authority of his Saxon predecessors that he was defending but his own right to meddle in politics and to dictate the secular opinions of his parishioners. Fredric Jameson asks why after April 1660 Milton never again mentions the Good Old Cause, and finds the answer in the 'political unconscious' of the poem and its author, in a deep refusal of the possibility of collective struggle for change (Barker 1986: 54); but it is possible, without denying the validity of this reading, to point to another explanation, at once simpler and more material: that after 1660 Milton and every other writer had to learn to work under a system of state censorship as pervasive and narrow-minded as anything since the abolition of the Star Chamber in the early forties, and a great deal more thorough and politically vindictive than that infamous institution had ever been. It is one of the ironies of the period that Milton, who wrote powerfully against censorship in *Areopagitica* (1644), had himself been a licenser of books in the fifties – a remarkably easy-going one, it must be said: there is no evidence that he ever banned or interfered with anything, and he was reported to have justified one particularly controversial decision on the grounds that 'men should refrain from forbidding books, and in approving of that book he had done no more than follow his conviction' (Parker 1968: II, 994). We can be sure that neither Tomkins nor his colleague, the furiously royalist civil licenser Roger L'Estrange, would have endorsed those libertarian principles; and it is likely that they took special pains to sniff out any hint of sedition in Milton's writings.

If they did, they must have been disappointed. The open appeal to republican ideals, the rallying activism of the *Ready and Easy Way* are not heard again in his work after the spring of 1660. But the 'fit audience . . . though few' that he seeks for *Paradise Lost* (VII, 31) need not be thought to be different from those 'men who set their minds on main matters' to whom he had addressed that earlier pamphlet, and of whom he had glumly said that 'in these most difficult times I find not many' (*SSPP* 147). The 'higher argument' of *Paradise Lost*, the 'better fortitude/Of patience and heroic martyrdom/ Unsung' that the poem offers in place of the 'Wars, hitherto the only argument/Heroic deem'd' of renaissance epic (IX, 28–33) represents not an escapist withdrawal from action into defeated passivity but a renewal of resistance in circumstances in which success can no longer be taken for granted and the way ahead, once so clear, can no longer be made out, 'In darkness and with dangers compass'd round' (*PL VII*, 27): an 'optimism of the will', to quote another revolutionary all too familiar with the experience of defeat, no less affirmative for being grounded in 'pessimism of the intelligence'.[3] The politics of *Paradise Lost* will be found not so much in direct references to rebellion or regicide, of the kind Tomkins was looking for. Rather, it is secreted in the poem's metaphors, its syntactical ambiguities, its puns, its entirely modern way – not found in any earlier epic – of commenting on its own structure and method, above all in the particular type and experience of reading that it incites, a reading watchful, self-conscious, increasingly alert as the text unfolds to the doubleness of language, the seductive treacheries of rhetoric, the deep perplexities of meaning. Such a reading might be called 'allegorical', if allegory had not acquired the diminished connotations of a simple cryptogram or *roman-à-clef.* Miltonic allegory (and I'm not thinking so much here of readings of the kind suggested, very interestingly, by Christopher Hill, who takes parts of the poem as a fairly close point-by-point allegory of the civil wars) is more like a continuous process of interpretation and reinterpretation, of comparison and revision, in which the boundaries between statement and metaphor, truth and fable, even the syntactical articulations of meaning itself are never fixed.

These features of the text can certainly be related to the conditions of censorship and political repression in which it was produced. Writers unable to express their convictions directly must either fall silent or find ways to express them indirectly. Ideas driven out of the public arena of the text may resurface strangely in its images, its syntax, its formal processes and marginal notations. Take the prefatory note on 'the Verse', added to later printings of the 1667 edition of *Paradise Lost.* Not even the most reactionary of Restoration hanging judges, I imagine, would have sent a poet to the gallows for preferring blank verse to rhyme; but who can doubt that just such an innocuously 'literary' issue carries for Milton a burden of political and moral conviction no less than, and no different from, that for which some of his contemporaries died at Tyburn and Charing Cross: 'this neglect then of rhyme so little is to be taken for a defect, though it may seem so perhaps to vulgar readers, that it rather is to be esteemed an example set, the first in English, of ancient liberty recovered to heroic poem from the troublesome and modern bondage of rhyming' (see p. 33). There is nothing fanciful about the language of this: it means exactly what it doesn't quite say. Rhyme, like monarchy, is unnecessary, artificial, *wasteful.* Blank verse restores the measured freedom enjoyed by the ancients, Greek and

Roman. And if that innovative and exemplary recovery, 'the first in English', of ancient liberty which Milton claims for his poem departs from the practice of renaissance epic (Spenser and the Italians wrote in rhyme), the poet might invoke the terms in which he had praised Charles Stuart's judges almost twenty years before: 'if the Parliament and military Council do what they do without precedent . . . it argues the more wisdom, virtue and magnanimity that they know themselves able to be a precedent to others' (*SSPP* 132). For a writer in a time of repression, questions of language, form and genre become crucial, carrying a significance that goes well beyond the narrowly linguistic, formal or generic. The politics of language assume paramount importance precisely at those times when the language of politics is no longer available.

Paradise Lost was first conceived, it seems, as a play. A manuscript notebook in the library of Trinity College, Cambridge contains sketches, probably dating from soon after Milton's return from Italy in 1639, for a sort of oratorio-cum-classical-tragedy called variously 'Adam in Banishment', 'Adam Unparadiz'd' and 'Paradise Lost' (*CPW* VIII, 554–85). His nephew Edward Phillips remembered being shown part of Satan's soliloquy at the beginning of the fourth book sometime in the early forties, when it was the opening scene of a tragedy (Darbishire 1932: 72-3). There is no reason to suppose that Milton intended the play to be performed on the stage, any more than *Samson Agonistes* later. The public theatres were closed by parliamentary order in 1642, and did not reopen until after the Restoration. In any case, Milton's few references to the contemporary stage do not suggest a very high opinion; and there are other examples in the period of plays written to be read rather than performed, or at most to be declaimed in a sort of concert performance, like the plays of the Roman tragedian Seneca.[4] But the drafts suggest nonetheless that for the young Milton drama, and specifically tragedy, represented (in Aristotle's words) 'the most serious and philosophical kind of poetry'. From the Ludlow *Masque* at the beginning of his career to *Samson* near the end, he chooses dramatic form for some of his most searching explorations of strength and virtue under trial. *Lycidas* is described as a 'monody', itself a dramatic genre. The biblical *Revelation* he compares to 'a high and stately tragedy'. *Paradise Lost* and its sequel *Paradise Regained* revolve, no less than the dramatic works, around confrontations too charged with vivid performative energies to be reduced to the staid 'debates' they are sometimes described as.

There is no way of knowing when the notion of a tragedy on the Fall was abandoned; but by 1658 ('about two years before the King came in', Phillips told the biographer John Aubrey) those earlier ideas and materials were being reworked into a heroic poem. Twenty years before, Milton had toyed with the notion of an epic based on the legendary pseudo-history of Geoffrey of Monmouth, perhaps tracing the descent of the ancient Britons from the Trojan Brutus and culminating in the exploits of Arthur against the Saxons. The project was soon abandoned; but both the choice of subject and Milton's inability to make anything of it say something important about the genre, as it was understood in the period. For if the tragic mode focuses on the struggles of the 'agonist', the embattled and lonely individual caught in a spotlit moment of triumph and disaster, the heroic (Milton prefers the term to 'epic') is historical, national, above all imperial: the explanatory myth of the nation-state on the threshold of a new *imperium*. For all the prestige of Homer, the *Aeneid* of Virgil was the real model here. Itself following close on a period of revolution, open class-conflict and civil war, it sets out to forge a new kind of national unity, at once ancient (Aeneas, like Homer's Odysseus, is a refugee from the destruction of Troy) and apocalyptically new (the poem gives visionary expression to the imperial destiny of Rome under Augustus). Plunging *in medias res*, into the heart of the story, with its great sweeps of retrospect and prospect, origin and destiny, the form has an intimate relationship with ideologies of nationhood; not a narrow, parochial chauvinism, but the broad consensual identification – Gramsci called it 'hegemony'[5] – that binds people, across differences of class and ethnicity, to a shared history and a common purpose.

Strong magic – if it works. Spenser's *Faerie Queene* had tried to do it, reworking Geoffrey's fanciful tales of Arthur and the ancient Britons to forge a sense of national unity around

Elizabeth; but the attempt had palpably failed long before he abandoned the poem half-finished. The social focus – the court and ruling elite of late Tudor England – is too narrow. The stories, organised around the frivolous pretence that the Tudors were descended from Arthur, and deployed with a scholarly antiquarianism that threatens constantly to degenerate into half-timbered tea-shoppe quaintness, simply cannot support the portentous allegorical and ideological load they are asked to carry. And the unity towards which the poem strains, a unity of crown and subjects, ancient and modern, feudal forms and capitalist energies, remains diagrammatic; it simply isn't there, in reality or imagination. Seeking to conjure a people out of the warring fractions of post-feudal England, the poem fails fatally to be popular.

Spenser had aspired, with a conscious sense of mission, to be the English Virgil. Milton, who admired him and shared his missionary ambitions, was never likely to repeat his mistakes, least of all the disastrous blunder of identifying the English people with the person of their monarch. (The supposed popularity of the Tudors and Stuarts was largely the work of professional propagandists, abetted by some later historians. As for our own sycophantic humbug about 'royalty', that is a Victorian invention). For a start, his intellectual formation and interests, expressed not only in his poetry and prose but in his work as 'Secretary for Foreign Tongues' under a Commonwealth notable for its expansionist foreign policy, were too European to waste much time on a narrowly ethnic idea of the 'British' epic. The polyglot poet who admired the Druids because (it was said) they wrote Greek outlined his plans for an Arthurian epic in a Latin poem addressed to an Italian acquaintance (*Mansus*, Carey 1971: 260–7). Second, his readings in early British history quickly persuaded him that the Brutus-to-Arthur story, a historical dead-end anyway after the collapse of the Tudor myth, wouldn't do, for the simple and devastating reason that it obviously wasn't true (see pp. 186–90). Third, the author of *Areopagitica*, increasingly caught up in the onrush of war and revolution, was coming to see the English people as the descendants (by analogy or symbol, at least) not of some shadowy Welsh chieftain but of the ancient civilisations of Greece, Italy and Palestine. Evelyn's comparison of the Restoration to 'the return of the Jews from the Babylonish captivity', like Milton's view of the same event as the people 'choosing them a captain back for Egypt' (*SSPP* 147), illustrates the period's fondness for scriptural parallelism. Often this amounts to little more than idle analogy-mongering or the exchange of biblical insults; but in its strongest form – and Milton certainly falls into this category – it provides the substance of a powerful historical myth. 'God's Englishmen', busy with the pious reforming of reformation at home and the building of a protestant and mercantile empire overseas, stand in direct providential succession both to the Old Testament Israelites and to the imperial Romans, and the poem that will tell their story must seek to unite the two traditions in terms of their living immediacy for the present. *Paradise Lost* does this in a variety of ways. Homer and Ovid jostle constantly in the poem's myriad intertextuality with *Job* and *Revelation*. Syncretic perspectives multiply vertiginously: the Greeks are descended from Noah (I, 508), the Roman Vulcan is the architect of the Satanic Pandemonium, his fall from Heaven described in images from Homer (I, 739-46), and Eve merges with Pandora, Proserpine and a panoply of near-eastern vegetation goddesses (IV, 269-71, IX, 393-6). But it unites them at a more fundamental level still, casting an Old Testament tale into a Virgilian form. Out of an ancient genre and an even older story, something absolutely new is made, a thing 'unattempted yet in prose or rhyme' (I, 16).

But what, in all this, of the supposedly national character of epic? The notion of the English as the new chosen people, successors to the biblical Israelites, provides part of the answer. That it is that gives the prophetic narrative of the twelfth book, ostensibly concerned with the early church, such powerful pertinence to Milton's own time: 'Who against faith and conscience can be heard/Infallible? Yet many will presume,/ Whence heavy persecution shall arise' (XII, 529-31). But the true 'Englishness' of *Paradise Lost* rests in something else, something so obvious that we are likely to overlook it altogether: the fact that it is written in English. The *Defences* of the 1650s, written in Latin, had given Milton a European reputation, and Latin remained, even in the later seventeenth century, the medium for any serious piece of writing that aspired to a more than parochial circulation. The decision to write in the mother-tongue is above all a political decision, an act of solidarity with a particular national culture and history (as it still is today, for a Nigerian or a Welsh or a Quebecois writer). Not a difficult decision to make, perhaps, in 1644, with the image of 'a noble and puissant nation rousing herself like a strong man after sleep' still untarnished by later disillusion and compromise. But by the end of the fifties Milton's hopes of the English people, the 'misguided and abused multitude' even now thronging the roadsides to welcome home the restored tyrant, had been drastically revised, and the prospect of a congenial readership of enlightened European intellectuals might have seemed an attractive alternative to the disappointments nearer home. In these circumstances, the decision to persist with a vernacular epic amounts to an affirmation of confidence, however qualified and deferred, in the regenerative potential of the English people, and in the continuing validity and relevance of the epic mode itself.

Clearly, then, the question of *language* is central, and it is no accident that some of the fiercest controversies about the poem have revolved around its language. Noting the 'persistent mutual interference of what is stated and what is shown, the contradictory entanglements of 'epic' immediacy and hermeneutic discourse, the fixing of significations at one level that produces a sliding of them at another', Terry Eagleton ascribes the 'offensiveness' of *Paradise Lost*, in the eyes of those critics and readers who look to literature for the sensual immediacy of a Keats ode or the conversational transparency and moral assurance of a novel by Jane Austen, to the fact that its wrought and self-conscious idiom is 'a labour that works athwart the "natural" texture of the senses, failing or refusing . . . to repress its own artifice'.[6] Oddly, it is precisely those features of the poem, the obtrusive 'writtenness' of its language, the shifting perspectives and vertiginous uncertainties of meaning induced by its extraordinary syntax and sentence-structure, that most strikingly assure its remarkable modernity, fully justifying T.S. Eliot's comparison with Joyce's *Finnegans Wake*, another linguistic and narrative *tour de force* that sets out to create not so much a story as a comprehensive and self-justifying *world.*[7] Such a claim for the poem's modernity may sound perversely improbable. What, after all, about Milton the great classicist, the scholarly revivalist of ancient forms like elegy, tragedy, epic? What about the notorious latinisms? The archaic convolutions of word-order? The schoolmasterly insistence on the etymological derivation of perfectly ordinary words? How can any of this be called modern? ''tis Latin, 'tis Greek English', enthused his eighteenth-century biographer Jonathan Richardson; 'not only the words, the phraseology, the transpositions, but the ancient idiom is seen in all he writes, so that a learned foreigner will think Milton the easiest to be understood of all the English writers'. The 'learned foreigner' criterion is unlikely to cut much ice nowadays as an argument for Milton's genius, and what Richardson intended as praise has served other critics as proof of a deadening antiquarianism 'such as a college easily supplies' (Johnson); 'a northern dialect', Keats, who had tried to imitate the Miltonic idiom, called it, 'accommodating itself to greek and roman inversions and intonations', and resolved 'to give myself up to other sensations', adding that 'life for him would be death for me' (Wittreich 1970: 561). Milton, declared F.R.Leavis with an air of settling the matter once and for all, 'invented a medium the distinction of which is to have denied itself the life of the living language' (Leavis 1952: 42).

It would be interesting to have Milton's response to the confusions, evasions and coercions lurking behind the deceptive simplicity of this last judgement. Earlier critics who remarked that he had invented a language of his own meant only that he had declined to employ the currently fashionable modes of literary language, such as the 'Horatian' style of conversational couplet-verse elaborated by Waller and Dryden or the flatulent 'heroic' bombast of restoration tragedy. When Richardson asserts that 'Milton's language is English, but 'tis Milton's English', he does not mean to set up some absolute standard of 'English' against which all writers can be judged. But Leavis's 'life of the living language', with its characteristic vagueness and tautology, seeks to impose and (in Leavisian idiom) 'enforce' just such a standard, one all the more insidious for being almost entirely meaningless. Is the 'living language' spoken or written? Does it mean the language of Milton's century or our own? The language of intellectuals, of merchants, of rural labourers? Of the church or the street? Of London or Glasgow, Norwich or Penzance? Of the kitchen, the nursery or the bedroom? The truth, of course, is that except in some uselessly general sense there is no such entity as 'the living language'. Language, any language, is historically, socially, culturally, functionally plural. The fundamental medium and material of identity and difference, inescapably woven into the variety, fluidity and conflict of the social world, language is, to use Voloshinov's word,[8] 'multiaccented', charged with the competing energies of dialogue, argument, struggle; and it is this multiaccentuality, the dimension of historical and social difference suppressed in Leavisian notions of organic unity, that Milton's writings put unavoidably on display. When Satan's arguments to Eve are countered by an admonitory comment, we observe not some deep disjunction between the moralist and the 'true poet' (Blake's view) or a revealing glimpse of authorial insecurity (as Waldock argues) but the collision and reciprocation of two languages, of impassioned persuasion and distanced commentary, the one immediate, the other retrospective, analytic, both functional. When a familiar English word is used in such a way that its etymological (Greek or Latin) sense is activated alongside the contemporary one (see pp.260–1), it is not Milton's pedantry that is summoned into view but the inescapable historicity of language and the provisional status of its meanings. And these features of the poem attest its modernity, indeed its precocious modernism, evoking not only Joyce but Pound and Eliot himself. The endlessly shifting points of view, the sexual panic and fascination with androgyny, the mingling of history and myth, past and present, the polyglot self-consciousness of the language, the search for logic and structure in a chaos of historical fragmentation and disorder: what do these evoke if not the *Cantos* and *The Waste Land* (Eliot's *Lycidas*, a meditation on 'death by water' coming midway between the ironic *Comus* of the *Prufrock* poems and the justification of the ways of

God attempted in the *Four Quartets*). 'Making strange', the formalists' term for the special property of poetic language, is nowhere more appropriate than with this strangest of poems, this odyssey of outer and inner space where nothing is as it seems and we encounter the most familiar words and things as if we were seeing them for the first time.

Paradise Lost was published in 1667. At its first appearance it was in ten books (for the second edition in 1674 Milton divided books seven and ten in two, to give twelve overall, the same number as the *Aeneid*), bare text without any explanatory material. Early readers evidently had some difficulties, because later copies of the first edition have an 'argument' (a summary of the action of the poem) and a note on the verse, which suggests that they found the story hard to follow without a map, and that they expected it to rhyme (blank verse being very unusual outside the theatre). Milton had published nothing for over seven years, and the poem must have looked a very odd fish indeed – a stranded leviathan, perhaps – in a year which also saw Dryden's *Annus Mirabilis*, an enthusiastically royalist poem in rhyming stanzas on the naval wars against the Dutch and the great fire of London, described by the poet as 'the most heroic subject which any poet could desire'. Despite all this, *Paradise Lost* sold rather well, the edition of 1300 copies selling out in less than two years and earning its author, now for the first time in his life in something like poverty, the impressive sum of ten pounds. In 1670 he published the *History of Britain* on which he had been working since the mid-forties, and the following year saw the publication, in a single volume, of the short epic *Paradise Regained* and the neoclassical tragedy *Samson Agonistes*, which may also have been started some time earlier. In 1673 appeared the brief treatise *Of True Religion* and a second edition of his shorter poems, adding the little pamphlet *Of Education* written thirty years earlier; and educational as well as financial considerations perhaps persuaded him to publish two other earlier works, a Latin *Grammar* (1669) and a *Logic* (1672). 1674 saw a collection of Latin letters, together with some writings from his university days, and the second (twelve-book) edition of *Paradise*

Lost, the last of his works to be published in his lifetime. He died in November, a month before his sixty-sixth birthday.

The history of Milton's reputation is unusually complex. Early readers, struggling to reconcile the 'heavenly muse' of the later poetry with the seditious impieties of the regicide pamphlets, betray a painful ambivalence. In most cases, the poetry wins, just (see *SSPP* 14–15); and by the middle of the eighteenth century *Paradise Lost*, at least, is well on the way, with a little discreet 'improvement',[9] to becoming a national monument. But the ambivalence lingers, resurfacing against a background of renewed social disorder and political agitation in Samuel Johnson's *Life* (1779), with its unconcealed hostility towards the 'surly and acrimonious republican' (Johnson had earlier collaborated with William Lauder in a fraudulent attempt to discredit Milton as a plagiarist). Tory disapproval finds its counterpart in a Whig mythology of Milton the incorruptible statesman-poet, with Milton posthumously conscripted as patron of the bourgeois 'glorious revolution' of 1688-9; a tradition, more vigorous overseas than at home, that played some part in formulating the political agenda of the American and French revolutions (Thomas Jefferson's commonplace-books are full of quotations from Milton, and Mirabeau's translation of *Areopagitica* went into four editions between 1788 and 1792), and that received its definitive expression in Macaulay's 1825 *Essay on Milton*. But there were always other Miltons, less assertive but perhaps more significant than the high-cultural consecration of the Christian Virgil or the noble patriot. Christopher Hill argues that Milton was closer to the plebeian radicalism of the Ranters, Muggletonians, Fifth Monarchists and early Quakers than his critics have allowed for (Hill 1977: 93-116); and through the eighteenth century his writings helped, in dissenting academies and corresponding societies, to nourish a dissident protestant counterculture that was to be the yeast of the popular radicalism of the revolutionary years and a vital constituent in what E.P. Thompson calls the 'making of the English working class'. William Godwin wrote warmly of the 'great talents and great energies' of the archetypal revolutionary, Satan, adding that such energies 'cannot flow but from a powerful sense of fitness and justice' (Shawcross 1972); and Joseph Wittreich has shown that women readers, including early feminists like Mary Astell and Mary Chudleigh, undeterred by the passages of patriarchalism and misogyny, read *Paradise Lost* and the pamphlets of the forties as the visionary manifestos of a still scarcely conceivable emancipation (Wittreich 1987). Godwin's daughter Mary read the *Tenure of Kings and Magistrates* shortly before starting to write *Frankenstein*, and while she worked on the novel, in which the unfortunate monster, abandoned by its creator, first comes to a full awareness of its predicament through overhearing *Paradise Lost* read aloud, her husband, the poet Shelley, was reading the poem to her in the evenings.

The importance of Milton to Shelley and the other romantic poets, whether as Blake's genial 'Awakener' or as the oppressive 'covering Cherub' of Harold Bloom's account (Bloom 1973), would be hard to overestimate. Joseph Wittreich's collection of romantic writings on Milton, by novelists and critics as well as poets (Wittreich 1970), is impressive testimony of a presence too actively disturbing to be called 'influence'. Chaucer, Spenser, Shakespeare were influences, admired and imitated. Milton entered the unconscious of the romantic imagination, surfacing not only in its waking language and imagery (Wordsworth's *Prelude*, for example, a conscious continuation of *Paradise Lost* with its initial determination to explore 'some British theme . . . by Milton left unsung', contains hundreds, perhaps thousands of quotations, allusions and verbal echoes of the earlier poet) but in its deepest desires and fears. Edmund Burke, for whom Milton was the outstanding example in English of literary 'sublimity', had described him as 'entirely possessed with the power of a well-managed darkness', and for Gothic novelists like Ann Radcliffe, Charles Maturin and Mary Shelley, Milton opened the way to a psychic underworld of crepuscular terrors, unacknowledged wishes and dark illuminations. Shelley's Monster, abandoned in fear and disgust by his creator Frankenstein, struggles to understand his own turbulent emotions through books. First he reads Plutarch's *Lives* and Goethe's *Werther*, but then, happening on *Paradise Lost*, he suddenly discovers 'different and far deeper emotions . . . It moved every feeling of wonder and awe that the picture of an omnipotent God warring with his creatures was capable of exciting'.[10] Blake, who told a friend that 'Milton loved me in childhood and shewed me his face', longed 'to have a continued dream, representing visually and audibly all Milton's Paradise Lost' (Wittreich 1970: 162). Coleridge, who wrote of 'my idol, Milton', described him in terms that seem more appropriate to the creator of the world than the author of *Paradise Lost*: 'Milton attracts all forms and things to himself, into the unity of his own ideal. All things and modes of action shape themselves anew in the being of Milton'.[11] Even Keats, who abandoned his Miltonic epic *Hyperion* and emerged from his shadow with the remark that 'life for him would be death for me', acknowledged a Promethean power and daring in the later writings: 'The evil days had come to him – he hit the new system of things a mighty mental blow – the exertion must have had or is yet to have some sequences' (Wittreich 1970: 556).

Through all this, still, run deep tensions and ambivalences. A presence so dominating cannot fail to arouse competing responses of admiration and repugnance, love and fear. In any case, we are confronted here not with a single 'romantic Milton' but with many. Against Blake's liberator and Shelley's revolutionary iconoclast we must set Wordsworth's Milton, an embodiment of traditional Englishness as conservative as Wordsworth himself. The Milton who 'attracts all forms and things to himself' provokes in all these writers what Harold Bloom calls a 'strong misreading', a formulation in Miltonic terms of their own deep needs and preoccupations. Nor is it only Milton's writings that evoke these responses, but the strikingly divergent traditions of interpretation through which they have been delivered, traditions that offer variously a high-bourgeois Milton, neoclassical, orthodox and patriarchal, a Whig Milton, enlightened, rational and English as roast beef and a popular-radical Milton, prophetic and antinomian. When Wordsworth thunders, in the preface to *Lyrical Ballads*, that 'the invaluable works of our elder writers, I had almost said the works of Shakespeare and Milton, are driven into neglect by frantic novels, sickly and stupid German tragedies, and deluges of idle and extravagant stories in verse',[12] his commitment to 'Shakespeare and Milton' as monuments of canonical high culture prevents him from seeing how deeply both writers, but especially Milton, have entered into the very novels, plays and poems he opposes them to. Blake's famous distinction between the conventional moralist writing 'in fetters' and the 'true poet' creating freely is a comment on Milton's eighteenth-century reputation as much as on the poet himself; and Shelley expressed the disjunction succinctly in his sardonic reminder that 'the sacred Milton' canonised by eighteenth-century literary culture had also been 'a republican, and a bold enquirer into morals and religion' (Shelley 1971: 206). Much more is at stake here, clearly, than a harmless difference of literary opinion. The attempt of some of Milton's early critics (and some of his more recent ones) to admire the poetry while suppressing their fear and hatred of the politics was inevitably doomed. His writings have always been, to a greater extent than with any other English writer, a battleground of competing ideologies.

Often this is explicit. The eighteen thirties and forties, the years of the People's Charter and the Communist Manifesto, saw a remarkable upsurge of Milton publishing for a popular readership. Biographies by Joseph Ivimey (1833) and William Carpenter (1836) set out to rescue the poet from the 'ultra-toryism and bigotry' of Johnson's *Life*, stressing his active republicanism and the visionary energies of his poetry. The chartist Thomas Cooper testified in his *Autobiography* to the influence of Milton on his political education, and G.J. Harney, friend of Marx and Engels, reviewing the prose works in 1850 for the chartist *Democratic Review*, thundered against 'the ban put upon them by the aristocracy, and the ill name given to them by royalist writers, and the literary toadies of monarchy and oligarchy'. Across the Atlantic, the American feminist Margaret Fuller praised Milton's 'primitive vitality', and his writings played their part in formulating the demands of the struggle for Black emancipation (Wittreich 1987: 4).

Against this celebration of a Milton embattled, partisan and popular, Matthew Arnold deplored the Hebraic 'narrowness and contentiousness' of the Puritan temper, and attempted to defuse the political impact and popular appeal of the writings by shifting attention, in a familiar classicising turn, to the style. Arnold's Milton is 'our great artist in style', source of a classless and depoliticised 'refining and elevation'; qualities, he adds, with an anxious eye on the resurgent suffrage and labour agitation of the 1860s, which 'no race needs . . . more than ours'. In the same vein, Mark Pattison, claiming Milton as the prime exemplar of the 'English man of letters', dismissed the prose as 'a record of the prostitution of genius to political party' and reclaimed the poems as the special preserve of a privileged minority – not, to be sure, the poet's own 'fit audience . . . though few', but an even more exclusive fraternity of chaps with 'taste', classics and the right school tie: 'the lofty strain which requires more effort to accompany, than the average reader is able to make . . . and a wealth of allusion demanding more literature than is possessed by any but the few whose life is lived with the poets' (Pattison 1879: 67, 215).

Confronted with this stuffily reverential academicism (what Harry Blamires calls 'the Milton of organ music and versified telephone directory', *Milton Encyclopedia* 4,139), we may feel that the debunking efforts of T.S. Eliot and F.R. Leavis, which the latter was to claim in 1936 had 'dislodged' Milton 'with remarkably little fuss', have a refreshing candour. But they, no less than Arnold and Pattison, were concerned to depoliticise Milton, to thwart the radical historical energies of the writing and to belittle the issues that animate it. They failed, and in retrospect the once-celebrated 'Milton controversy' looks comically self-important, a parochial squabble among literary critics about the 'great tradition' of academic English, reminiscent of the 'surplice-brabbles and tippet-scuffles' of the Anglican prelates that Milton had satirised in the 1640s (*SSPP* 71). But as so often in Milton criticism, the real issues lie deeper, and the hidden agenda of the Eliot-Leavis onslaught, as of the defence mounted by C.S. Lewis and the 'neo-Christians', is much more interesting than anything they actually wrote.[13] For both sides, Milton serves as a symbol of something much wider: for Eliot and Leavis, of a 'dissociation of sensibility' evident everywhere in a society that has supposedly lost contact with its organic and traditional roots; for Lewis and Douglas Bush, of the immutable simplicities of Christian orthodoxy, given lapidary expression by a poet 'to whom good and evil are distinct polarities . . . who sees in human life an eternal contest between irreligious pride and religious humility' (Bush, in Barker 1965: 174). There is little to choose here; for what both sides in the argument are concerned to reject or deny in Milton's writings is their disconcerting *modernity*.

Milton, Fredric Jameson writes, is 'the greatest English political poet', and the hero of his greatest poem is not Satan but Adam, 'the commoner, the first bourgeois', prototype of 'that extraordinary mutation which is middle-class man' (Barker 1986: 52). The son of a scrivener (that is, a money-lender and investment-broker), Milton defines liberty and virtue in competitive and individualistic terms. The arguments against censorship in *Areopagitica* advocate a free market in knowledge. The Lady in *Comus* defends her chastity as a kind of thrift and good husbandry, anticipating the open commercialisation of virginity in Restoration comedy and eighteenth-century fiction. Eve and Adam are not the aristocratic heroes of classical or renaissance epic but Everywoman and Everyman, and Paradise before the fall idealises the middle-class household. *Paradise Lost* and *Samson*, with their self-tormenting interiority, their preoccupation with self-knowledge and the labyrinthine perplexities of motive and action, their focal stress on family relationships and their unheroic protagonists struggling to grasp the elusive meaning and logic of history, are closer in most important respects to *Middlemarch* and *War and Peace*, *The Rainbow* and *The Golden Notebook*, than they are to the *Iliad*, the *Aeneid* or *The Faerie Queene*. To look at Milton's impact, not on literary critics but on novelists and poets, is to see his writings as one of the key vectors of modernity, shaping images and concepts for a society that was still, in his own lifetime, struggling into being.

Raymond Williams's term for cultural forms reaching out for new articulations of meaning and response – inevitably a difficult and contradictory process, since they must do so with the very same traditional languages and structures that they seek to transcend – is 'emergent'[14]; and the idea of emergence recalls the exuberantly imagined episode in *Paradise Lost* when, on the sixth and last day of creation, the earth is commanded to bring forth 'cattle and creeping things, and beast of th'earth,/ Each in their kind'.

> The earth obey'd, and straight
> Op'ning her fertile womb teem'd at a birth
> Innumerous living creatures, perfect forms,
> Limb'd and full-grown. Out of the ground up rose
> As from his lair the wild beast where he wons
> In forest wild, in thicket, brake or den;
> Among the trees in pairs they rose, they walk'd,
> The cattle in the fields and meadows green,
> Those rare and solitary, these in flocks
> Pasturing at once, and in broad herds upsprung.
> The grassy clods now calv'd; now half appear'd
> The tawny lion, pawing to get free
> His hinder parts, then springs as broke from bonds
> And rampant shakes his brinded mane; the ounce,
> The libbard and the tiger, as the mole
> Rising, the crumbled earth above them threw
> In hillocks; the swift stag from underground
> Bore up his branching head; scarce from his mould
> Behemoth, biggest born of earth, upheav'd
> His vastness;
>
> (VII, 453-72)

Behemoth, the biblical elephant, gave Hobbes the title of his study of the causes of the Civil Wars; but although the whole episode, in which the ant figures as a 'pattern of just equality perhaps/Hereafter', is open to an allegorical reading (what isn't, in this poem?), what impresses and moves above all is the playful, fantastic and wholly positive celebration of new and emergent life. In just such terms had Milton welcomed the bewildering proliferation of pamphlet literature in the London of the 1640s, satire, polemic, visionary prophecy, 'each in their kind': 'The shop of war hath not there more anvils and hammers waking, to fashion out the plates and instruments of armed Justice in defence of beleaguered Truth, than there be pens and heads there sitting by their studious lamps, musing, searching, revolving new notions and ideas wherewith to present as with their homage and fealty the approaching reformation . . . Where there is much desire to learn, there of necessity will be much argument, much writing, many opinions; for opinion in good men is but knowledge in the making . . . Should ye suppress all this flowery crop of knowledge and new light sprung up and yet springing daily in this city?' (*SSPP* 101–4); and *Areopagitica*'s revolutionary England 'rising like a strong man from sleep and shaking her invincible locks' (103) is not a more compelling image of the 'rousing motions' of resurgent creative power than the lion who, 'half appear'd' and 'pawing to get free/His hinder parts, then springs as broke from bonds/And rampant shakes his brinded mane'.

Such passages give strong support to Frank Kermode's contention that Milton's 'radical topic' is 'the power of joy and its loss'; joy, he adds, cautioning against too theological a reading of the poems, which is 'very much a matter of the senses' (Kermode 1960: 101–3). The image of the joyless puritan patriarch, abusing his daughters and browbeating his readers, still persists in some quarters, and the suggestion that Milton's writings, for all their fierce moral and political argumentativeness, are committed at root to the pleasures of the senses may seem an improbable one. But it was the arch-intellectual Milton, not Keats or Lawrence, who defined poetry as 'simple, sensuous and passionate', and his own poetry explores and develops its meanings at least as much through the sensualities of sound and rhythm and the evocation of smell, taste, sight, and movement as through the logic and structure of its arguments. In any case, the distinction between sensation (physical) and argument (intellectual) is misleading. 'Poetry is written in the brain', Dannie Abse has said; 'but the brain is bathed in blood';[15] and Milton, who rejected the Platonic and Augustinian separation of soul and body, would undoubtedly have agreed. We think with our bodies, just as we feel with our minds, and in the baroque synaesthesia[16] of Milton's text an idea can be as luminous, as fragrant, as sensuously provocative as ripe fruit or warm flesh.

'Love Virtue, she alone is free'. Love, Virtue, Freedom: the triad of Miltonic Graces invoked at the end of the Ludlow masque rewrites the 'faith, hope and charity' of Pauline orthodoxy. Virtue (integrity, self-knowledge, justice) is politicised, as the only route to freedom; but it is also sensualised, as the only goal of love, the ultimate object of desire. The bitter lessons of 1660 forced Milton to rethink the meaning of love, virtue and freedom, and the relations between them, in a world darkened by disappointment and defeat. The writings that result from that rethinking may indeed, as Jameson suggests, 'anticipate the social impoverishment of the modern world', its privatisation of hope, its collective internalisation of failure (Barker 1986: 54). But they offer too some of the most compelling accounts we have of the rousing motions of change, the sheer unpredictability of the emergent. Whether they also successfully 'assert eternal providence/And justify the ways of God to men' is a question for their modern readers to decide for ourselves, if we care to. Speaking for myself, I don't believe that they do; but then the question isn't one that interests me very much. What does strike me, writing these sentences and looking around at our world, at China or Latin America or Eastern Europe, is that history has lost none of its power to astonish and confound since Milton's day, that people caught up in it can still be moved by the love of virtue (though they might not call it that) and the hope of freedom to turn the world upside down, and that his own writings continue to testify with undiminished eloquence to that hope and that possibility.

NOTES

1 'An Horatian Ode On Cromwell's Return From Ireland', lines 119-20, in *Marvell: Selected Poems and Prose*, ed. Robert Wilcher, London, Methuen (1986), 60.

2 Sir Thomas Browne, *Religio Medici*, London, Dent (1965), 10-11.

3 Antonio Gramsci, *Selections from the Prison Notebooks*, ed. Quintin Hoare and Geoffrey Nowell Smith, London, Lawrence & Wishart (1971), 175. Gramsci, Sardinian leader of the Italian Communist Party, was arrested on Mussolini's orders in November 1926, and spent the last ten years of his life in prison. The phrase is a quotation from the French socialist writer Romain Rolland.

4 On the other hand, one of the drafts begins with a prologue explaining that Adam and Eve are invisible to mortal eyes until after the fall, which looks like an ingenious way of getting round the problem of prelapsarian nudity and wouldn't be necessary unless some sort of performance was envisaged.

5 Gramsci, *Prison Notebooks*, 242ff. 'Hegemony', for Gramsci, means not just political leadership but the creation of common objectives and a common socio-national identity for different social classes and groups.

6 Terry Eagleton, *Walter Benjamin*, London, Verso (1981), 12.

7 T.S. Eliot, 'Milton II', in *On Poetry and Poets*, London, Faber & Faber (1957), 157. See also p. 143.

8 V. Voloshinov, *Marxism and the Philosophy of Language*, New York, Seminar Press (1973).

9 For example, John Wesley's *Paradise Lost Improved* (1763) and James Buchanan's *Paradise Lost Rendered Into Grammatical Construction* (1773).

10 Mary Shelley, *Frankenstein*, in *Three Gothic Novels*, Harmondsworth, Penguin (1968), 396.

11 Samuel Coleridge, *Biographia Literaria* (1817), ch. 15.

12 William Wordsworth, *Poems*, Harmondsworth, Penguin (1977), vol. 1, p. 873.

13 There is a review of the 'Milton controversy' by Bernard Bergonzi in Kermode (1960), 162–80.

14 Raymond Williams, *Marxism and Literature*, Oxford University Press (1977), 123: 'By "emergent" I mean, first, that new meanings and values, new practices, new relationships and kinds of relationship are continually being created. But it is exceptionally difficult to distinguish between those which are really elements of some new phase of the dominant culture . . . and those which are substantially alternative or oppositional to it.' On my reading, Satan would fall into the first category, Eve into the second; but Milton would have agreed that it is 'exceptionally difficult to distinguish' between them.

15 In an interview in *The Observer*, 3 June 1990, p. 61.

16 Margaret Bottrall defines baroque in terms of 'audacity',

'figures hurtling through space', 'amplitude and richness', 'exaggerated contrast and counterpoise', 'the fusion of classical and biblical materials' and 'synaesthesia', the running-together of the different senses ('The baroque element in Milton', *English Miscellany I*, 31–42).

A NOTE ON THE TEXT

I have used the 1674 (twelve-book) text of *Paradise Lost* (with a couple of generally-accepted emendations, recorded in the notes), the 1670 text of the *History of Britain*, the 1671 text of *Samson Agonistes*, with modernised spelling and (very sparingly) punctuation. The great temptation for an editor of Milton is to over-punctuate, in a misguided attempt to nail down the meaning of his great, serpentine verse-paragraphs. I hope I've avoided that (if anything, the text is more lightly punctuated than the original), but Milton's commas, semi-colons, colons and even full-stops have a different weight and significance from our own, and I've tried to 'translate' them into their closest modern equivalents where necessary. Of course that involves decisions about what the 'weight and significance' of a particular passage is, but that is a responsibility an editor has to take. Readers who want to see what the original texts look like will find them transcribed in Helen Darbishire's edition (*The Poetical Works of John Milton*, 2 vols, Oxford University Press 1952–5). As in the *Selected Shorter Poems and Prose* (Routledge 1988), I have, in the poems only, elided the final 'e' of a past participle or participial adjective ('high overarch'd embower'), of 'the' before a vowel ('th'Etrurian shades', 'th'archangel') and of a few other words (e.g. 'o'er'), where the metre requires it. It follows that '-ed' fully written out is always voiced as a syllable.

The 'arguments' or prose summaries added during the printing of the first edition of *Paradise Lost* will be found in the notes, at the head of the relevant book, with the arguments of the other six books (III, V, VI, VIII, X and XI) inserted at the appropriate point to provide a linking narrative.

JOHN MILTON

Selected Longer Poems and Prose

Paradise Lost

The verse

The measure is English heroic verse without rhyme, as that of Homer in Greek, and of Virgil in Latin; rhyme being no necessary adjunct or true ornament of poem or good verse, in longer works especially, but the invention of a barbarous age, to set off wretched matter and lame metre; graced indeed since by the use of some famous modern poets, carried away by custom, but much to their own vexation, hindrance, and constraint to express many things otherwise, and for the most part worse than else they would have expressed them. Not without cause therefore some both Italian and Spanish poets of prime note have rejected rhyme both in longer and shorter works, as have also long since our best English tragedies, as a thing of itself, to all judicious ears, trivial and of no true musical delight; which consists only in apt numbers, fit quantity of syllables, and the sense variously drawn out from one verse into another, not in the jingling sound of like endings, a fault avoided by the learned ancients both in poetry and all good oratory. This neglect then of rhyme so little is to be taken for a defect, though it may seem so perhaps to vulgar readers, that it rather is to be esteemed an example set, the first in English, of ancient liberty recovered to heroic poem from the troublesome and modern bondage of rhyming.

BOOK I

Of man's first disobedience, and the fruit
Of that forbidden tree whose mortal taste
Brought death into the world, and all our woe,
With loss of Eden, till one greater man
Restore us and regain that blissful seat,
Sing, heavenly Muse, that on the secret top
Of Oreb or of Sinai didst inspire
That shepherd who first taught the chosen seed
In the beginning how the heavens and earth
Rose out of chaos; or if Sion hill
Delight thee more, and Siloa's brook that flow'd
Fast by the oracle of God, I thence
Invoke thy aid to my advent'rous song,
That with no middle flight intends to soar
Above th'Aonian mount while it pursues
Things unattempted yet in prose or rhyme.
And chiefly thou, O Spirit, that dost prefer
Before all temples the upright heart and pure,
Instruct me, for thou know'st; thou from the first
Wast present, and with mighty wings outspread
Dove-like sat'st brooding on the vast abyss
And mad'st it pregnant. What in me is dark
Illumine, what is low raise and support,
That to the height of this great argument
I may assert eternal providence,
And justify the ways of God to men.
  Say first, for heaven hides nothing from thy view
Nor the deep tract of hell, say first what cause
Mov'd our grand parents in that happy state,
Favour'd of heaven so highly, to fall off
From their creator, and transgress his will
For one restraint, lords of the world besides?
Who first seduc'd them to that foul revolt?
Th' infernal serpent; he it was whose guile
Stirr'd up with envy and revenge deceiv'd
The mother of mankind, what time his pride

* Numbers in square brackets refer to pages on which notes may be found

Had cast him out from heaven with all his host
Of rebel angels, by whose aid aspiring
To set himself in glory above his peers
He trusted to have equall'd the most high
If he oppos'd, and with ambitious aim
Against the throne and monarchy of God
Rais'd impious war in heaven and battle proud
With vain attempt. Him the almighty power
Hurl'd headlong flaming from th'etherial sky
With hideous ruin and combustion down
To bottomless perdition, there to dwell
In adamantine chains and penal fire
Who durst defy th'omnipotent to arms.—
Nine times the space that measures day and night
To mortal men he with his horrid crew
Lay vanquish'd, rolling in the fiery gulf,
Confounded though immortal; but his doom
Reserv'd him to more wrath, for now the thought
Both of lost happiness and lasting pain
Torments him. Round he throws his baleful eyes
That witness'd huge affliction and dismay
Mix'd with obdurate pride and steadfast hate.
At once as far as angels ken he views
The dismal situation waste and wild:
A dungeon horrible on all sides round
As one great furnace flam'd, yet from those flames
No light but rather darkness visible
Serv'd only to discover sights of woe,
Regions of sorrow, doleful shades, where peace
And rest can never dwell, hope never comes
That comes to all, but torture without end
Still urges, and a fiery deluge fed
With ever-burning sulphur unconsum'd.
Such place eternal justice had prepar'd
For these rebellious, here their prison ordain'd
In utter darkness, and their portion set
As far remov'd from God and light of heaven
As from the centre thrice to th'utmost pole.
O how unlike the place from whence they fell!

There the companions of his fall o'erwhelm'd
With floods and whirlwinds of tempestuous fire
He soon discerns, and weltering by his side
One next himself in power and next in crime,
Long after known in Palestine and nam'd
Beelzebub; to whom th'arch-enemy,
And thence in heaven call'd Satan, with bold words
Breaking the horrid silence thus began.
  If thou beest he – but O how fall'n! how chang'd
From him who in the happy realms of light
Cloth'd with transparent brightness didst outshine
Myriads though bright; if he whom mutual league,
United thoughts and counsels, equal hope
And hazard in the glorious enterprise
Join'd with me once, now misery hath join'd
In equal ruin; into what pit thou seest
From what height fall'n, so much the stronger prov'd
He with his thunder; and till then who knew
The force of those dire arms? Yet not for those,
Nor what the potent victor in his rage
Can else inflict, do I repent or change,
Though chang'd in outward lustre, that fix'd mind
And high disdain from sense of injur'd merit
That with the mightiest rais'd me to contend,
And to the fierce contention brought along
Innumerable force of spirits arm'd
That durst dislike his reign and, me preferring,
His utmost power with adverse power oppos'd
In dubious battle on the plains of heaven
And shook his throne. What though the field be lost?
All is not lost: th' unconquerable will
And study of revenge, immortal hate,
And courage never to submit or yield,
And what is else not to be overcome.
That glory never shall his wrath or might
Extort from me. To bow and sue for grace
With suppliant knee, and deify his power
Who from the terror of this arm so late

Doubted his empire, that were low indeed;
That were an ignominy and shame beneath
This downfall. Since by fate the strength of gods
And this empyreal substance cannot fail,
Since through experience of this great event
In arms not worse, in foresight much advanc'd,
We may with more successful hope resolve
To wage by force or guile eternal war
Irreconcilable to our grand foe,
Who now triumphs and in th'excess of joy
Sole reigning holds the tyranny of heaven.
  So spake th'apostate angel, though in pain,
Vaunting aloud, but rack'd with deep despair;
And him thus answer'd soon his bold compeer.
  O Prince, O chief of many throned powers
That led th'embattl'd seraphim to war
Under thy conduct, and in dreadful deeds
Fearless endanger'd heaven's perpetual king
And put to proof his high supremacy,
Whether upheld by strength or chance or fate,
Too well I see and rue the dire event
That with sad overthrow and foul defeat
Hath lost us heaven, and all this mighty host
In horrible destruction laid thus low,
As far as gods and heavenly essences
Can perish; for the mind and spirit remains
Invincible, and vigour soon returns,
Though all our glory extinct and happy state
Here swallow'd up in endless misery.
But what if he our conqueror (whom I now
Of force believe almighty, since no less
Than such could have o'erpower'd such force as ours)
Have left us this our spirit and strength entire
Strongly to suffer and support our pains,
That we may so suffice his vengeful ire,
Or do him mightier service as his thralls
By right of war, whate'er his business be
Here in the heart of hell, to work in fire
Or do his errands in the gloomy deep?

What can it then avail though yet we feel
Strength undiminish'd, or eternal being
To undergo eternal punishment?
Whereto with speedy words the fiend repli'd.
  Fall'n cherub, to be weak is miserable,
Doing or suffering; but of this be sure,
To do aught good never will be our task,
But ever to do ill our sole delight,
As being the contrary to his high will
Whom we resist. If then his providence
Out of our evil seek to bring forth good,
Our labour must be to pervert that end
And out of good still to find means of evil;
Which oft-times may succeed, so as perhaps
To grieve him, if I fail not, and disturb
His inmost counsels from their destin'd aim.
But see, the angry victor hath recall'd
His ministers of vengeance and pursuit
Back to the gates of heaven. The sulphurous hail
Shot after us in storm o'erblown hath laid
The fiery surge that from the precipice
Of heaven receiv'd us falling, and the thunder,
Wing'd with red lightning and impetuous rage,
Perhaps hath spent his shafts, and ceases now
To bellow through the vast and boundless deep.
Let us not slip th'occasion, whether scorn
Or satiate fury yield it from our foe.
Seest thou yon dreary plain forlorn and wild,
The seat of desolation, void of light
Save what the glimmering of these livid flames
Casts pale and dreadful? Thither let us tend
From off the tossing of these fiery waves,
There rest, if any rest can harbour there,
And reassembling our afflicted powers
Consult how we may henceforth most offend
Our enemy, our own loss how repair,
How overcome this dire calamity,
What reinforcement we may gain from hope,
If not what resolution from despair.

Thus Satan, talking to his dearest mate
With head uplift above the wave and eyes
That sparkling blaz'd; his other parts besides
Prone on the flood extended long and large
Lay floating many a rood, in bulk as huge
As whom the fables name of monstrous size,
Titanian or Earth-born, that warr'd on Jove:
Briareus or Typhon, whom the den
By ancient Tarsus held, or that sea-beast
Leviathan, which God of all his works
Created hugest that swim the ocean stream.
Him haply slumb'ring on the Norway foam
The pilot of some small night-founder'd skiff
Deeming some island oft, as seamen tell,
With fixed anchor in his scaly rind
Moors by his side under the lee, while night
Invests the sea and wished morn delays.
So stretch'd out huge in length the arch-fiend lay
Chain'd on the burning lake, nor ever thence
Had ris'n or heav'd his head but that the will
And high permission of all-ruling heaven
Left him at large to his own dark designs,
That with reiterated crimes he might
Heap on himself damnation while he sought
Evil to others, and enrag'd might see
How all his malice serv'd but to bring forth
Infinite goodness, grace and mercy shown
On man by him seduc'd, but on himself
Treble confusion, wrath and vengeance pour'd.
Forthwith upright he rears from off the pool
His mighty stature. On each hand the flames
Driv'n backward slope their pointing spires, and roll'd
In billows leave i'the midst a horrid vale.
Then with expanded wings he steers his flight
Aloft, incumbent on the dusky air
That felt unusual weight, till on dry land
He lights, if it were land that ever burn'd
With solid as the lake with liquid fire,
And such appear'd in hue as when the force

Of subterranean wind transports a hill
Torn from Pelorus or the shatter'd side
Of thundering Etna, whose combustible
And fuell'd entrails, thence conceiving fire,
Sublim'd with mineral fury aid the winds
And leave a singed bottom, all involv'd
With stench and smoke: such resting found the sole
Of unbless'd feet. Him follow'd his next mate,
Both glorying to have scap'd the Stygian flood
As gods, and by their own recover'd strength,
Not by the sufferance of supernal power.
Is this the region, this the soil, the clime,
Said then the lost archangel, this the seat
That we must change for heaven, this mournful gloom
For that celestial light? Be it so, since he
Who now is sovereign can dispose and bid
What shall be right. Furthest from him is best
Whom reason hath equall'd, force hath made supreme
Above his equals. Farewell, happy fields
Where joy for ever dwells; hail horrors, hail
Infernal world, and thou, profoundest hell,
Receive thy new possessor, one who brings
A mind not to be chang'd by place or time.
The mind is its own place, and in itself
Can make a heaven of hell, a hell of heaven.
What matter where, if I be still the same
And what I should be, all but less than he
Whom thunder hath made greater? Here at least
We shall be free. Th'almighty hath not built
Here for his envy, will not drive us hence.
Here we may reign secure, and in my choice
To reign is worth ambition though in hell:
Better to reign in hell than serve in heaven.
But wherefore let we then our faithful friends,
Th' associates and copartners of our loss,
Lie thus astonish'd on th'oblivious pool,
And call them not to share with us their part
In this unhappy mansion, or once more

With rallied arms to try what may be yet
Regain'd in heaven, or what more lost in hell?
  So Satan spake, and him Beelzebub
Thus answer'd. Leader of those armies bright
Which but th'omnipotent none could have foil'd,
If once they hear that voice, their liveliest pledge
Of hope in fears and dangers, heard so oft
In worst extremes and on the perilous edge
Of battle when it rag'd, in all assaults
Their surest signal, they will soon resume
New courage and revive, though now they lie
Grovelling and prostrate on yon lake of fire,
As we erewhile, astounded and amaz'd;
No wonder, fall'n such a pernicious height.
  He scarce had ceas'd when the superior fiend
Was moving toward the shore, his ponderous shield,
Ethereal temper, massy, large and round
Behind him cast. The broad circumference
Hung on his shoulders like the moon, whose orb
Through optic glass the Tuscan artist views
At evening from the top of Fesole,
Or in Valdarno, to descry new lands,
Rivers or mountains in her spotty globe.
His spear, to equal which the tallest pine,
Hewn on Norwegian hills to be the mast
Of some great ammiral, were but a wand,
He walked with to support uneasy steps
Over the burning marl, not like those steps
On heaven's azure; and the torrid clime
Smote on him sore besides, vaulted with fire.
Natheless he so endur'd till on the beach
Of that inflamed sea he stood and call'd
His legions, angel forms, who lay entranc'd
Thick as autumnal leaves that strew the brooks
In Vallombrosa, where th'Etrurian shades
High overarch'd imbower, or scatter'd sedge
Afloat, when with fierce winds Orion arm'd
Hath vex'd the Red Sea coast, whose waves o'erthrew
Busiris and his Memphian chivalry

While with perfidious hatred they pursu'd
The sojourners of Goshen, who beheld
From the safe shore their floating carcasses
And broken chariot wheels; so thick bestrewn,
Abject and lost lay these, covering the flood,
Under amazement of their hideous change.
He call'd so loud that all the hollow deep
Of hell resounded. Princes, potentates,
Warriors, the flower of heaven once yours, now lost
If such astonishment as this can seize
Eternal spirits; or have ye chos'n this place
After the toil of battle to repose
Your weari'd virtue, for the ease you find
To slumber here, as in the vales of heaven?
Or in this abject posture have ye sworn
To adore the conqueror? who now beholds
Cherub and seraph rolling in the flood
With scatter'd arms and ensigns, till anon
His swift pursuers from heaven gates discern
Th' advantage and descending tread us down
Thus drooping, or with linked thunderbolts
Transfix us to the bottom of this gulf.
Awake, arise, or be for ever fallen.
  They heard and were abash'd, and up they sprung
Upon the wing, as when men wont to watch,
On duty sleeping found by whom they dread,
Rouse and bestir themselves ere well awake.
Nor did they not perceive the evil plight
In which they were, or the fierce pains not feel,
Yet to their general's voice they soon obey'd
Innumerable; as when the potent rod
Of Amram's son, in Egypt's evil day
Wav'd round the coast, up call'd a pitchy cloud
Of locusts warping on the eastern wind,
That o'er the realm of impious Pharaoh hung
Like night and darken'd all the land of Nile,
So numberless were those bad angels seen
Hovering on wing under the cope of hell
'Twixt upper, nether and surrounding fires,

Till, as a signal giv'n th'uplifted spear
Of their great sultan waving to direct
Their course, in even balance down they light
On the firm brimstone, and fill all the plain;
A multitude like which the populous north
Pour'd never from her frozen loins to pass
Rhene or the Danaw, when her barbarous sons
Came like a deluge on the south and spread
Beneath Gibraltar to the Lybian sands.
Forthwith from every squadron and each band
The heads and leaders thither haste where stood
Their great commander, godlike shapes and forms
Excelling human, princely dignities
And powers that erst in heaven sat on thrones,
Though of their names in heavenly records now
Be no memorial, blotted out and raz'd
By their rebellion from the book of life.
Nor had they yet among the sons of Eve
Got them new names, till wandering o'er the earth
Through God's high sufferance for the trial of man,
By falsities and lies the greatest part
Of mankind they corrupted to forsake
God their creator, and th'invisible
Glory of him that made them, to transform
Oft to the image of a brute, adorn'd
With gay religions full of pomp and gold
And devils to adore for deities.
Then were they known to men by various names
And various idols through the heathen world.
Say, Muse, their names then known, who first, who last,
Rous'd from the slumber on that fiery couch
At their great emperor's call, as next in worth,
Came singly where he stood on the bare strand,
While the promiscuous crowd stood yet aloof.
The chief were those who from the pit of hell
Roaming to seek their prey on earth durst fix
Their seats, long after, next the seat of God,
Their altars by his altar, gods ador'd
Among the nations round, and durst abide

Jehovah thundering out of Sion, thron'd
Between the cherubim; yea, often plac'd
Within his sanctuary itself their shrines,
Abominations, and with cursed things
His holy rites and solemn feasts profan'd,
And with their darkness durst affront his light.
First Moloch, horrid king, besmear'd with blood
Of human sacrifice and parents' tears,
Though for the noise of drums and timbrels loud
Their children's cries unheard that pass'd through fire
To his grim idol. Him the Ammonite
Worshipp'd in Rabba and her watery plain,
In Argob and in Basan to the stream
Of utmost Arnon; nor content with such
Audacious neighbourhood, the wisest heart
Of Solomon he led by fraud to build
His temple right against the temple of God
On that opprobrious hill, and made his grove
The pleasant valley of Hinnom, Tophet thence
And black Gehenna call'd, the type of hell.
Next Chemos, th'obscene dread of Moab's sons
From Aroar to Nebo and the wild
Of southmost Abarim, in Hesebon
And Horonaim, Seon's realm, beyond
The flowery dale of Sibma clad with vines,
And Eleale to th'asphaltic pool;
Peor his other name, when he entic'd
Israel in Sittim, on their march from Nile,
To do him wanton rites, which cost them woe.
Yet thence his lustful orgies he enlarg'd
Ev'n to that hill of scandal by the grove
Of Moloch homicide, lust hard by hate,
Till good Josiah drove them thence to hell.
With these came they who from the bordering flood
Of old Euphrates to the brook that parts
Egypt from Syrian ground had general names
Of Baalim and Ashtaroth, those male,
These feminine; for spirits, when they please,

Can either sex assume or both, so soft
And uncompounded is their essence pure,
Not ti'd or manacl'd with joint or limb,
Nor founded on the brittle strength of bones
Like cumbrous flesh, but in what shape they choose,
Dilated or condens'd, bright or obscure,
Can execute their airy purposes
And works of love or enmity fulfil.
For those the race of Israel oft forsook
Their living strength and unfrequented left
His righteous altar, bowing lowly down
To bestial gods, for which their heads as low
Bow'd down in battle, sunk before the spear
Of despicable foes. With these in troop
Came Astoreth, whom the Phoenicians call'd
Astarte, queen of heaven, with crescent horns,
To whose bright image nightly by the moon
Sidonian virgins paid their vows and songs:
In Sion also not unsung, where stood
Her temple on th'offensive mountain, built
By that uxorious king whose heart, though large,
Beguil'd by fair idolatresses fell
To idols foul. Thammuz came next behind,
Whose annual wound in Lebanon allur'd
The Syrian damsels to lament his fate
In amorous ditties all a summer's day,
While smooth Adonis from his native rock
Ran purple to the sea, suppos'd with blood
Of Thammuz yearly wounded. The love-tale
Infected Sion's daughters with like heat,
Whose wanton passions in the sacred porch
Ezekiel saw when by the vision led
His eye survey'd the dark idolatries
Of alienated Judah. Next came one
Who mourn'd in earnest when the captive ark
Main'd his brute image, head and hands lopp'd off
In his own temple, on the groundsel edge
Where he fell flat and sham'd his worshippers;
Dagon his name, sea monster, upward man

And downward fish, yet had his temple high
Rear'd in Azotus, dreaded through the coast
Of Palestine, in Gath and Ascalon
And Accaron and Gaza's frontier bounds.
Him follow'd Rimmon, whose delightful seat
Was fair Damascus on the fertile banks
Of Abbana and Pharphar, lucid streams.
He also against the house of God was bold:
A leper once he lost and gain'd a king,
Ahaz, his sottish conqueror, whom he drew
God's altar to disparage and displace
For one of Syrian mode whereon to burn
His odious offerings and adore the gods
Whom he had vanquish'd. After these appear'd
A crew who under names of old renown,
Osiris, Isis, Orus and their train,
With monstrous shapes and sorceries abus'd
Fanatic Egypt and her priests to seek
Their wandering gods disguis'd in brutish forms
Rather than human; nor did Israel scape
Th'infection when their borrow'd gold compos'd
The calf in Oreb; and the rebel king
Doubl'd that sin in Bethel and in Dan,
Lik'ning his maker to the grazed ox,
Jehovah, who in one night when he pass'd
From Egypt marching equall'd with one stroke
Both her first-born and all her bleating gods.
Belial came last, than whom a spirit more lewd
Fell not from heaven, or more gross to love
Vice for itself. To him no temple stood
Or altar smok'd; yet who more oft than he
In temples and at altars when the priest
Turns atheist, as did Eli's sons, who fill'd
With lust and violence the house of God.
In courts and palaces he also reigns,
And in luxurious cities, where the noise
Of riot ascends above their loftiest towers,
And injury and outrage; and when night
Darkens the streets, then wander forth the sons

Of Belial, flown with insolence and wine.
Witness the streets of Sodom, and that night
In Gibeah when the hospitable door
Expos'd a matron to avoid worse rape.
These were the prime in order and in might.
The rest were long to tell, though far renown'd,
Th'Ionian gods, of Javan's issue held
Gods, yet confess'd later than Heaven and Earth,
Their boasted parents: Titan, Heaven's first-born,
With his enormous brood, and birthright seiz'd
By younger Saturn, he from mightier Jove,
His own and Rhea's son, like measure found;
So Jove usurping reign'd. These first in Crete
And Ida known, thence on the snowy top
Of cold Olympus rul'd the middle air,
Their highest heaven, or on the Delphian cliff
Or in Dodona and through all the bounds
Of Doric land; or who with Saturn old
Fled over Adria to th'Hesperian fields,
And o'er the Celtic roam'd the utmost isles.
All these and more came flocking, but with looks
Downcast and damp, yet such wherein appear'd
Obscure some glimpse of joy t'have found their chief
Not in despair, t'have found themselves not lost
In loss itself, which on his countenance cast
Like doubtful hue; but he his wonted pride
Soon recollecting with high words, that bore
Semblance of worth, not substance, gently rais'd
Their fainting courage and dispell'd their fears,
Then straight commands that at the warlike sound
Of trumpets loud and clarions be uprear'd
His mighty standard. That proud honour claim'd
Azazel as his right, a cherub tall,
Who forthwith from the glittering staff unfurl'd
Th'imperial ensign, which full high advanc'd
Shone like a meteor streaming to the wind
With gems and golden lustre rich emblaz'd,
Seraphic arms and trophies, all the while
Sonorous metal blowing martial sounds;

At which the universal host upsent
A shout that tore hell's concave, and beyond
Frighted the realm of Chaos and old Night.
All in a moment through the gloom were seen
Ten thousand banners rise into the air
With orient colours waving. With them rose
A forest huge of spears, and thronging helms
Appear'd, and serried shields in thick array
Of depth immeasurable. Anon they move
In perfect phalanx to the Dorian mood
Of flutes and soft recorders, such as rais'd
To height of noblest temper heroes old
Arming to battle, and instead of rage
Deliberate valour breath'd, firm and unmov'd
With dread of death to flight or foul retreat;
Nor wanting power to mitigate and suage
With solemn touches troubl'd thoughts, and chase
Anguish and doubt and fear and sorrow and pain
From mortal or immortal minds. Thus they
Breathing united force with fixed thought
Mov'd on in silence to soft pipes that charm'd
Their painful steps o'er the burnt soil; and now
Advanc'd in view they stand, a horrid front
Of dreadful length and dazzling arms, in guise
Of warriors old with order'd spear and shield,
Awaiting what command their mighty chief
Had to impose. He through the armed files
Darts his experienc'd eye, and soon traverse
The whole battalion views, their order due,
Their visages and stature as of gods,
Their number last he sums. And now his heart
Distends with pride, and hard'ning in his strength
Glories; for never since created man
Met such embodi'd force as nam'd with these
Could merit more than that small infantry
Warr'd on by cranes, though all the giant brood
Of Phlegra with th'heroic race were join'd
That fought at Thebes and Ilium, on each side

Mix'd with auxiliar gods, and what resounds
In fable or romance of Uther's son
Begirt with British and Armoric knights,
And all who since, baptiz'd or infidel,
Jousted in Aspramont or Montalban,
Damasco or Marocco or Trebizond,
Or whom Biserta sent from Afric shore
When Charlemagne with all his peerage fell
By Fontarabbia: thus far these beyond
Compare of mortal prowess yet observ'd
Their dread commander. He above the rest
In shape and gesture proudly eminent
Stood like a tower; his form had not yet lost
All its original brightness, nor appear'd
Less than archangel ruin'd and th'excess
Of glory obscur'd, as when the sun new risen
Looks through the horizontal misty air
Shorn of his beams, or from behind the moon
In dim eclipse disastrous twilight sheds
On half the nations, and with fear of change
Perplexes monarchs. Darken'd so, yet shone
Above them all th'archangel; but his face
Deep scars of thunder had entrench'd, and care
Sat on his faded cheek, but under brows
Of dauntless courage and considerate pride
Waiting revenge; cruel his eye, but cast
Signs of remorse and passion to behold
The fellows of his crime, the followers rather,
Far other once beheld in bliss, condemn'd
For ever now to have their lot in pain,
Millions of spirits for his fault amerc'd
Of heaven and from eternal splendours flung
For his revolt, yet faithful how they stood,
Their glory wither'd, as when heaven's fire
Hath scath'd the forest oaks or mountain pines,
With singed top their stately growth though bare
Stands on the blasted heath. He now prepar'd
To speak, whereat their doubled ranks they bend
From wing to wing and half enclose him round

With all his peers; attention held them mute.
Thrice he essay'd, and thrice, in spite of scorn,
Tears such as angels weep burst forth; at last
Words interwove with sighs found out their way.
  O myriads of immortal spirits, O powers
Matchless but with th'almighty, and that strife
Was not inglorious, though th' event was dire,
As this place testifies, and this dire change
Hateful to utter; but what power of mind,
Foreseeing or presaging from the depth
Of knowledge past and present, could have fear'd
How such united force of gods, how such
As stood like these, could ever know repulse?
For who can yet believe, though after loss,
That all these puissant legions, whose exile
Hath empti'd heaven, shall fail to reascend
Self-rais'd and repossess their native seat?
For me be witness all the host of heaven
If counsels different or danger shunn'd
By me have lost our hopes. But he who reigns
Monarch in heaven till then as one secure
Sat on his throne, upheld by old repute,
Consent or custom, and his regal state
Put forth at full, but still his strength conceal'd,
Which tempted our attempt and wrought our fall.
Henceforth his might we know, and know our own,
So as not either to provoke or dread
New war, provok'd. Our better part remains
To work in close design, by fraud and guile,
What force effected not, that he no less
At length from us may find who overcomes
By force hath overcome but half his foe.
Space may produce new worlds; whereof so rife
There went a fame in heaven that he ere long
Intended to create, and therein plant
A generation whom his choice regard
Should favour equal to the sons of heaven.
Thither, if but to pry, shall be perhaps

Our first eruption, thither or elsewhere;
For this infernal pit shall never hold
Celestial spirits in bondage, nor th' abyss
Long under darkness cover. But these thoughts
Full counsel must mature. Peace is despair'd,
For who can think submission? War then, war
Open or understood must be resolv'd.
  He spake, and to confirm his words out flew
Millions of flaming swords, drawn from the thighs
Of mighty cherubim. The sudden blaze
Far round illumin'd hell; highly they rag'd
Against the highest, and fierce with grasped arms
Clash'd on their sounding shields the din of war,
Hurling defiance toward the vault of heaven.
  There stood a hill not far whose grisly top
Belch'd fire and rolling smoke; the rest entire
Shone with a glossy scurf, undoubted sign
That in his womb was hid metallic ore,
The work of sulphur. Thither wing'd with speed
A num'rous brigade hasten'd, as when bands
Of pioneers with spade and pickaxe arm'd
Forerun the royal camp to trench a field
Or cast a rampart. Mammon led them on,
Mammon, the least erected spirit that fell
From heaven, for ev'n in heaven his looks and thoughts
Were always downward bent, admiring more
The riches of heaven's pavement, trodden gold,
Than ought divine or holy else enjoy'd
In vision beatific. By him first
Men also, and by his suggestion taught,
Ransack'd the centre, and with impious hands
Rifled the bowels of their mother earth
For treasures better hid. Soon had his crew
Open'd into the hill a spacious wound
And digg'd out ribs of gold. Let none admire
That riches grow in hell; that soil may best
Deserve the precious bane. And here let those
Who boast in mortal things, and wondering tell

Of Babel and the works of Memphian kings,
Learn how their greatest monuments of fame
And strength and art are easily outdone
By spirits reprobate, and in an hour
What in an age they with incessant toil
And hands innumerable scarce perform.
Nigh on the plain, in many cells prepar'd
That underneath had veins of liquid fire
Sluic'd from the lake, a second multitude
With wondrous art founded the massy ore,
Severing each kind, and scumm'd the bullion dross.
A third as soon had form'd within the ground
A various mould, and from the boiling cells
By strange conveyance fill'd each hollow nook,
As in an organ from one blast of wind
To many a row of pipes the sound-board breathes.
Anon out of the earth a fabric huge
Rose like an exhalation, with the sound
Of dulcet symphonies and voices sweet,
Built like a temple, where pilasters round
Were set and Doric pillars, overlaid
With golden architrave; nor did there want
Cornice or frieze with bossy sculptures graven;
The roof was fretted gold. Not Babylon
Nor great Alcairo such magnificence
Equall'd in all their glories, to enshrine
Belus or Serapis their gods, or seat
Their kings, when Egypt with Assyria strove
In wealth and luxury. Th' ascending pile
Stood fix'd her stately height, and straight the doors
Op'ning their brazen folds discover wide
Within her ample spaces o'er the smooth
And level pavement. From the arched roof
Pendent by subtle magic many a row
Of starry lamps and blazing cressets fed
With naphtha and asphaltus yielded light
As from a sky. The hasty multitude
Admiring enter'd, and the work some praise
And some the architect; his hand was known

In heaven by many a tower'd structure high
Where scepter'd angels held their residence
And sat as princes, whom the supreme king
Exalted to such power and gave to rule,
Each in his hierarchy, the orders bright.
Nor was his name unheard or unador'd
In ancient Greece, and in Ausonian land
Men call'd him Mulciber, and how he fell
From heaven they fabled, thrown by angry Jove
Sheer o'er the crystal battlements; from morn
To noon he fell, from noon to dewy eve,
A summer's day, and with the setting sun
Dropp'd from the zenith like a falling star
On Lemnos th'Aegaean isle: thus they relate,
Erring; for he with this rebellious rout
Fell long before, nor aught avail'd him now
T'have built in heaven high towers, nor did he scape
By all his engines, but was headlong sent
With his industrious crew to build in hell.
Meanwhile the winged heralds by command
Of sovereign power with awful ceremony
And trumpet's sound throughout the host proclaim
A solemn council forthwith to be held
At Pandaemonium, the high capital
Of Satan and his peers. Their summons call'd
From every band and squared regiment
By place or choice the worthiest; they anon
With hundreds and with thousands trooping came
Attended. All access was throng'd, the gates
And porches wide, but chief the spacious hall
(Though like a cover'd field where champions bold
Wont ride in arm'd, and at the soldan's chair
Defi'd the best of paynim chivalry
To mortal combat or career with lance)
Thick swarm'd both on the ground and in the air,
Brush'd with the hiss of rustling wings, as bees
In springtime, when the sun with Taurus rides,
Pour forth their populous youth about the hive
In clusters; they among fresh dews and flowers

Fly to and fro, or on the smoothed plank,
The suburb of their straw-built citadel
New-rubb'd with balm, expatiate and confer
Their state affairs. So thick the airy crowd
Swarm'd and were straiten'd, till the signal given,
Behold a wonder! they but now who seem'd
In bigness to surpass Earth's giant sons
Now less than smallest dwarfs in narrow room
Throng numberless, like that pygmean race
Beyond the Indian mount, or faerie elves
Whose midnight revels by a forest side
Or fountain some belated peasant sees,
Or dreams he sees, while overhead the moon
Sits arbitress and nearer to the earth
Wheels her pale course, they on their mirth and dance
Intent with jocund music charm his ear;
At once with joy and fear his heart rebounds.
Thus incorporeal spirits to smallest forms
Reduc'd their shapes immense, and were at large
Though without number still amidst the hall
Of that infernal court. But far within,
And in their own dimensions like themselves,
The great seraphic lords and cherubim
In close recess and secret conclave sat,
A thousand demi-gods on golden seats,
Frequent and full. After short silence then
And summons read, the great consult began.

BOOK II

High on a throne of royal state which far
Outshone the wealth of Ormus and of Ind,
Or where the gorgeous East with richest hand
Showers on her kings barbaric pearl and gold,
Satan exalted sat, by merit rais'd
To that bad eminence; and from despair
Thus high uplifted beyond hope aspires
Beyond thus high, insatiate to pursue

Vain war with heaven, and by success untaught
His proud imaginations thus display'd.
  Powers and dominions, deities of heaven,
For since no deep within her gulf can hold
Immortal vigour, though oppress'd and fallen,
I give not heaven for lost. From this descent
Celestial virtues rising will appear
More glorious and more dread than from no fall,
And trust themselves to fear no second fate.
Me though just right and the fix'd laws of heaven
Did first create your leader, next free choice,
With what besides in counsel or in fight
Hath been achiev'd of merit, yet this loss,
Thus far at least recover'd, hath much more
Establish'd in a safe unenvi'd throne
Yielded with full consent. The happier state
In heaven which follows dignity might draw
Envy from each inferior; but who here
Will envy whom the highest place exposes
Foremost to stand against the thunderer's aim
Your bulwark, and condemns to greatest share
Of endless pain? Where there is then no good
For which to strive, no strife can grow up there
From faction; for none sure will claim in hell
Precedence, none whose portion is so small
Of present pain with that ambitious mind
Will covet more. With this advantage then
To union, and firm faith and firm accord
More than can be in heaven, we now return
To claim our just inheritance of old,
Surer to prosper than prosperity
Could have assur'd us; and by what best way,
Whether of open war or covert guile,
We now debate. Who can advise may speak.
  He ceas'd, and next him Moloch, sceptr'd king,
Stood up, the strongest and the fiercest spirit
That fought in heaven, now fiercer by despair.
His trust was with th'eternal to be deem'd
Equal in strength, and rather than be less

Car'd not to be at all. With that care lost
Went all his fear: of God or hell or worse
He reck'd not, and these words thereafter spake.
  My sentence is for open war. Of wiles
More unexpert I boast not; them let those
Contrive who need, or when they need, not now.
For while they sit contriving, shall the rest,
Millions that stand in arms and longing wait
The signal to ascend, sit lingering here
Heaven's fugitives, and for their dwelling place
Accept this dark opprobrious den of shame,
The prison of his tyranny who reigns
By our delay? No, let us rather choose
Arm'd with hell flames and fury all at once
O'er heaven's high towers to force resistless way,
Turning our tortures into horrid arms
Against the torturer, when to meet the noise
Of his almighty engine he shall hear
Infernal thunder, and for lightning see
Black fire and horror shot with equal rage
Among his angels, and his throne itself
Mix'd with Tartarean sulphur and strange fire,
His own invented torments. But perhaps
The way seems difficult and steep to scale
With upright wing against a higher foe?
Let such bethink them, if the sleepy drench
Of that forgetful lake benumb not still,
That in our proper motion we ascend
Up to our native seat: descent and fall
To us is adverse. Who but felt of late,
When the fierce foe hung on our broken rear
Insulting and pursu'd us through the deep,
With what compulsion and laborious flight
We sunk thus low? The ascent is easy, then;
The event is fear'd: should we again provoke
Our stronger, some worse way his wrath may find
To our destruction, if there be in hell
Fear to be worse destroy'd. What can be worse
Than to dwell here, driv'n out from bliss, condemn'd

In this abhorred deep to utter woe,
Where pain of unextinguishable fire
Must exercise us without hope of end,
The vassals of his anger, when the scourge
Inexorably and the torturing hour
Call us to penance? More destroy'd than thus
We should be quite abolish'd and expire.
What fear we then? What doubt we to incense
His utmost ire, which to the height enrag'd
Will either quite consume us and reduce
To nothing this essential, happier far
Than miserable to have eternal being,
Or if our substance be indeed divine
And cannot cease to be, we are at worst
On this side nothing? And by proof we feel
Our power sufficient to disturb his heaven,
And with perpetual inroads to alarm,
Though inaccessible, his fatal throne;
Which, if not victory, is yet revenge.
He ended, frowning, and his look denounc'd
Desperate revenge and battle dangerous
To less than gods. On th' other side up rose
Belial, in act more graceful and humane.
A fairer person lost not heaven; he seem'd
For dignity compos'd and high exploit.
But all was false and hollow, though his tongue
Dropp'd manna and could make the worse appear
The better reason, to perplex and dash
Maturest counsels, for his thoughts were low,
To vice industrious but to nobler deeds
Timorous and slothful. Yet he pleas'd the ear,
And with persuasive accent thus began.
I should be much for open war, O peers,
As not behind in hate, if what was urg'd
Main reason to persuade immediate war
Did not dissuade me most, and seem to cast
Ominous conjecture on the whole success,
When he who most excels in fact of arms,
In what he counsels and in what excels

Mistrustful, grounds his courage on despair
And utter dissolution as the scope
Of all his aim, after some dire revenge.
First, what revenge? The towers of heaven are fill'd
With armed watch that render all access
Impregnable; oft on the bordering deep
Encamp their legions, or with obscure wing
Scout far and wide into the realm of night,
Scorning surprise. Or could we break our way
By force, and at our heels all hell should rise
With blackest insurrection to confound
Heaven's purest light, yet our great enemy
All incorruptible would on his throne
Sit unpolluted, and th'ethereal mould,
Incapable of stain, would soon expel
Her mischief and purge off the baser fire
Victorious. Thus repuls'd, our final hope
Is flat despair: we must exasperate
Th'almighty victor to spend all his rage,
And that must end us, that must be our cure,
To be no more. Sad cure, for who would lose
Though full of pain this intellectual being,
Those thoughts that wander through eternity,
To perish rather, swallow'd up and lost
In the wide womb of uncreated night,
Devoid of sense and motion. And who knows,
Let this be good, whether our angry foe
Can give it, or will ever? How he can
Is doubtful; that he never will is sure.
Will he, so wise, let loose at once his ire,
Belike through impotence or unaware,
To give his enemies their wish and end
Then in his anger, whom his anger saves
To punish endless? Wherefore cease we then?
Say they who counsel war, we are decreed,
Reserv'd and destin'd to eternal woe;
Whatever doing, what can we suffer more,
What can we suffer worse? Is this then worst,

Thus sitting, thus consulting, thus in arms?
What when we fled amain, pursu'd and struck
With heaven's afflicting thunder, and besought
The deep to shelter us? This hell then seem'd
A refuge from those wounds. Or when we lay
Chain'd on the burning lake? That sure was worse.
What if the breath that kindled those grim fires
Awak'd should blow them into sevenfold rage
And plunge us in the flames? Or from above
Should intermitted vengeance arm again
His red right hand to plague us? What if all
Her stores were open'd, and this firmament
Of hell should spout her cataracts of fire,
Impendent horrors, threatening hideous fall
One day upon our heads, while we, perhaps
Designing or exhorting glorious war,
Caught in a fiery tempest shall be hurl'd,
Each on his rock transfix'd, the sport and prey
Of racking whirlwinds, or for ever sunk
Under yon boiling ocean, wrapp'd in chains,
There to converse with everlasting groans
Unrespited, unpitied, unrepriev'd
Ages of hopeless end? This would be worse.
War therefore open or conceal'd alike
My voice dissuades; for what can force or guile
With him, or who deceive his mind, whose eye
Views all things at one view? He from heaven's height
All these our motions vain sees and derides,
Not more almighty to resist our might
Than wise to frustrate all our plots and wiles.
Shall we then live thus vile, the race of heaven
Thus trampl'd, thus expell'd to suffer here
Chains and these torments? Better these than worse
By my advice, since fate inevitable
Subdues us and omnipotent decree,
The victor's will. To suffer, as to do,
Our strength is equal, nor the law unjust
That so ordains; this was at first resolv'd

If we were wise, against so great a foe
Contending, and so doubtful what might fall.
I laugh when those who at the spear are bold
And vent'rous, if that fail them, shrink and fear
What yet they know must follow, to endure
Exile or ignominy or bonds or pain,
The sentence of their conqueror. This is now
Our doom, which if we can sustain and bear,
Our supreme foe in time may much remit
His anger and perhaps, thus far remov'd,
Not mind us not offending, satisfi'd
With what is punish'd; whence these raging fires
Will slacken, if his breath stir not their flames.
Our purer essence then will overcome
Their noxious vapour, or inur'd not feel,
Or chang'd at length and to the place conform'd
In temper and in nature will receive
Familiar the fierce heat and void of pain.
This horror will grow mild, this darkness light;
Besides what hope the never-ending flight
Of future days may bring, what chance, what change
Worth waiting, since our present lot appears
For happy though but ill, for ill not worst
If we procure not to ourselves more woe.
  Thus Belial with words cloth'd in reason's garb
Counsell'd ignoble ease and peaceful sloth,
Not peace; and after him thus Mammon spake.
  Either to disenthrone the king of heaven
We war, if war be best, or to regain
Our own right lost. Him to unthrone we then
May hope when everlasting fate shall yield
To fickle chance, and Chaos judge the strife.
The former vain to hope argues as vain
The latter, for what place can be for us
Within heaven's bound unless heaven's lord supreme
We overpower? Suppose he should relent
And publish grace to all on promise made
Of new subjection? With what eyes could we
Stand in his presence humble and receive

Strict laws impos'd, to celebrate his throne
With warbled hymns and to his godhead sing
Forc'd hallelujahs, while he lordly sits
Our envied sovereign and his altar breathes
Ambrosial odours and ambrosial flowers,
Our servile offerings? This must be our task
In heaven, this our delight; how wearisome
Eternity so spent in worship paid
To whom we hate. Let us not then pursue
By force impossible, by leave obtain'd
Unacceptable though in heaven, our state
Of splendid vassalage, but rather seek
Our own good from ourselves and from our own
Live to ourselves, though in this vast recess,
Free and to none accountable, preferring
Hard liberty before the easy yoke
Of servile pomp. Our greatness will appear
Then most conspicuous when great things of small,
Useful of hurtful, prosperous of adverse
We can create, and in what place soe'er
Thrive under evil and work ease out of pain
Through labour and endurance. This deep world
Of darkness do we dread? How oft amidst
Thick clouds and dark doth heaven's all-ruling sire
Choose to reside, his glory unobscur'd,
And with the majesty of darkness round
Covers his throne, from whence deep thunders roar
Mustering their rage, and heaven resembles hell?
As he our darkness, cannot we his light
Imitate when we please? This desert soil
Wants not her hidden lustre, gems and gold;
Nor want we skill and art from whence to raise
Magnificence; and what can heaven show more?
Our torments also may in length of time
Become our elements, these piercing fires
As soft as now severe, our temper chang'd
Into their temper, which must needs remove
The sensible of pain. All things invite

To peaceful counsels and the settl'd state
Of order, how in safety best we may
Compose our present evils, with regard
Of what we are and where, dismissing quite
All thoughts of war. Ye have what I advise.
  He scarce had finish'd when such murmur fill'd
Th'assembly as when hollow rocks retain
The sound of blust'ring winds which all night long
Had rous'd the sea, now with hoarse cadence lull
Seafaring men o'erwatch'd, whose bark by chance
Or pinnace anchors in a craggy bay
After the tempest; such applause was heard
As Mammon ended, and his sentence pleas'd,
Advising peace. For such another field
They dreaded worse than hell, so much the fear
Of thunder and the sword of Michaël
Wrought still within them, and no less desire
To found this nether empire, which might rise
By policy and long process of time
In emulation opposite to heaven.
Which when Beelzebub perceiv'd, than whom,
Satan except, none higher sat, with grave
Aspect he rose, and in his rising seem'd
A pillar of state. Deep on his front engraven
Deliberation sat and public care,
And princely counsel in his face yet shone,
Majestic though in ruin. Sage he stood
With Atlantean shoulders fit to bear
The weight of mightiest monarchies. His look
Drew audience and attention still as night
Or summer's noontide air while thus he spake.
  Thrones and imperial powers, offspring of heaven,
Ethereal virtues – or these titles now
Must we renounce, and changing style be call'd
Princes of hell? For so the popular vote
Inclines, here to continue and build up here
A growing empire, doubtless; while we dream,
And know not that the king of heaven hath doom'd
This place our dungeon, not our safe retreat

Beyond his potent arm, to live exempt
From heaven's high jurisdiction, in new league
Banded against his throne, but to remain
In strictest bondage though thus far remov'd,
Under th'inevitable curb reserv'd
His captive multitude. For he, be sure,
In height or depth still first and last will reign
Sole king, and of his kingdom lose no part
By our revolt, but over hell extend
His empire and with iron sceptre rule
Us here as with his golden those in heaven.
What sit we then projecting peace and war?
War hath determin'd us and foil'd with loss
Irreparable, terms of peace yet none
Vouchsaf'd or sought; for what peace will be given
To us enslav'd, but custody severe
And stripes and arbitrary punishment
Inflicted? And what peace can we return,
But to our power hostility and hate,
Untam'd reluctance, and revenge though slow
Yet ever plotting how the conqueror least
May reap his conquest and may least rejoice
In doing what we most in suffering feel?
Nor will occasion want, nor shall we need
With dangerous expedition to invade
Heav'n, whose high walls fear no assault or siege
Or ambush from the deep. What if we find
Some easier enterprise? There is a place
(If ancient and prophetic fame in heaven
Err not), another world, the happy seat
Of some new race call'd Man, about this time
To be created like to us, though less
In power and excellence, but favour'd more
Of him who rules above: so was his will
Pronounc'd among the gods, and by an oath
That shook heaven's whole circumference confirm'd.
Thither let us bend all our thoughts, to learn
What creatures there inhabit, of what mould
Or substance, how endu'd, and what their power,

And where their weakness, how attempted best,
By force or subtlety. Though heaven be shut
And heaven's high arbitrator sit secure
In his own strength, this place may lie expos'd
The utmost border of his kingdom, left
To their defence who hold it. Here perhaps
Some advantageous act may be achiev'd
By sudden onset, either with hell fire
To waste his whole creation or possess
All as our own, and drive as we were driven
The puny habitants; or if not drive,
Seduce them to our party, that their God
May prove their foe and with repenting hand
Abolish his own works. This would surpass
Common revenge, and interrupt his joy
In our confusion and our joy upraise
In his disturbance, when his darling sons,
Hurl'd headlong to partake with us, shall curse
Their frail original and faded bliss,
Faded so soon. Advise if this be worth
Attempting, or to sit in darkness here
Hatching vain empires. Thus Beelzebub
Pleaded his devilish counsel, first devis'd
By Satan and in part propos'd; for whence
But from the author of all ill could spring
So deep a malice, to confound the race
Of mankind in one root and earth with hell
To mingle and involve, done all to spite
The great creator? But their spite still serves
His glory to augment. The bold design
Pleas'd highly those infernal states, and joy
Sparkled in all their eyes. With full assent
They vote, whereat his speech he thus renews.
Well have ye judg'd, well ended long debate,
Synod of gods, and like to what ye are,
Great things resolv'd, which from the lowest deep
Will once more lift us up in spite of fate
Nearer our ancient seat, perhaps in view

Of those bright confines, whence with neighbouring arms
And opportune excursion we may chance
Re-enter heav'n, or else in some mild zone
Dwell not unvisited of heaven's fair light
Secure, and at the brightening orient beam
Purge off this gloom; the soft delicious air
To heal the scar of these corrosive fires
Shall breathe her balm. But first, whom shall we send
In search of this new world, whom shall we find
Sufficient? Who shall tempt with wand'ring feet
The dark unbottom'd infinite abyss,
And through the palpable obscure find out
His uncouth way, or spread his airy flight
Upborne with indefatigable wings
Over the vast abrupt ere he arrive
The happy isle? What strength, what art can then
Suffice, or what evasion bear him safe
Through the strict senteries and stations thick
Of angels watching round? Here he had need
All circumspection, and we now no less
Choice in our suffrage; for on whom we send
The weight of all and our last hope relies.
  This said, he sat, and expectation held
His look suspense, awaiting who appear'd
To second or oppose, or undertake
The perilous attempt; but all sat mute,
Pond'ring the danger with deep thoughts, and each
In other's count'nance read his own dismay
Astonish'd. None among the choice and prime
Of those heaven-warring champions could be found
So hardy as to proffer or accept
Alone the dreadful voyage; till at last
Satan, whom now transcendent glory rais'd
Above his fellows, with monarchal pride
Conscious of highest worth unmov'd thus spake.
  O progeny of heaven, empyreal thrones,
With reason hath deep silence and demur
Seiz'd us, though undismay'd. Long is the way

And hard that out of hell leads up to light.
Our prison strong, this huge convex of fire
Outrageous to devour, immures us round
Ninefold, and gates of burning adamant
Barr'd over us prohibit all egress.
These pass'd, if any pass, the void profound
Of unessential night receives him next
Wide gaping and with utter loss of being
Threatens him, plung'd in that abortive gulf.
If thence he scape into whatever world
Or unknown region, what remains him less
Than unknown dangers and as hard escape?
But I should ill become this throne, O peers,
And this imperial sovereignty adorn'd
With splendour, arm'd with power, if aught propos'd
And judg'd of public moment in the shape
Of difficulty or danger could deter
Me from attempting. Wherefore do I assume
These royalties and not refuse to reign,
Refusing to accept as great a share
Of hazard as of honour, due alike
To him who reigns, and so much to him due
Of hazard more as he above the rest
High honour'd sits? Go therefore, mighty powers,
Terror of heaven though fall'n; intend at home,
While here shall be our home, what best may ease
The present misery and render hell
More tolerable, if there be cure or charm
To respite or deceive or slack the pain
Of this ill mansion. Intermit no watch
Against a wakeful foe, while I abroad
Through all the coasts of dark destruction seek
Deliverance for us all. This enterprise
None shall partake with me. Thus saying rose
The monarch, and prevented all reply;
Prudent, lest from his resolution rais'd
Others among the chief might offer now
(Certain to be refus'd) what erst they fear'd,
And so refus'd might in opinion stand

His rivals, winning cheap the high repute
Which he through hazard huge must earn. But they
Dreaded not more th'adventure than his voice
Forbidding, and at once with him they rose.
Their rising all at once was as the sound
Of thunder heard remote. Towards him they bend
With awful reverence prone, and as a god
Extol him equal to the highest in heaven.
Nor fail'd they to express how much they prais'd
That for the general safety he despis'd
His own; for neither do the spirits damn'd
Lose all their virtue, lest bad men should boast
Their specious deeds on earth, which glory excites
Or close ambition varnish'd o'er with zeal.
Thus they their doubtful consultations dark
Ended rejoicing in their matchless chief;
As when from mountain-tops the dusky clouds
Ascending, while the north wind sleeps, o'erspread
Heaven's cheerful face, the louring element
Scowls o'er the darken'd landscape snow or shower,
If chance the radiant sun with farewell sweet
Extend his evening beam, the fields revive,
The birds their notes renew, and bleating herds
Attest their joy that hill and valley rings.
O shame to men! Devil with devil damn'd
Firm concord holds; men only disagree
Of creatures rational, though under hope
Of heavenly grace, and God proclaiming peace
Yet live in hatred, enmity and strife
Among themselves, and levy cruel wars,
Wasting the earth each other to destroy,
As if (which might induce us to accord)
Man had not hellish foes enough besides
That day and night for his destruction wait.
The Stygian counsel thus dissolv'd, and forth
In order came the grand infernal peers;
Midst came their mighty paramount, and seem'd

Alone th'antagonist of heaven, nor less
Than hell's dread emperor with pomp supreme
And god-like imitated state. Him round
A globe of fiery seraphim enclos'd
With bright emblazonry and horrent arms.
Then of their session ended they bid cry
With trumpets' regal sound the great result.
Toward the four winds four speedy cherubim
Put to their mouths the sounding alchemy
By herald's voice explain'd; the hollow abyss
Heard far and wide, and all the host of hell
With deafening shout return'd them loud acclaim.
Thence more at ease their minds and somewhat rais'd
By false presumptuous hope the ranged powers
Disband, and wandering each his several way
Pursues as inclination or sad choice
Leads him perplex'd where he may likeliest find
Truce to his restless thoughts, and entertain
The irksome hours till his great chief return.
Part on the plain or in the air sublime
Upon the wing or in swift race contend
As at th'Olympian games or Pythian fields;
Part curb their fiery steeds, or shun the goal
With rapid wheels, or fronted brigades form,
As when, to warn proud cities, war appears
Wag'd in the troubled sky, and armies rush
To battle in the clouds; before each van
Prick forth the airy knights and couch their spears
Till thickest legions close; with feats of arms
From either end of heaven the welkin burns.
Others with vast Typhoean rage more fell
Rend up both rocks and hills and ride the air
In whirlwind; hell scarce holds the wild uproar,
As when Alcides, from Oechalia crown'd
With conquest, felt th'envenom'd robe and tore
Through pain up by the roots Thessalian pines,
And Lichas from the top of Oeta threw
Into th'Euboeic sea. Others more mild,
Retreated in a silent valley, sing

With notes angelical to many a harp
Their own heroic deeds and hapless fall
By doom of battle, and complain that fate
Free virtue should enthral to force or chance.
Their song was partial, but the harmony
(What could it less when spirits immortal sing?)
Suspended hell, and took with ravishment
The thronging audience. In discourse more sweet
(For eloquence the soul, song charms the sense)
Others apart sat on a hill retir'd
In thoughts more elevate, and reason'd high
Of providence, foreknowledge, will and fate,
Fix'd fate, free will, foreknowledge absolute,
And found no end, in wandering mazes lost.
Of good and evil much they argu'd then,
Of happiness and final misery,
Passion and apathy, and glory and shame;
Vain wisdom all and false philosophy,
Yet with a pleasing sorcery could charm
Pain for a while or anguish, and excite
Fallacious hope or arm th'obdured breast
With stubborn patience as with triple steel.
Another part in squadrons and gross bands
On bold adventure to discover wide
That dismal world, if any clime perhaps
Might yield them easier habitation, bend
Four ways their flying march along the banks
Of four infernal rivers that disgorge
Into the burning lake their baleful streams:
Abhorred Styx the flood of deadly hate,
Sad Acheron of sorrow, black and deep,
Cocytus, nam'd of lamentation loud
Heard on the rueful stream, fierce Phlegethon
Whose waves of torrent fire inflame with rage.
Far off from these a slow and silent stream,
Lethe the river of oblivion, rolls
Her watery labyrinth, whereof who drinks
Forthwith his former state and being forgets,
Forgets both joy and grief, pleasure and pain.

Beyond this flood a frozen continent
Lies dark and wild, beat with perpetual storms
Of whirlwind and dire hail which on firm land
Thaws not, but gathers heap, and ruin seems
Of ancient pile; all else deep snow and ice,
A gulf profound as that Serbonian bog
Betwixt Damiata and Mount Casius old
Where armies whole have sunk. The parching air
Burns frore, and cold performs th'effect of fire.
Thither by Harpy-footed Furies hal'd
At certain revolutions all the damn'd
Are brought, and feel by turns the bitter change
Of fierce extremes, extremes by change more fierce,
From beds of raging fire to starve in ice
Their soft ethereal warmth, and there to pine
Immovable, infix'd and frozen round
Periods of time, thence hurri'd back to fire;
They ferry over this Lethean sound
Both to and fro, their sorrow to augment,
And wish and struggle as they pass to reach
The tempting stream, with one small drop to lose
In sweet forgetfulness all pain and woe,
All in one moment, and so near the brink;
But fate withstands, and to oppose th' attempt
Medusa with Gorgonian terror guards
The ford, and of itself the water flies
All taste of living wight, as once it fled
The lip of Tantalus. Thus roving on
In confus'd march forlorn th'adventurous bands
With shuddering horror pale and eyes aghast
View'd first their lamentable lot, and found
No rest. Through many a dark and dreary vale
They pass'd and many a region dolorous,
O'er many a frozen, many a fiery alp,
Rocks, caves, lakes, fens, bogs, dens, and shades of death,
A universe of death which God by curse
Created evil, for evil only good,
Where all life dies, death lives, and nature breeds
Perverse all monstrous, all prodigious things,

Abominable, inutterable, and worse
Than fables yet have feign'd or fear conceiv'd,
Gorgons and Hydras and Chimeras dire.
  Meanwhile th'adversary of God and man,
Satan, with thoughts inflam'd of highest design
Puts on swift wings and towards the gates of hell
Explores his solitary flight. Sometimes
He scours the right hand coast, sometimes the left,
Now shaves with level wing the deep, then soars
Up to the fiery concave towering high.
As when far off at sea a fleet descri'd
Hangs in the clouds, by equinoctial winds
Close sailing from Bengala or the isles
Of Ternate and Tidore, whence merchants bring
Their spicy drugs, they on the trading flood
Through the wide Ethiopian to the Cape
Ply stemming nightly toward the pole, so seem'd
Far off the flying fiend. At last appear
Hell bounds high reaching to the horrid roof,
And thrice threefold the gates; three folds were brass,
Three iron, three of adamantine rock,
Impenetrable, impal'd with circling fire
Yet unconsum'd. Before the gates there sat
On either side a formidable shape.
The one seem'd woman to the waist, and fair,
But ended foul in many a scaly fold
Voluminous and vast, a serpent arm'd
With mortal sting. About her middle round
A cry of hell hounds never ceasing bark'd
With wide Cerberean mouths full loud and rung
A hideous peal; yet, when they list, would creep,
If aught disturb'd their noise, into her womb
And kennel there, yet there still bark'd and howl'd
Within unseen. Far less abhorr'd than these
Vex'd Scylla bathing in the sea that parts
Calabria from the hoarse Trinacrian shore;
Nor uglier follow the night-hag when, call'd
In secret, riding through the air she comes

Lur'd with the smell of infant blood to dance
With Lapland witches, while the labouring moon
Eclipses at their charms. The other shape,
If shape it might be call'd that shape had none
Distinguishable in member, joint or limb,
Or substance might be call'd that shadow seem'd,
For each seem'd either, black it stood as night,
Fierce as ten Furies, terrible as hell,
And shook a dreadful dart; what seem'd his head
The likeness of a kingly crown had on.
Satan was now at hand, and from his seat
The monster moving onward came as fast
With horrid strides; hell trembled as he strode.
Th'undaunted fiend what this might be admir'd
(Admir'd, not fear'd: God and his son except,
Created thing nought valu'd he nor shunn'd)
And with disdainful look thus first began.
  Whence and what art thou, execrable shape,
That dar'st, though grim and terrible, advance
Thy miscreated foot athwart my way
To yonder gates? Through them I mean to pass,
That be assur'd, without leave ask'd of thee.
Retire, or taste thy folly and learn by proof,
Hell-born, not to contend with spirits of heaven.
  To whom the goblin, full of wrath, repli'd,
Art thou that traitor angel, art thou he
Who first broke peace in heaven and faith till then
Unbroken, and in proud rebellious arms
Drew after him the third part of heaven's sons
Conjur'd against the highest, for which both thou
And they outcast from God are here condemn'd
To waste eternal days in woe and pain?
And reckon'st thou thyself with spirits of heaven,
Hell-doom'd, and breath'st defiance here and scorn
Where I reign king, and, to enrage thee more,
Thy king and lord? Back to thy punishment,
False fugitive, and to thy speed add wings,
Lest with a whip of scorpions I pursue
Thy lingering, or with one stroke of this dart

Strange horror seize thee and pangs unfelt before.
  So spake the grisly terror, and in shape
So speaking and so threat'ning grew tenfold
More dreadful and deform. On th'other side
Incens'd with indignation Satan stood
Unterrifi'd. and like a comet burn'd
That fires the length of Ophiuchus huge
In th'Arctic sky, and from his horrid hair
Shakes pestilence and war. Each at the head
Levell'd his deadly aim. Their fatal hands
No second stroke intend, and such a frown
Each cast at th'other as when two black clouds
With heaven's artillery fraught come rattling on
Over the Caspian, then stand front to front
Hovering a space, till winds the signal blow
To join their dark encounter in mid air.
So frown'd the mighty combatants that hell
Grew darker at their frown, so match'd they stood;
For never but once more was either like
To meet so great a foe. And now great deeds
Had been achiev'd, whereof all hell had rung,
Had not the snaky sorceress that sat
Fast by hell gate and kept the fatal key
Ris'n and with hideous outcry rush'd between.
  O father, what intends thy hand, she cri'd,
Against thy only son? What fury, O son,
Possesses thee to bend that mortal dart
Against thy father's head? And know'st for whom?
For him who sits above and laughs the while
At thee ordain'd his drudge, to execute
Whate'er his wrath, which he calls justice, bids;
His wrath which one day will destroy ye both.
  She spake, and at her words the hellish pest
Forbore; then these to her Satan return'd.
  So strange thy outcry and thy words so strange
Thou interposest that my sudden hand
Prevented spares to tell thee yet by deeds
What it intends, till first I know of thee
What thing thou art, thus double-form'd, and why

In this infernal vale first met thou call'st
Me father, and that phantasm call'st my son.
I know thee not, nor ever saw till now
Sight more detestable than him and thee.
  T'whom thus the portress of hell gate repli'd,
Hast thou forgot me, then, and do I seem
Now in thine eye so foul, once deem'd so fair
In heaven, when at th'assembly and in sight
Of all the seraphim with thee combin'd
In bold conspiracy against heaven's king,
All on a sudden miserable pain
Surpris'd thee? Dim thine eyes and dizzy swum
In darkness, while thy head flames thick and fast
Threw forth, till on the left side op'ning wide,
Likest to thee in shape and countenance bright,
Then shining heavenly fair, a goddess arm'd
Out of thy head I sprung. Amazement seiz'd
All th'host of heaven. Back they recoil'd afraid
At first, and call'd me Sin, and for a sign
Portentous held me; but familiar grown
I pleas'd and with attractive graces won
The most averse, thee chiefly, who full oft
Thyself in me thy perfect image viewing
Becam'st enamour'd, and such joy thou took'st
With me in secret that my womb conceiv'd
A growing burden. Meanwhile war arose,
And fields were fought in heaven, wherein remain'd
(For what could else?) to our almighty foe
Clear victory, to our part loss and rout
Through all the empyrean; down they fell
Driv'n headlong from the pitch of heaven down
Into this deep, and in the general fall
I also; at which time this powerful key
Into my hand was given, with charge to keep
These gates for ever shut, which none can pass
Without my opening. Pensive here I sat
Alone, but long I sat not till my womb,
Pregnant by thee and now excessive grown,
Prodigious motion felt and rueful throes.

At last this odious offspring whom thou seest,
Thine own begotten, breaking violent way
Tore through my entrails, that with fear and pain
Distorted all my nether shape thus grew
Transform'd; but he, my inbred enemy,
Forth issu'd brandishing his fatal dart
Made to destroy. I fled, and cri'd out Death.
Hell trembled at the hideous name and sigh'd
From all her caves, and back resounded Death.
I fled, but he pursu'd, though more it seems
Inflam'd with lust than rage, and swifter far
Me overtook, his mother all dismay'd,
And in embraces forcible and foul
Engendering with me, of that rape begot
These yelling monsters that with ceaseless cry
Surround me, as thou saw'st, hourly conceiv'd
And hourly born, with sorrow infinite
To me, for when they list, into the womb
That bred them they return, and howl and gnaw
My bowels, their repast, then bursting forth
Afresh with conscious terrors vex me round,
That rest or intermission none I find.
Before mine eyes in opposition sits
Grim Death, my son and foe, who sets them on,
And me his parent would full soon devour
For want of other prey, but that he knows
His end with mine involv'd, and knows that I
Should prove a bitter morsel and his bane
Whenever that shall be; so fate pronounc'd.
But thou, O father, I forewarn thee, shun
His deadly arrow, neither vainly hope
To be invulnerable in those bright arms,
Though temper'd heavenly, for that mortal dint
Save he who reigns above none can resist.
She finish'd, and the subtle fiend, his lore
Soon learn'd, now milder and thus answer'd smooth.
Dear daughter, since thou claim'st me for thy sire,
And my fair son here show'st me, the dear pledge

Of dalliance had with thee in heaven and joys
Then sweet, now sad to mention through dire change
Befall'n us unforeseen, unthought of, know
I come no enemy but to set free
From out this dark and dismal house of pain
Both him and thee and all the heavenly host
Of spirits that in our just pretences arm'd
Fell with us from on high. From them I go
This uncouth errand sole, and one for all
Myself expose, with lonely steps to tread
Th'unfounded deep and through the void immense
To search with wandering quest a place foretold
Should be, and by concurring signs ere now
Created vast and round, a place of bliss
In the purlieus of heaven, and therein plac'd
A race of upstart creatures, to supply
Perhaps our vacant room, though more remov'd
Lest heaven, surcharg'd with potent multitude,
Might hap to move new broils. Be this or aught
Than this more secret now design'd I haste
To know, and this once known shall soon return
And bring ye to the place where thou and Death
Shall dwell at ease, and up and down unseen
Wing silently the buxom air embalm'd
With odours; there shall ye be fed and fill'd
Immeasurably, all things shall be your prey.
He ceas'd, for both seem'd highly pleas'd, and Death
Grinn'd horribly a ghastly smile to hear
His famine should be fill'd, and bless'd his maw
Destin'd to that good hour; no less rejoic'd
His mother bad, and thus bespake her sire.
  The key of this infernal pit by due
And by command of heaven's all-powerful king
I keep, by him forbidden to unlock
These adamantine gates; against all force
Death ready stands to interpose his dart,
Fearless to be o'ermatch'd by living might.
But what owe I to his commands above
Who hates me and hath hither thrust me down

Into this gloom of Tartarus profound
To sit in hateful office here confin'd,
Inhabitant of heaven and heavenly born,
Here in perpetual agony and pain,
With terrors and with clamours compass'd round
Of mine own brood that on my bowels feed?
Thou art my father, thou my author, thou
My being gav'st me: whom should I obey
But thee, whom follow? Thou wilt bring me soon
To that new world of light and bliss, among
The gods who live at ease, where I shall reign
At thy right hand voluptuous, as beseems
Thy daughter and thy darling, without end.
  Thus saying from her side the fatal key,
Sad instrument of all our woe, she took,
And towards the gate rolling her bestial train
Forthwith the huge portcullis high updrew
Which but herself, not all the Stygian powers,
Could once have mov'd; then in the keyhole turns
Th' intricate wards, and every bolt and bar
Of massy iron or solid rock with ease
Unfastens. On a sudden open fly
With impetuous recoil and jarring sound
Th' infernal doors and on their hinges grate
Harsh thunder that the lowest bottom shook
Of Erebus. She open'd, but to shut
Excell'd her power; the gates wide open stood,
That with extended wings a banner'd host
Under spread ensigns marching might pass through
With horse and chariots rank'd in loose array;
So wide they stood, and like a furnace mouth
Cast forth redounding smoke and ruddy flame.
Before their eyes in sudden view appear
The secrets of the hoary deep, a dark
Illimitable ocean without bound,
Without dimension, where length, breadth and height
And time and place are lost, where eldest Night
And Chaos, ancestors of Nature, hold
Eternal anarchy amidst the noise

Of endless wars, and by confusion stand.
For hot, cold, moist and dry, four champions fierce,
Strive here for mastery and to battle bring
Their embryon atoms; they around the flag
Of each his faction, in their several clans,
Light-arm'd or heavy, sharp, smooth, swift or slow,
Swarm populous, unnumber'd as the sands
Of Barca or Cyrene's torrid soil,
Levied to side with warring winds and poise
Their lighter wings. To whom these most adhere,
He rules a moment; Chaos umpire sits,
And by decision more embroils the fray,
By which he reigns; next him high arbiter
Chance governs all. Into this wild abyss,
The womb of nature and perhaps her grave,
Of neither sea nor shore nor air nor fire
But all these in their pregnant causes mix'd
Confus'dly, and which thus must ever fight
Unless th'almighty maker them ordain
His dark materials to create more worlds,
Into this wild abyss the wary fiend
Stood on the brink of hell and look'd awhile,
Pondering his voyage, for no narrow frith
He had to cross. Nor was his ear less peal'd
With noises loud and ruinous (to compare
Great things with small) than when Bellona storms
With all her battering engines bent to raze
Some capital city, or less than if this frame
Of heaven were falling and these elements
In mutiny had from her axle torn
The steadfast earth. At last his sail-broad vans
He spreads for flight and in the surging smoke
Uplifted spurns the ground, thence many a league
As in a cloudy chair ascending rides
Audacious, but that seat soon failing meets
A vast vacuity. All unawares
Fluttering his pennons vain plumb down he drops
Ten thousand fathom deep, and to this hour
Down had been falling had not by ill chance

The strong rebuff of some tumultuous cloud
Instinct with fire and nitre hurri'd him
As many miles aloft. That fury stay'd,
Quench'd in a boggy Syrtis, neither sea
Nor good dry land, nigh founder'd on he fares
Treading the crude consistence, half on foot,
Half flying; behoves him now both oar and sail.
As when a gryphon through the wilderness
With winged course o'er hill or moory dale
Pursues the Arimaspian, who by stealth
Had from his wakeful custody purloin'd
The guarded gold, so eagerly the fiend
O'er bog or steep, through straight, rough, dense or rare,
With head, hand, wings or feet pursues his way,
And swims or sinks or wades or creeps or flies.
At length a universal hubbub wild
Of stunning sounds and voices all confus'd
Borne through the hollow dark assaults his ear
With loudest vehemence. Thither he plies,
Undaunted to meet there whatever power
Or spirit of the nethermost abyss
Might in that noise reside, of whom to ask
Which way the nearest coast of darkness lies
Bordering on light, when straight behold the throne
Of Chaos, and his dark pavilion spread
Wide on the wasteful deep. With him enthron'd
Sat sable-vested Night, eldest of things,
The consort of his reign, and by them stood
Orcus and Ades, and the dreaded name
Of Demogorgon; Rumour next, and Chance,
And Tumult and Confusion all embroil'd,
And Discord with a thousand various mouths;
T' whom Satan turning boldly, thus. Ye powers
And spirits of this nethermost abyss,
Chaos and ancient Night, I come no spy
With purpose to explore or to disturb
The secrets of your realm, but by constraint
Wandering this darksome desert, as my way

Lies through your spacious empire up to light,
Alone and without guide, half lost, I seek
What readiest path leads where your gloomy bounds
Confine with heaven; or if some other place
From your dominion won th'ethereal king
Possesses lately, thither to arrive
I travel this profound. Direct my course;
Directed no mean recompense it brings
To your behoof, if I that region lost,
All usurpation thence expell'd, reduce
To her original darkness and your sway,
Which is my present journey, and once more
Erect the standard there of ancient Night.
Yours be th'advantage all, mine the revenge.
Thus Satan; and him thus the anarch old
With falt'ring speech and visage incompos'd
Answer'd. I know thee, stranger, who thou art,
That mighty leading angel who of late
Made head against heaven's king, though overthrown.
I saw and heard, for such a numerous host
Fled not in silence through the frighted deep
With ruin upon ruin, rout on rout,
Confusion worse confounded, and heaven gates
Pour'd out by millions her victorious bands
Pursuing. I upon my frontiers here
Keep residence, if all I can will serve
That little which is left so to defend,
Encroach'd on still through your intestine broils
Weak'ning the sceptre of old Night; first hell
Your dungeon stretching far and wide beneath,
Now lately heaven and earth, another world
Hung o'er my realm, link'd in a golden chain
To that side heaven from whence your legions fell.
If that way be your walk, you have not far,
So much the nearer danger. Go, and speed;
Havoc and spoil and ruin are my gain.
He ceas'd, and Satan stay'd not to reply,
But glad that now his sea should find a shore
With fresh alacrity and force renew'd

Springs upward like a pyramid of fire
Into the wild expanse, and through the shock
Of fighting elements on all sides round
Environ'd wins his way, harder beset
And more endanger'd than when Argo pass'd
Through Bosphorus, betwixt the jostling rocks,
Or when Ulysses on the larboard shunn'd
Charybdis and by th'other whirlpool steer'd.
So he with difficulty and labour hard
Mov'd on, with difficulty and labour he;
But he once past, soon after, when man fell,
Strange alteration! Sin and Death amain
Following his track (such was the will of heaven)
Pav'd after him a broad and beaten way
Over the dark abyss, whose boiling gulf
Tamely endur'd a bridge of wondrous length
From hell continu'd reaching th'utmost orb
Of this frail world, by which the spirits perverse
With easy intercourse pass to and fro
To tempt or punish mortals, except whom
God and good angels guard by special grace.
But now at last the sacred influence
Of light appears, and from the walls of heaven
Shoots far into the bosom of dim Night
A glimmering dawn. Here Nature first begins
Her farthest verge, and Chaos to retire
As from her outmost works a broken foe
With tumult less and with less hostile din,
That Satan with less toil and now with ease
Wafts on the calmer wave by dubious light,
And like a weather-beaten vessel holds
Gladly the port, though shrouds and tackle torn,
Or in the emptier waste, resembling air,
Weighs his spread wings at leisure to behold
Far off th'empyreal heaven extended wide
In circuit, undetermin'd square or round,
With opal towers and battlements adorn'd
Of living sapphire, once his native seat;
And fast by, hanging in a golden chain,

This pendant world, in bigness as a star
Of smallest magnitude close by the moon.
Thither full fraught with mischievous revenge
Accurs'd and in a cursed hour he hies.

BOOK IV

O for that warning voice, which he who saw
Th'apocalypse heard cry in heaven aloud
Then when the dragon, put to second rout,
Came furious down to be reveng'd on men,
"Woe to th'inhabitants on earth!", that now
While time was our first parents had been warn'd
The coming of their secret foe, and scap'd,
Haply so scap'd his mortal snare. For now
Satan, now first inflam'd with rage, came down,
The tempter ere th'accuser of mankind,
To wreak on innocent frail man his loss
Of that first battle and his flight to hell,
Yet not rejoicing in his speed, though bold,
Far off and fearless, nor with cause to boast
Begins his dire attempt, which, nigh the birth
Now rolling, boils in his tumultuous breast
And like a devilish engine back recoils
Upon himself. Horror and doubt distract
His troubled thoughts and from the bottom stir
The hell within him, for within him hell
He brings, and round about him, nor from hell
One step no more than from himself can fly
By change of place. Now conscience wakes despair
That slumber'd, wakes the bitter memory
Of what he was, what is, and what must be
Worse: of worse deeds worse suffering must ensue.
Sometimes towards Eden, which now in his view
Lay pleasant, his griev'd look he fixes sad,
Sometimes towards heaven and the full-blazing sun
Which now sat high in his meridian tower;
Then, much revolving, thus in sighs began.

O thou that with surpassing glory crown'd
Look'st from thy sole dominion like the god
Of this new world, at whose sight all the stars
Hide their diminish'd heads, to thee I call,
But with no friendly voice, and add thy name,
O sun, to tell thee how I hate thy beams
That bring to my remembrance from what state
I fell, how glorious once above thy sphere,
Till pride and worse ambition threw me down,
Warring in heaven against heaven's matchless king;
Ah, wherefore? He deserv'd no such return
From me, whom he created what I was
In that bright eminence, and with his good
Upbraided none. Nor was his service hard:
What could be less than to afford him praise,
The easiest recompense, and pay him thanks,
How due? Yet all his good prov'd ill in me
And wrought but malice; lifted up so high
I 'sdeign'd subjection, and thought one step higher
Would set me highest and in a moment quit
The debt immense of endless gratitude
So burdensome still paying, still to owe,
Forgetful what from him I still receiv'd,
And understood not that a grateful mind
By owing owes not but still pays, at once
Indebted and discharg'd, what burden then?
O had his powerful destiny ordain'd
Me some inferior angel, I had stood
Then happy; no unbounded hope had rais'd
Ambition. Yet why not? Some other power
As great might have aspir'd, and me though mean
Drawn to his part. But other powers as great
Fell not, but stand unshaken, from within
Or from without to all temptations arm'd.
Hadst thou the same free will and power to stand?
Thou hadst; whom hast thou then or what to accuse
But heaven's free love, dealt equally to all?
Be then his love accurs'd, since, love or hate
To me alike, it deals eternal woe.

Nay, curs'd be thou, since against his thy will
Chose freely what it now so justly rues.
Me miserable! Which way shall I fly
Infinite wrath and infinite despair?
Which way I fly is hell, myself am hell,
And in the lowest deep a lower deep
Still threat'ning to devour me opens wide,
To which the hell I suffer seems a heaven.
O then at last relent. Is there no place
Left for repentance, none for pardon left?
None left but by submission, and that word
Disdain forbids me and my dread of shame
Among the spirits beneath, whom I seduc'd
With other promises and other vaunts
Than to submit, boasting I could subdue
Th' omnipotent. Ay me, they little know
How dearly I abide that boast so vain,
Under what torments inwardly I groan.
While they adore me on the throne of hell
With diadem and sceptre high advanc'd,
The lower still I fall, only supreme
In misery. Such joy ambition finds.
But say I could repent, and could obtain
By act of grace my former state, how soon
Would height recall high thoughts, how soon unsay
What feign'd submission swore? Ease would recant
Vows made in pain as violent and void,
For never can true reconcilement grow
Where wounds of deadly hate have pierc'd so deep;
Which would but lead me to a worse relapse
And heavier fall. So should I purchase dear
Short intermission bought with double smart.
This knows my punisher; therefore as far
From granting he as I from begging peace.
All hope excluded thus, behold in stead
Of us outcast, exil'd, his new delight
Mankind created, and for him this world.
So farewell hope, and with hope farewell fear,

Farewell remorse. All good to me is lost.
Evil be thou my good; by thee at least
Divided empire with heaven's king I hold
By thee, and more than half perhaps will reign,
As man ere long and this new world shall know.
  Thus while he spake, each passion dimm'd his face
Thrice-chang'd with pale, ire, envy and despair,
Which marr'd his borrow'd visage and betray'd
Him counterfeit, if any eye beheld,
For heavenly minds from such distempers foul
Are ever clear. Whereof he soon aware
Each perturbation smooth'd with outward calm,
Artificer of fraud, and was the first
That practis'd falsehood, under saintly show
Deep malice to conceal, couch'd with revenge;
Yet not enough had practis'd to deceive
Uriel, once warn'd, whose eye pursu'd him down
The way he went, and on th'Assyrian mount
Saw him disfigur'd more than could befall
Spirit of happy sort. His gestures fierce
He mark'd and mad demeanour, then alone,
As he suppos'd, all unobserv'd, unseen.
So on he fares and to the border comes
Of Eden, where delicious Paradise
Now nearer crowns with her enclosure green
As with a rural mound the champaign head
Of a steep wilderness, whose hairy sides
With thicket overgrown, grotesque and wild,
Access deni'd; and overhead up grew
Insuperable height of loftiest shade,
Cedar and pine and fir and branching palm,
A sylvan scene, and, as the ranks ascend
Shade above shade, a woody theatre
Of stateliest view. Yet higher than their tops
The verdurous wall of Paradise up sprung,
Which to our general sire gave prospect large
Into his nether empire neighbouring round;
And higher than that wall a circling row
Of goodliest trees loaden with fairest fruit,

Blossoms and fruits at once of golden hue
Appear'd, with gay enamell'd colours mix'd,
On which the sun more glad impress'd his beams
Than in fair evening cloud or humid bow
When God hath shower'd the earth. So lovely seem'd
That landscape; and of pure now purer air
Meets his approach, and to the heart inspires
Vernal delight and joy, able to drive
All sadness but despair. Now gentle gales
Fanning their odoriferous wings dispense
Native perfumes, and whisper whence they stole
Those balmy spoils, as when to them who sail
Beyond the Cape of Hope and now are past
Mozambique off at sea north-east winds blow
Sabean odours from the spicy shore
Of Araby the blest; with such delay
Well pleas'd they slack their course, and many a league
Cheer'd with the grateful smell old Ocean smiles.
So entertain'd those odorous sweets the fiend
Who came their bane, though with them better pleas'd
Than Asmodeus with the fishy fume
That drove him though enamour'd from the spouse
Of Tobit's son, and with a vengeance sent
From Media post to Egypt, there fast bound.
  Now to th' ascent of that steep savage hill
Satan had journey'd on, pensive and slow,
But further way found none, so thick entwin'd
As one continu'd brake the undergrowth
Of shrubs and tangling bushes had perplex'd
All path of man or beast that pass'd that way.
One gate there only was, and that look'd east
On th'other side, which when th' arch-felon saw
Due entrance he disdain'd and in contempt
At one slight bound high over-leap'd all bound
Of hill or highest wall, and sheer within
Lights on his feet. As when a prowling wolf
Whom hunger drives to seek new haunt for prey,
Watching where shepherds pen their flocks at eve
In hurdl'd cotes amid the field secure,

Leaps o'er the fence with ease into the fold,
Or as a thief, bent to unhoard the cash
Of some rich burgher whose substantial doors,
Cross-barr'd and bolted fast, fear no assault,
In at the window climbs or o'er the tiles,
So clomb this first grand thief into God's fold;
So since into his church lewd hirelings climb.
Thence up he flew, and on the tree of life,
The middle tree and highest there that grew,
Sat like a cormorant; yet not true life
Thereby regain'd, but sat devising death
To them who liv'd, nor on the virtue thought
Of that life-giving plant, but only us'd
For prospect what well us'd had been the pledge
Of immortality. So little knows
Any but God alone to value right
The good before him, but perverts best things
To worst abuse, or to their meanest use.
Beneath him with new wonder now he views
To all delight of human sense expos'd
In narrow room nature's whole wealth, yea more,
A heaven on earth, for blissful Paradise
Of God the garden was, by him in th'east
Of Eden planted. Eden stretch'd her line
From Auran eastward to the royal towers
Of great Seleucia, built by Grecian kings,
Or where the sons of Eden long before
Dwelt in Telassar. In this pleasant soil
His far more pleasant garden God ordain'd;
Out of the fertile ground he caus'd to grow
All trees of noblest kind for sight, smell, taste,
And all amid them stood the tree of life
High eminent, blooming ambrosial fruit
Of vegetable gold; and next to life
Our death, the tree of knowledge, grew fast by,
Knowledge of good bought dear by knowing ill.
Southward through Eden went a river large,
Nor chang'd his course, but through the shaggy hill
Pass'd underneath engulf'd, for God had thrown

That mountain as his garden mould high-rais'd
Upon the rapid current, which through veins
Of porous earth with kindly thirst up drawn
Rose a fresh fountain and with many a rill
Water'd the garden, thence united fell
Down the steep glade, and met the nether flood
Which from his darksome passage now appears,
And now divided into four main streams
Runs diverse, wand'ring many a famous realm
And country whereof here needs no account;
But rather to tell how, if art could tell,
How from that sapphire fount the crisped brooks
Rolling on orient pearl and sands of gold
With mazy error under pendant shades
Ran nectar, visiting each plant, and fed
Flowers worthy of Paradise, which not nice art
In beds and curious knots but nature boon
Pour'd forth profuse on hill and dale and plain,
Both where the morning sun first warmly smote
The open field and where the unpierced shade
Embrown'd the noontide bowers. Thus was this place,
A happy rural seat of various view:
Groves whose rich trees wept odorous gums and balm;
Others whose fruit burnish'd with golden rind
Hung amiable, Hesperian fables true,
If true, here only, and of delicious taste;
Betwixt them lawns or level downs and flocks
Grazing the tender herb were interpos'd,
Or palmy hillock or the flowery lap
Of some irriguous valley spread her store,
Flowers of all hue and without thorn the rose;
Another side umbrageous grots and caves
Of cool recess, o'er which the mantling vine
Lays forth her purple grape and gently creeps
Luxuriant; meanwhile murmuring waters fall
Down the slope hills dispers'd, or in a lake,
That to the fringed bank with myrtle crown'd
Her crystal mirror holds, unite their streams;

The birds their choir apply; airs, vernal airs
Breathing the smell of field and grove attune
The trembling leaves, while universal Pan
Knit with the Graces and the Hours in dance
Led on th'eternal spring. Not that fair field
Of Enna, where Proserpine gathering flowers
Herself a fairer flower by gloomy Dis
Was gather'd, which cost Ceres all that pain
To seek her through the world, nor that sweet grove
Of Daphne, by Orontes and th'inspir'd
Castalian spring, might with this Paradise
Of Eden strive, nor that Nyseian isle
Girt with the river Triton where old Cham,
Whom Gentiles Ammon call and Libyan Jove,
Hid Amalthea and her florid son
Young Bacchus from his stepdame Rhea's eye;
Nor where Abassin kings their issue guard,
Mount Amara, though this by some suppos'd
True Paradise, under the Ethiop line
By Nilus' head, enclos'd with shining rock
A whole day's journey high; but wide remote
From this Assyrian garden, where the fiend
Saw undelighted all delight, all kind
Of living creatures new to sight and strange.
Two of far nobler shape, erect and tall,
Godlike erect, with naked honour clad
In naked majesty seem'd lords of all,
And worthy seem'd, for in their looks divine
The image of their glorious maker shone,
Truth, wisdom, sanctitude severe and pure,
Severe but in true filial freedom plac'd,
Whence true authority in men; though both
Not equal, as their sex not equal seem'd:
For contemplation he and valour form'd,
For softness she and sweet attractive grace,
He for God only, she for God in him.
His fair large front and eye sublime declar'd
Absolute rule, and hyacinthine locks
Round from his parted forelock manly hung

Clustering, but not beneath his shoulders broad;
She as a veil down to the slender waist
Her unadorned golden tresses wore
Dishevell'd, but in wanton ringlets wav'd
As the vine curls her tendrils, which impli'd
Subjection, but requir'd with gentle sway
And by her yielded, by him best receiv'd
Yielded with coy submission, modest pride
And sweet reluctant amorous delay.
Nor those mysterious parts were then conceal'd,
Then was not guilty shame; dishonest shame
Of nature's works, honour dishonourable,
Sin-bred, how have ye troubl'd all mankind
With shows instead, mere shows of seeming pure,
And banish'd from man's life his happiest life,
Simplicity and spotless innocence.
So pass'd they naked on, nor shunn'd the sight
Of God or angel, for they thought no ill;
So hand in hand they pass'd, the loveliest pair
That ever since in love's embraces met,
Adam the goodliest man of men since born
His sons, the fairest of her daughters Eve.
Under a tuft of shade that on a green
Stood whispering soft by a fresh fountain side
They sat them down, and after no more toil
Of their sweet gardening labour than suffic'd
To recommend cool zephyr and made ease
More easy, wholesome thirst and appetite
More grateful, to their supper fruits they fell,
Nectarine fruits which the compliant boughs
Yielded them, sidelong as they sat recline
On the soft downy bank damask'd with flowers.
The savoury pulp they chew, and in the rind
Still as they thirsted scoop the brimming stream;
Nor gentle purpose nor endearing smiles
Wanted, nor youthful dalliance, as beseems
Fair couple link'd in happy nuptial league
Alone as they. About them frisking play'd

All beasts of th'earth, since wild and of all chase
In wood or wilderness, forest or den.
Sporting the lion ramp'd, and in his paw
Dandl'd the kid; bears, tigers, ounces, pards
Gamboll'd before them; th'unwieldy elephant
To make them mirth us'd all his might, and wreath'd
His lithe proboscis; close the serpent sly
Insinuating wove with Gordian twine
His braided train, and of his fatal guile
Gave proof unheeded. Others on the grass
Couch'd, and now fill'd with pasture gazing sat
Or bedward ruminating; for the sun
Declin'd was hasting now with prone career
To th'Ocean isles, and in th'ascending scale
Of heaven the stars that usher evening rose,
When Satan still in gaze, as first he stood,
Scarce thus at length fail'd speech recover'd sad.
  O hell! What do mine eyes with grief behold?
Into our room of bliss thus high advanc'd
Creatures of other mould, earth-born perhaps,
Not spirits, yet to heavenly spirits bright
Little inferior, whom my thoughts pursue
With wonder, and could love, so lively shines
In them divine resemblance and such grace
The hand that form'd them on their shape hath pour'd.
Ah gentle pair, ye little think how nigh
Your change approaches, when all these delights
Will vanish and deliver ye to woe,
More woe, the more your taste is now of joy;
Happy, but for so happy ill-secur'd
Long to continue, and this high seat your heaven
Ill-fenc'd for heaven to keep out such a foe
As now is enter'd; yet no purpos'd foe
To you, whom I could pity thus forlorn,
Though I unpiti'd. League with you I seek
And mutual amity so strait, so close
That I with you must dwell or you with me
Henceforth. My dwelling haply may not please

Like this fair Paradise your sense, yet such
Accept your maker's work; he gave it me,
Which I as freely give. Hell shall unfold
To entertain you two her widest gates
And send forth all her kings; there will be room,
Not like these narrow limits, to receive
Your numerous offspring. If no better place,
Thank him who puts me loth to this revenge
On you who wrong'd me not for him who wrong'd;
And should I at your harmless innocence
Melt, as I do, yet public reason just,
Honour, and empire with revenge enlarg'd
With conquering this new world compels me now
To do what else though damn'd I should abhor.
So spake the fiend, and with necessity,
The tyrant's plea, excus'd his devilish deeds.
Then from his lofty stand on that high tree
Down he alights among the sportful herd
Of those four-footed kinds, himself now one,
Now other, as their shape serv'd best his end
Nearer to view his prey and unespi'd
To mark what of their state he more might learn
By word or action mark'd. About them round
A lion now he stalks with fiery glare,
Then as a tiger, who by chance hath spi'd
In some purlieu two gentle fawns at play,
Straight couches close, then rising changes oft
His couchant watch, as one who chose his ground
Whence rushing he might surest seize them both
Grip'd in each paw; when Adam first of men
To first of women Eve thus moving speech
Turn'd him all ear to hear new utterance flow.
Sole partner and sole part of all these joys,
Dearer thyself than all, needs must the power
That made us, and for us this ample world,
Be infinitely good, and of his good
As liberal and free as infinite,
That rais'd us from the dust and plac'd us here
In all this happiness who at his hand

Have nothing merited nor can perform
Aught whereof he hath need, he who requires
From us no other service than to keep
This one, this easy charge, of all the trees
In Paradise that bear delicious fruit
So various, not to taste that only tree
Of knowledge, planted by the tree of life.
So near grows death to life, what e'er death is;
Some dreadful thing, no doubt, for well thou know'st
God hath pronounc'd it death to taste that tree,
The only sign of our obedience left
Among so many signs of power and rule
Conferr'd upon us and dominion given
Over all other creatures that possess
Earth, air and sea. Then let us not think hard
One easy prohibition, who enjoy
Free leave so large to all things else, and choice
Unlimited of manifold delights,
But let us ever praise him and extol
His bounty, following our delightful task
To prune these growing plants and tend these flowers,
Which were it toilsome, yet with thee were sweet.
To whom thus Eve repli'd. O thou for whom
And from whom I was form'd flesh of thy flesh
And without whom am to no end, my guide
And head, what thou hast said is just and right,
For we to him indeed all praises owe
And daily thanks, I chiefly who enjoy
So far the happier lot, enjoying thee
Pre-eminent by so much odds, while thou
Like consort to thyself canst nowhere find.
That day I oft remember, when from sleep
I first awak'd and found myself repos'd
Under a shade of flowers, much wondering where
And what I was, whence thither brought and how.
Not distant far from thence a murmuring sound
Of waters issu'd from a cave and spread
Into a liquid plain, then stood unmov'd
Pure as th'expanse of heaven; I thither went

With unexperienc'd thought, and laid me down
On the green bank to look into the clear
Smooth lake that to me seem'd another sky.
As I bent down to look, just opposite
A shape within the watery gleam appear'd
Bending to look on me; I started back,
It started back, but pleas'd I soon return'd,
Pleas'd it return'd as soon with answering looks
Of sympathy and love. There I had fix'd
Mine eyes till now and pin'd with vain desire,
Had not a voice thus warn'd me, What thou seest,
What there thou seest, fair creature, is thyself,
With thee it came and goes; but follow me
And I will bring thee where no shadow stays
Thy coming and thy soft embraces. He
Whose image thou art, him thou shalt enjoy
Inseparably thine, to him shalt bear
Multitudes like thyself, and thence be call'd
Mother of human race. What could I do
But follow straight, invisibly thus led?
Till I espi'd thee, fair indeed and tall,
Under a platan, yet methought less fair,
Less winning soft, less amiably mild
Than that smooth watery image. Back I turn'd,
Thou following cri'dst aloud, Return, fair Eve,
Whom fly'st thou? Whom thou fly'st, of him thou art,
His flesh, his bone. To give thee being I lent
Out of my side to thee nearest my heart
Substantial life, to have thee by my side
Henceforth an individual solace dear.
Part of my soul I seek thee, and thee claim
My other half. With that thy gentle hand
Seiz'd mine, I yielded, and from that time see
How beauty is excell'd by manly grace
And wisdom, which alone is truly fair.
So spake our general mother, and with eyes
Of conjugal attraction unreprov'd
And meek surrender half-embracing lean'd
On our first father; half her swelling breast

Naked met his under the flowing gold
Of her loose tresses hid. He in delight
Both of her beauty and submissive charms
Smil'd with superior love, as Jupiter
On Juno smiles when he impregns the clouds
That shed May flowers, and press'd her matron lip
With kisses pure. Aside the devil turn'd
For envy, yet with jealous leer malign
Ey'd them askance, and to himself thus plain'd.
  Sight hateful, sight tormenting! Thus these two
Imparadis'd in one another's arms,
The happier Eden, shall enjoy their fill
Of bliss on bliss while I to hell am thrust,
Where neither joy nor love but fierce desire,
Among our other torments not the least,
Still unfulfill'd with pain of longing pines.
Yet let me not forget what I have gain'd
From their own mouths. All is not theirs, it seems.
One fatal tree there stands, of knowledge call'd,
Forbidden them to taste. Knowledge forbidden?
Suspicious, reasonless. Why should their lord
Envy them that? Can it be sin to know?
Can it be death? And do they only stand
By ignorance, is that their happy state,
The proof of their obedience and their faith?
O fair foundation laid whereon to build
Their ruin! Hence I will excite their minds
With more desire to know, and to reject
Envious commands, invented with design
To keep them low whom knowledge might exalt
Equal with gods. Aspiring to be such,
They taste and die; what likelier can ensue?
But first with narrow search I must walk round
This garden, and no corner leave unspi'd;
A chance, but chance may lead where I may meet
Some wand'ring spirit of heaven, by fountain side
Or in thick shade retir'd, from him to draw
What further would be learn'd. Live while ye may,

Yet happy pair; enjoy till I return
Short pleasures, for long woes are to succeed.
So saying, his proud step he scornful turn'd,
But with sly circumspection, and began
Through wood, through waste, o'er hill, o'er dale his roam.
Meanwhile in utmost longitude, where heaven
With earth and ocean meets, the setting sun
Slowly descended and with right aspect
Against the eastern gate of Paradise
Levell'd his evening rays. It was a rock
Of alabaster, pil'd up to the clouds,
Conspicuous far, winding with one ascent
Accessible from earth, one entrance high;
The rest was craggy cliff that overhung
Still as it rose, impossible to climb.
Betwixt these rocky pillars Gabriel sat,
Chief of th'angelic guards, awaiting night.
About him exercis'd heroic games
Th'unarmed youth of heaven, but nigh at hand
Celestial armoury, shields, helms and spears,
Hung high with diamond flaming and with gold.
Thither came Uriel gliding through the even
On a sunbeam, swift as a shooting star
In autumn thwarts the night, when vapours fir'd
Impress the air, and shows the mariner
From what point of his compass to beware
Impetuous winds. He thus began in haste.
Gabriel, to thee thy course by lot hath giv'n
Charge and strict watch that to this happy place
No evil thing approach or enter in.
This day at height of noon came to my sphere
A spirit, zealous, as he seem'd, to know
More of th'almighty's works, and chiefly man,
God's latest image. I describ'd his way
Bent all on speed, and mark'd his airy gait,
But in the mount that lies from Eden north,
Where he first lighted, soon discern'd his looks
Alien from heaven, with passions foul obscur'd.
Mine eye pursu'd him still, but under shade

Lost sight of him. One of the banish'd crew
I fear hath ventur'd from the deep to raise
New troubles; him thy care must be to find.
  To whom the winged warrior thus return'd.
Uriel, no wonder if thy perfect sight
Amid the sun's bright circle where thou sitst
See far and wide. In at this gate none pass
The vigilance here plac'd but such as come
Well known from heaven, and since meridian hour
No creature thence. If spirit of other sort
So minded have o'erleap'd these earthy bounds
On purpose, hard thou knowst it to exclude
Spiritual substance with corporeal bar.
But if within the circuit of these walks
In whatsoever shape he lurk of whom
Thou tell'st, by morrow dawning I shall know.
  So promis'd he, and Uriel to his charge
Return'd on that bright beam, whose point now rais'd
Bore him slope downward to the sun now fallen
Beneath th'Azores, whither the prime orb,
Incredible how quick, had thither roll'd
Diurnal, or this less voluble earth
By shorter flight to th'east had left him there
Arraying with reflected purple and gold
The clouds that on his western throne attend.
Now came still evening on, and twilight grey
Had in her sober livery all things clad;
Silence accompanied, for beast and bird,
They to their grassy couch, these to their nests
Were slunk, all but the wakeful nightingale;
She all night long her amorous descant sung.
Silence was pleas'd. Now glow'd the firmament
With living sapphires; Hesperus that led
The starry host rode brightest, till the moon,
Rising in clouded majesty, at length
Apparent queen unveil'd her peerless light
And o'er the dark her silver mantle threw;
When Adam thus to Eve. Fair consort, th' hour
Of night and all things now retir'd to rest

Mind us of like repose, since God hath set
Labour and rest as day and night to men
Successive, and the timely dew of sleep
Now falling with soft slumbrous weight inclines
Our eyelids. Other creatures all day long
Rove idle unemploy'd, and less need rest.
Man hath his daily work of body or mind
Appointed, which declares his dignity
And the regard of heaven on all his ways,
While other animals unactive range
And of their doings God takes no account.
Tomorrow, ere fresh morning streak the east
With first approach of light, we must be ris'n
And at our pleasant labour, to reform
Yon flowery arbours, yonder alleys green,
Our walk at noon, with branches overgrown
That mock our scant manuring and require
More hands than ours to lop their wanton growth.
Those blossoms also and those dropping gums
That lie bestrewn unsightly and unsmooth
Ask riddance, if we mean to tread with ease.
Meanwhile, as nature wills, night bids us rest.
  To whom thus Eve, with perfect beauty adorn'd.
My author and disposer, what thou bidd'st
Unargu'd I obey. So God ordains;
God is thy law, thou mine. To know no more
Is woman's happiest knowledge and her praise.
With thee conversing I forget all time,
All seasons and their change, all please alike.
Sweet is the breath of morn, her rising sweet
With charm of earliest birds; pleasant the sun
When first on this delightful land he spreads
His orient beams, on herb, tree, fruit and flower
Glist'ring with dew; fragrant the fertile earth
After soft showers, and sweet the coming on
Of grateful evening mild, then silent night
With this her solemn bird and this fair moon
And these the gems of heaven, her starry train.
But neither breath of morn when she ascends

With charm of earliest birds, nor rising sun
On this delightful land, nor herb, fruit, flower
Glist'ring with dew, nor fragrance after showers,
Nor grateful evening mild, nor silent night
With this her solemn bird, nor walk by moon
Or glittering starlight without thee is sweet.
But wherefore all night long shine these, for whom
This glorious sight, when sleep hath shut all eyes?
  To whom our general ancestor repli'd.
Daughter of God and man, accomplish'd Eve,
Those have their course to finish round the earth
By morrow evening, and from land to land
In order, though to nations yet unborn
Minist'ring light prepar'd, they set and rise,
Lest total darkness should by night regain
Her old possession and extinguish life
In nature and all things, which these soft fires
Not only enlighten but with kindly heat
Of various influence foment and warm,
Temper or nourish or in part shed down
Their stellar virtue on all kinds that grow
On earth, made apter hereby to receive
Perfection from the sun's more potent ray.
These then, though unbeheld in deep of night,
Shine not in vain; nor think, though men were none,
That heaven would want spectators, God want praise.
Millions of spiritual creatures walk the earth
Unseen, both when we wake and when we sleep;
All these with ceaseless praise his works behold
Both day and night. How often from the steep
Of echoing hill or thicket have we heard
Celestial voices to the midnight air,
Sole or responsive each to other's note,
Singing their great creator? Oft in bands
While they keep watch or nightly rounding walk,
With heavenly touch of instrumental sounds
In full harmonic number join'd their songs
Divide the night, and lift our thoughts to heaven.

Thus talking hand in hand alone they pass'd
On to their blissful bower. It was a place
Chos'n by the sovereign planter when he fram'd
All things to man's delightful use; the roof
Of thickest covert was inwoven shade,
Laurel and myrtle and what higher grew
Of firm and fragrant leaf; on either side
Acanthus and each odorous bushy shrub
Fenc'd up the verdant wall; each beauteous flower,
Iris all hues, roses and jessamine
Rear'd high their flourish'd heads between and wrought
Mosaic; underfoot the violet,
Crocus and hyacinth with rich inlay
Broider'd the ground, more colour'd than with stone
Of costliest emblem. Other creature here,
Beast, bird, insect or worm durst enter none,
Such was their awe of man. In shady bower
More sacred and sequester'd, though but feign'd,
Pan or Silvanus never slept, nor nymph
Nor Faunus haunted. Here in close recess
With flowers, garlands and sweet-smelling herbs
Espoused Eve deck'd first her nuptial bed,
And heavenly choirs the hymenean sung
What day the genial angel to our sire
Brought her in naked beauty more adorn'd,
More lovely than Pandora, whom the gods
Endow'd with all their gifts; and O, too like
In sad event, when to th'unwiser son
Of Japhet brought by Hermes she ensnar'd
Mankind with her fair looks, to be aveng'd
On him who had stole Jove's authentic fire.
  Thus at their shady lodge arriv'd both stood,
Both turn'd, and under open sky ador'd
The God that made both sky, air, earth and heaven
Which they beheld, the moon's resplendent globe
And starry pole: Thou also mad'st the night,
Maker omnipotent, and thou the day
Which we in our appointed work employ'd
Have finish'd happy in our mutual help

And mutual love, the crown of all our bliss
Ordain'd by thee, and this delicious place
For us too large, where thy abundance wants
Partakers and uncropp'd falls to the ground.
But thou hast promis'd from us two a race
To fill the earth, who shall with us extol
Thy goodness infinite both when we wake
And when we seek, as now, thy gift of sleep.
  This said unanimous, and other rites
Observing none but adoration pure
Which God likes best, into their inmost bower
Handed they went and, eas'd the putting off
These troublesome disguises which we wear,
Straight side by side were laid; nor turn'd I ween
Adam from his fair spouse, nor Eve the rites
Mysterious of connubial love refus'd,
Whatever hypocrites austerely talk
Of purity and place and innocence,
Defaming as impure what God declares
Pure and commands to some, leaves free to all.
Our maker bids increase, who bids abstain
But our destroyer, foe to God and man?
Hail wedded love, mysterious law, true source
Of human offspring, sole propriety
In Paradise of all things common else.
By thee adulterous lust was driv'n from men
Among the bestial herds to range; by thee
Founded in reason, loyal, just and pure
Relations dear and all the charities
Of father, son and brother first were known.
Far be it that I should write thee sin or blame
Or think thee unbefitting holiest place,
Perpetual fountain of domestic sweets,
Whose bed is undefil'd and chaste pronounc'd
Present or past, as saints and patriarchs us'd.
Here Love his golden shafts employs, here lights
His constant lamp and waves his purple wings,
Reigns here and revels, not in the bought smile
Of harlots, loveless, joyless, unendear'd

Casual fruition, nor in court amours,
Mix'd dance or wanton mask or midnight ball,
Or serenade which the starv'd lover sings
To his proud fair, best quitted with disdain.
These lull'd by nightingales embracing slept,
And on their naked limbs the flowery roof
Shower'd roses, which the morn repair'd. Sleep on,
Bless'd pair, and O yet happiest if ye seek
No happier state, and know to know no more.
  Now had night measur'd with her shadowy cone
Half way uphill this vast sublunar vault,
And from their ivory port the cherubim
Forth issuing at th'accustom'd hour stood arm'd
To their night watches in warlike parade,
When Gabriel to his next in power thus spake.
  Uzziel, half these draw off and coast the south
With strictest watch; these other wheel the north,
Our circuit meets full west. As flame they part,
Half wheeling to the shield, half to the spear.
From these, two strong and subtle spirits he call'd
That near him stood, and gave them thus in charge.
  Ithuriel and Zephon, with wing'd speed
Search through this garden, leave unsearch'd no nook,
But chiefly where those two fair creatures lodge,
Now laid perhaps asleep secure of harm.
This evening from the sun's decline arriv'd
Who tells of some infernal spirit seen
Hitherward bent (who could have thought?) escap'd
The bars of hell, on errand bad no doubt.
Such where ye find seize fast, and hither bring.
  So saying, on he led his radiant files,
Dazzling the moon. These to the bower direct
In search of whom they sought, him there they found
Squat like a toad, close at the ear of Eve,
Assaying by his devilish art to reach
The organs of her fancy and with them forge
Illusions as he list, phantasms and dreams,
Or if, inspiring venom, he might taint
The animal spirits that from pure blood arise

Like gentle breaths from rivers pure, thence raise
At least distemper'd, discontented thoughts,
Vain hopes, vain aims, inordinate desires
Blown up with high conceits engend'ring pride.
Him thus intent Ithuriel with his spear
Touch'd lightly; for no falsehood can endure
Touch of celestial temper, but returns
Of force to its own likeness. Up he starts
Discover'd and surpris'd; as when a spark
Lights on a heap of nitrous powder, laid
Fit for the tun some magazine to store
Against a rumour'd war, the smutty grain
With sudden blaze diffus'd inflames the air,
So started up in his own shape the fiend.
Back stepp'd those two fair angels, half amaz'd
So sudden to behold the grisly king,
Yet thus, unmov'd with fear, accost him soon.
  Which of those rebel spirits adjudg'd to hell
Com'st thou escap'd thy prison, and transform'd
Why sat'st thou like an enemy in wait
Here watching at the head of these that sleep?
  Know ye not then, said Satan, fill'd with scorn,
Know ye not me? Ye knew me once no mate
For you, there sitting where ye durst not soar.
Not to know me argues yourselves unknown,
The lowest of your throng; or if ye know,
Why ask ye, and superfluous begin
Your message, like to end as much in vain?
To whom thus Zephon, answering scorn with scorn.
Think not, revolted spirit, thy shape the same
Or undiminish'd brightness, to be known
As when thou stood'st in heaven upright and pure.
That glory then when thou no more wast good
Departed from thee, and thou resemblest now
Thy sin and place of doom obscure and foul.
But come, for thou, be sure, shalt give account
To him who sent us, whose charge is to keep
This place inviolable and these from harm.

So spake the cherub, and his grave rebuke
Severe in youthful beauty added grace
Invincible. Abash'd the devil stood,
And felt how awful goodness is, and saw
Virtue in her shape how lovely; saw, and pin'd
His loss, but chiefly to find here observ'd
His lustre visibly impair'd; yet seem'd
Undaunted. If I must contend, said he,
Best with the best, the sender not the sent,
Or all at once; more glory will be won
Or less be lost. Thy fear, said Zephon bold,
Will save us trial what the least can do
Single against thee wicked, and thence weak.
The fiend repli'd not, overcome with rage,
But like a proud steed rein'd went haughty on,
Champing his iron curb. To strive or fly
He held it vain; awe from above had quell'd
His heart, not else dismay'd. Now drew they nigh
The western point, where those half-rounding guards
Just met and closing stood in squadron join'd
Awaiting next command; to whom their chief
Gabriel from the front thus call'd aloud.
O friends, I hear the tread of nimble feet
Hasting this way, and now by glimpse discern
Ithuriel and Zephon through the shade;
And with them comes a third of regal port
But faded splendour wan, who by his gait
And fierce demeanour seems the prince of hell,
Not likely to part hence without contest.
Stand firm, for in his look defiance lours.
He scarce had ended when those two approach'd
And brief related whom they brought, where found,
How busi'd, in what form and posture couch'd;
To whom with stern regard thus Gabriel spake.
Why hast thou, Satan, broke the bounds prescrib'd
To thy transgressions and disturb'd the charge
Of others, who approve not to transgress
By thy example, but have power and right
To question thy bold entrance on this place,

Employ'd it seems to violate sleep and those
Whose dwelling God hath planted here in bliss?
To whom thus Satan, with contemptuous brow.
  Gabriel, thou hadst in heaven th'esteem of wise,
And such I held thee; but this question ask'd
Puts me in doubt. Lives there who loves his pain?
Who would not, finding way, break loose from hell,
Though thither doom'd? Thou wouldst thyself, no doubt,
And boldly venture to whatever place
Farthest from pain, where thou mightst hope to change
Torment with ease and soonest recompense
Dole with delight, which in this place I sought;
To thee no reason, who know'st only good,
But evil hast not tri'd. And wilt object
His will who bound us? Let him surer bar
His iron gates if he intends our stay
In that dark durance. Thus much what was ask'd.
The rest is true, they found me where they say;
But that implies not violence or harm.
  Thus he in scorn. The warlike angel, mov'd,
Disdainfully half smiling thus replied.
  O loss of one in heaven to judge of wise
Since Satan fell, whom folly overthrew,
And now returns him from his prison scap'd,
Gravely in doubt whether to hold them wise
Or not who ask what boldness brought him hither
Unlicens'd from his bounds in hell prescrib'd.
So wise he judges it to fly from pain
However, and to scape his punishment.
So judge thou still, presumptuous, till the wrath
Which thou incurr'st by flying meet thy flight
Sevenfold, and scourge that wisdom back to hell
Which taught thee yet no better that no pain
Can equal anger infinite provok'd.
But wherefore thou alone? Wherefore with thee
Came not all hell broke loose? Is pain to them
Less pain, less to be fled, or thou than they
Less hardy to endure? Courageous chief,

The first in flight from pain, hadst thou alleg'd
To thy deserted host this cause of flight,
Thou surely hadst not come sole fugitive.
To which the fiend thus answer'd frowning stern.
  Not that I less endure or shrink from pain,
Insulting angel; well thou know'st I stood
Thy fiercest, when in battle to thy aid
The blasting volley'd thunder made all speed
And seconded thy else not dreaded spear.
But still thy words at random, as before,
Argue thy inexperience what behoves
From hard assays and ill successes past
A faithful leader, not to hazard all
Through ways of danger by himself untri'd.
I therefore, I alone first undertook
To wing the desolate abyss and spy
This new-created world, whereof in hell
Fame is not silent, here in hope to find
Better abode, and my afflicted powers
To settle here on earth or in mid air,
Though for possession put to try once more
What thou and thy gay legions dare against,
Whose easier business were to serve their lord
High up in heaven, with songs to hymn his throne
And practis'd distances to cringe, not fight.
To whom the warrior angel soon repli'd.
  To say and straight unsay, pretending first
Wise to fly pain, professing next the spy,
Argues no leader but a liar trac'd,
Satan; and couldst thou faithful add? O name,
O sacred name of faithfulness profan'd!
Faithful to whom? To thy rebellious crew?
Army of fiends, fit body to fit head.
Was this your discipline and faith engag'd,
Your military obedience, to dissolve
Allegiance to th'acknowledg'd power supreme?
And thou, sly hypocrite, who now wouldst seem
Patron of liberty, who more than thou

Once fawn'd and cring'd and servilely ador'd
Heaven's awful monarch? Wherefore but in hope
To dispossess him, and thyself to reign?
But mark what I aread thee now: avaunt,
Fly thither whence thou fled'st; if from this hour
Within these hallow'd limits thou appear,
Back to th'infernal pit I drag thee chain'd,
And seal thee so, as henceforth not to scorn
The facile gates of hell too slightly barr'd.
  So threaten'd he; but Satan to no threats
Gave heed, but waxing more in rage repli'd.
  Then when I am thy captive talk of chains,
Proud limitary cherub, but ere then
Far heavier load thyself expect to feel
From my prevailing arm, though heaven's king
Ride on thy wings, and thou with thy compeers,
Us'd to the yoke, draw'st his triumphal wheels
In progress through the road of heaven star-pav'd.
  While thus he spake th'angelic squadron bright
Turn'd fiery red, sharp'ning in mooned horns
Their phalanx, and began to hem him round
With ported spears as thick as when a field
Of Ceres ripe for harvest waving bends
Her bearded grove of ears which way the wind
Sways them; the careful ploughman doubting stands
Lest on the threshing-floor his hopeful sheaves
Prove chaff. On th'other side Satan alarm'd
Collecting all his might dilated stood
Like Teneriffe or Atlas unremov'd.
His stature reach'd the sky, and on his crest
Sat horror plum'd; nor wanted in his grasp
What seem'd both spear and shield. Now dreadful deeds
Might have ensu'd, nor only Paradise
In this commotion but the starry cope
Of heaven perhaps or all the elements
At least had gone to wrack, disturb'd and torn
With violence of this conflict, had not soon
Th'eternal to prevent such horrid fray

Hung forth in heaven his golden scales, yet seen
Betwixt Astrea and the Scorpion sign,
Wherein all things created first he weigh'd,
The pendulous round earth with balanc'd air
In counterpoise, now ponders all events,
Battles and realms. In these he put two weights,
The sequel each of parting and of fight.
The latter quick up flew and kick'd the beam;
Which Gabriel spying thus bespake the fiend.
  Satan, I know thy strength and thou know'st mine,
Neither our own, but giv'n. What folly then
To boast what arms can do, since thine no more
Than heaven permits, nor mine, though doubled now
To trample thee as mire. For proof, look up
And read thy lot in yon celestial sign,
Where thou art weigh'd and shown how light, how weak
If thou resist. The fiend look'd up and knew
His mounted scale aloft; nor more, but fled
Murmuring, and with him fled the shades of night.

BOOK VII

Descend from heaven, Urania, by that name
If rightly thou art call'd, whose voice divine
Following above th' Olympian hill I soar,
Above the flight of Pegasean wing.
The meaning, not the name I call; for thou
Nor of the Muses nine, nor on the top
Of old Olympus dwell'st, but heavenly born,
Before the hills appear'd or fountain flow'd
Thou with eternal Wisdom didst converse,
Wisdom thy sister, and with her didst play
In presence of th'almighty Father pleas'd
With thy celestial song. Up led by thee
Into the heaven of heavens I have presum'd,
An earthly guest, and drawn empyreal air,
Thy tempering; with like safety guided down
Return me to my native element,

Lest from this flying steed unrein'd (as once
Bellerophon, though from a lower clime)
Dismounted on th' Aleian field I fall,
Erroneous there to wander and forlorn.
Half yet remains unsung, but narrower bound
Within the visible diurnal sphere;
Standing on earth, not rapt above the pole,
More safe I sing with mortal voice unchang'd
To hoarse or mute, though fall'n on evil days,
On evil days though fall'n and evil tongues,
In darkness and with dangers compass'd round
And solitude, yet not alone while thou
Visit'st my slumbers nightly, or when morn
Purples the east; still govern thou my song,
Urania, and fit audience find, though few.
But drive far off the barbarous dissonance
Of Bacchus and his revellers, the race
Of that wild rout that tore the Thracian bard
In Rhodope, where woods and rocks had ears
To rapture, till the savage clamour drown'd
Both harp and voice, nor could the Muse defend
Her son. So fail not thou who thee implores;
For thou art heavenly, she an empty dream.
  Say, goddess, what ensu'd when Raphael,
The affable archangel, had forewarn'd
Adam by dire example to beware
Apostasy, by what befell in heaven
To those apostates, lest the like befall
In Paradise to Adam or his race,
Charg'd not to touch the interdicted tree,
If they transgress and slight that sole command
So easily obey'd amid the choice
Of all tastes else to please their appetite,
Though wand'ring. He with his consorted Eve
The story heard attentive, and was fill'd
With admiration and deep muse to hear
Of things so high and strange, things to their thought
So unimaginable as hate in heaven
And war so near the peace of God in bliss

With such confusion; but the evil soon
Driv'n back redounded as a flood on those
From whom it sprung, impossible to mix
With blessedness. Whence Adam soon repeal'd
The doubts that in his heart arose, and now
Led on, yet sinless, with desire to know
What nearer might concern him, how this world
Of heaven and earth conspicuous first began,
When and whereof created, for what cause,
What within Eden or without was done
Before his memory, as one whose drouth
Yet scarce allay'd still eyes the current stream
Whose liquid murmur heard new thirst excites,
Proceeded thus to ask his heavenly guest.
Great things, and full of wonder in our ears,
Far differing from this world thou hast reveal'd,
Divine interpreter, by favour sent
Down from the empyrean to forewarn
Us timely of what might else have been our loss,
Unknown, which human knowledge could not reach,
For which to th' infinitely good we owe
Immortal thanks, and his admonishment
Receive with solemn purpose to observe
Immutably his sovereign will, the end
Of what we are. But since thou hast vouchsaf'd
Gently for our instruction to impart
Things above earthly thought which yet concern'd
Our knowing, as to highest wisdom seem'd,
Deign to descend now lower and relate
What may no less perhaps avail us known,
How first began this heaven which we behold
Distant so high, with moving fires adorn'd
Innumerable, and this which yields or fills
All space, the ambient air wide interfus'd
Embracing round this florid earth, what cause
Mov'd the creator in his holy rest
Through all eternity so late to build
In chaos, and the work begun, how soon

Absolv'd, if unforbid thou mayst unfold
What we not to explore the secrets ask
Of his eternal empire, but the more
To magnify his works, the more we know.
And the great light of day yet wants to run
Much of his race though steep, suspense in heaven
Held by thy voice, thy potent voice he hears,
And longer will delay to hear thee tell
His generation and the rising birth
Of nature from the unapparent deep;
Or if the star of evening and the moon
Haste to thy audience, night with her will bring
Silence, and sleep list'ning to thee will watch,
Or we can bid his absence till thy song
End, and dismiss thee ere the morning shine.
  Thus Adam his illustrious guest besought,
And thus the godlike angel answer'd mild.
  This also thy request with caution ask'd
Obtain, though to recount almighty works
What words or tongue of seraph can suffice,
Or heart of man suffice to comprehend?
Yet what thou canst attain, which best may serve
To glorify the maker and infer
Thee also happier, shall not be withheld
Thy hearing. Such commission from above
I have receiv'd, to answer thy desire
Of knowledge within bounds; beyond abstain
To ask, nor let thine own inventions hope
Things not reveal'd, which th' invisible king
Only omniscient hath suppress'd in night,
To none communicable in earth or heaven.
Enough is left besides to search and know.
But knowledge is as food, and needs no less
Her temperance over appetite, to know
In measure what the mind may well contain,
Oppresses else with surfeit, and soon turns
Wisdom to folly as nourishment to wind.
Know then that after Lucifer from heaven
(So call him, brighter once amidst the host

Of angels than that star the stars among)
Fell with his flaming legions through the deep
Into his place, and the great Son return'd
Victorious with his saints, th'omnipotent
Eternal Father from his throne beheld
Their multitude, and to his Son thus spake.
At least our envious foe hath fail'd, who thought
All like himself rebellious, by whose aid
This inaccessible high strength, the seat
Of deity supreme, us dispossess'd,
He trusted to have seiz'd, and into fraud
Drew many whom their place knows here no more;
Yet far the greater part have kept, I see,
Their station; heaven yet populous retains
Number sufficient to possess her realms
Though wide, and this high temple to frequent
With ministeries due and solemn rites.
But lest his heart exalt him in the harm
Already done, to have dispeopled heaven,
My damage fondly deem'd, I can repair
That detriment, if such it be to lose
Self-lost, and in a moment will create
Another world, out of one man a race
Of men innumerable there to dwell,
Not here, till by degrees of merit rais'd
They open to themselves at length the way
Up hither, under long obedience tri'd,
And earth be chang'd to heaven, and heaven to earth,
One kingdom, joy and union without end.
Meanwhile inhabit lax, ye powers of heaven;
And thou, my Word, begotten Son, by thee
This I perform. Speak thou, and be it done.
My overshadowing spirit and might with thee
I send along; ride forth, and bid the deep
Within appointed bounds be heaven and earth,
Boundless the deep, because I am who fill
Infinitude, nor vacuous the space
Though I uncircumscrib'd my self retire
And put not forth my goodness, which is free

To act or not; necessity and chance
Approach me not, and what I will is fate.
  So spake th'almighty, and to what he spake
His Word, the filial Godhead, gave effect.
Immediate are the acts of God, more swift
Than time or motion, but to human ears
Cannot without process of speech be told,
So told as earthly notion can receive.
Great triumph and rejoicing was in heaven
When such was heard declar'd th' almighty's will;
Glory they sung to the most high, good will
To future men and in their dwellings peace,
Glory to him whose just avenging ire
Had driven out th' ungodly from his sight
And th' habitations of the just, to him
Glory and praise whose wisdom had ordain'd
Good out of evil to create, in stead
Of spirits malign a better race to bring
Into their vacant room, and thence diffuse
His good to worlds and ages infinite.
So sang the hierarchies; meanwhile the Son
On his great expedition now appear'd,
Girt with omnipotence, with radiance crown'd
Of majesty divine, sapience and love
Immense, and all his father in him shone.
About his chariot numberless were pour'd
Cherub and seraph, potentates and thrones
And virtues, winged spirits, and chariots wing'd
From th'armoury of God, where stand of old
Myriads between two brazen mountains lodg'd
Against a solemn day, harness'd at hand,
Celestial equipage, and now come forth
Spontaneous, for within them spirits liv'd
Attendant on their lord. Heaven open'd wide
Her ever-during gates, harmonious sound
Of golden hinges moving, to let forth
The king of glory in his powerful Word
And Spirit coming to create new worlds.
On heavenly ground they stood, and from the shore

They view'd the vast immeasurable abyss
Outrageous as a sea, dark, wasteful, wild,
Up from the bottom turn'd by furious winds
And surging waves as mountains to assault
Heaven's height and with the centre mix the pole.
  Silence, ye troubled waves, and thou deep, peace,
Said then th'omnific Word, your discord end;
Nor stay'd, but on the wings of cherubim
Uplifted in paternal glory rode
Far into Chaos and the world unborn,
For Chaos heard his voice. Him all his train
Follow'd in bright procession to behold
Creation and the wonders of his might.
Then stay'd the fervid wheels, and in his hand
He took the golden compasses, prepar'd
In God's eternal store to circumscribe
The universe and all created things;
One foot he centred, and the other turn'd
Round through the vast profundity obscure
And said, Thus far extend, thus far thy bounds,
This be thy just circumference, O world.
Thus God the heaven created, thus the earth,
Matter unform'd and void. Darkness profound
Cover'd th' abyss, but on the watery calm
His brooding wings the Spirit of God outspread
And vital virtue infus'd and vital warmth
Throughout the fluid mass, but downward purg'd
The black tartareous cold infernal dregs
Adverse to life; then founded, then conglob'd
Like things to like, the rest to several place
Disparted, and between spun out the air,
And earth self balanc'd on her centre hung.
  Let there be light, said God, and forthwith light
Ethereal, first of things, quintessence pure
Sprung from the deep and from her native east
To journey through the airy gloom began
Spher'd in a radiant cloud, for yet the sun
Was not; she in a cloudy tabernacle

Sojourn'd the while. God saw the light was good,
And light from darkness by the hemisphere
Divided; light the day, and darkness night
He nam'd. Thus was the first day ev'n and morn;
Nor pass'd uncelebrated nor unsung
By the celestial choirs, when orient light
Exhaling first from darkness they beheld,
Birthday of heaven and earth. With joy and shout
The hollow universal orb they fill'd,
And touch'd their golden harps and hymning prais'd
God and his works, creator him they sung,
Both when first evening was and when first morn.
Again God said, Let there be firmament
Amid the waters, and let it divide
The waters from the waters; and God made
The firmament, expanse of liquid pure,
Transparent elemental air diffus'd
In circuit to the uttermost convex
Of this great round, partition firm and sure,
The waters underneath from those above
Dividing; for as earth, so he the world
Built on circumfluous waters calm in wide
Crystalline ocean, and the loud misrule
Of Chaos far remov'd, lest fierce extremes
Contiguous might distemper the whole frame;
And heaven he nam'd the firmament. So ev'n
And morning chorus sung the second day.
The earth was form'd, but in the womb as yet
Of waters, embryon immature involv'd,
Appear'd not. Over all the face of earth
Main ocean flow'd; not idle, but with warm
Prolific humour soft'ning all her globe
Fermented the great mother to conceive,
Satiate with genial moisture, when God said,
Be gather'd now ye waters under heaven
Into one place, and let dry land appear.
Immediately the mountains huge appear
Emergent, and their broad bare backs upheave
Into the clouds; their tops ascend the sky.

So high as heav'd the tumid hills, so low
Down sunk a hollow bottom broad and deep,
Capacious bed of waters; thither they
Hasted with glad precipitance, uproll'd
As drops on dust conglobing from the dry.
Part rise in crystal wall or ridge direct
For haste, such flight the great command impress'd
On the swift floods; as armies at the call
Of trumpet (for of armies thou hast heard)
Troop to their standard, so the watery throng,
Wave rolling after wave where way they found,
If steep, with torrent rapture, if through plain,
Soft ebbing, nor withstood them rock or hill
But they or underground or circuit wide
With serpent error wandering found their way,
And on the washy ooze deep channels wore,
Easy ere God had bid the ground be dry,
All but within those banks where rivers now
Stream and perpetual draw their humid train.
The dry land earth, and the great receptacle
Of congregated waters he call'd seas,
And saw that it was good, and said, Let th' earth
Put forth the verdant grass, herb yielding seed
And fruit tree yielding fruit after her kind,
Whose seed is in herself upon the earth.
He scarce had said when the bare earth, till then
Desert and bare, unsightly, unadorn'd,
Brought forth the tender grass, whose verdure clad
Her universal face with pleasant green,
Then herbs of every leaf that sudden flower'd,
Op'ning their various colours, and made gay
Her bosom smelling sweet; and these scarce blown
Forth flourish'd thick the clust'ring vine, forth crept
The swelling gourd, up stood the corny reed
Embattl'd in her field; add th' humble shrub,
And bush with frizzl'd hair implicit; last
Rose as in dance the stately trees, and spread
Their branches hung with copious fruit, or gemm'd
Their blossoms; with high woods the hills were crown'd,

With tufts the valleys and each fountain-side,
With borders long the rivers, that earth now
Seem'd like to heaven, a seat where gods might dwell
Or wander with delight, and love to haunt
Her sacred shades; though God had yet not rain'd
Upon the earth, and man to till the ground
None was, but from the earth a dewy mist
Went up and water'd all the ground and each
Plant of the field which ere it was in th' earth
God made, and every herb before it grew
On the green stem. God saw that it was good.
So ev'n and morn recorded the third day.
  Again th' almighty spake, Let there be lights
High in th' expanse of heaven to divide
The day from night, and let them be for signs,
For seasons, and for days, and circling years,
And let them be for lights as I ordain
Their office in the firmament of heaven
To give light on the earth; and it was so.
And God made two great lights, great for their use
To man, the greater to have rule by day,
The less by night altern; and made the stars
And set them in the firmament of heaven
T' illuminate the earth, and rule the day
In their vicissitude and rule the night,
And light from darkness to divide. God saw,
Surveying his great work, that it was good;
For of celestial bodies first the sun
A mighty sphere he fram'd, unlightsome first
Though of ethereal mould; then form'd the moon
Globose, and every magnitude of stars,
And sow'd with stars the heaven thick as a field.
Of light by far the greater part he took,
Transplanted from her cloudy shrine and plac'd
In the sun's orb, made porous to receive
And drink the liquid light, firm to retain
Her gather'd beams, great palace now of light.
Hither as to their fountain other stars
Repairing in their golden urns draw light,

And hence the morning planet gilds her horns;
By tincture or reflection they augment
Their small peculiar, though from human sight
So far remote with diminution seen.
First in his east the glorious lamp was seen,
Regent of day, and all th'horizon round
Invested with bright rays, jocund to run
His longitude through heaven's high road; the grey
Dawn and the Pleiades before him danc'd
Shedding sweet influence. Less bright the moon
But opposite in levell'd west was set
His mirror, with full face borrowing her light
From him, for other light she needed none
In that aspect, and still that distance keeps
Till night, then in the east her turn she shines
Revolv'd on heaven's great axle, and her reign
With thousand lesser lights dividual holds,
With thousand thousand stars that then appear'd
Spangling the hemisphere. Then first adorn'd
With their bright luminaries that set and rose,
Glad ev'ning and glad morn crown'd the fourth day.
  And God said, Let the waters generate
Reptile with spawn abundant, living soul,
And let fowl fly above the earth with wings
Display'd on th' open firmament of heaven.
And God created the great whales, and each
Soul living, each that crept, which plenteously
The waters generated by their kinds,
And every bird of wing after his kind,
And saw that it was good, and bless'd them, saying,
Be fruitful, multiply, and in the seas
And lakes and running streams the waters fill,
And let the fowl be multipli'd on th' earth.
Forthwith the sounds and seas, each creek and bay
With fry innumerable swarm, and shoals
Of fish that with their fins and shining scales
Glide under the green wave in schools that oft
Bank the mid sea; part single or with mate

Graze the sea-weed, their pasture, and through groves
Of coral stray, or sporting with quick glance
Show to the sun their wav'd coats dropp'd with gold,
Or in their pearly shells at ease attend
Moist nutriment, or under rocks their food
In jointed armour watch. On smooth the seal
And bended dolphins play; part huge of bulk,
Wallowing unwieldy, enormous in their gait
Tempest the ocean; there leviathan,
Hugest of living creatures, on the deep
Stretch'd like a promontory sleeps or swims
And seems a moving land, and at his gills
Draws in and at his trunk spouts out a sea.
Meanwhile the tepid caves and fens and shores
Their brood as numerous hatch from th' egg that soon
Bursting with kindly rupture forth disclos'd
Their callow young; but feather'd soon and fledge
They summ'd their pens, and soaring th'air sublime
With clang despis'd the ground, under a cloud
In prospect. There the eagle and the stork
On cliffs and cedar tops their eyries build.
Part loosely wing the region, part more wise
In common rang'd in figure wedge their way
Intelligent of seasons, and set forth
Their airy caravan high over seas
Flying, and over lands with mutual wing
Easing their flight. So steers the prudent crane
Her annual voyage, borne on winds. The air
Floats as they pass, fann'd with unnumber'd plumes.
From branch to branch the smaller birds with song
Solac'd the woods and spread their painted wings
Till ev'n; nor then the solemn nightingale
Ceas'd warbling, but all night tun'd her soft lays.
Others on silver lakes and rivers bath'd
Their downy breast; the swan with arched neck
Between her white wings mantling proudly rows
Her state with oary feet. Yet oft they quit
The dank, and rising on stiff pennons tower
The mid aërial sky. Others on ground

Walk'd firm, the crested cock whose clarion sounds
The silent hours, and th'other whose gay train
Adorns him colour'd with the florid hue
Of rainbows and starry eyes. The waters thus
With fish replenish'd and the air with fowl,
Ev'ning and morn solemnis'd the fifth day.
  The sixth and of creation last arose
With evening harps and matin, when God said,
Let th' earth bring forth soul living in her kind,
Cattle and creeping things and beast of th' earth,
Each in their kind. The earth obey'd, and straight
Op'ning her fertile womb teem'd at a birth
Innumerous living creatures, perfect forms,
Limb'd and full-grown. Out of the ground up rose
As from his lair the wild beast where he wons
In forest wild, in thicket, brake or den;
Among the trees in pairs they rose, they walk'd,
The cattle in the fields and meadows green,
Those rare and solitary, these in flocks
Pasturing at once, and in broad herds upsprung.
The grassy clods now calv'd; now half appear'd
The tawny lion, pawing to get free
His hinder parts, then springs as broke from bonds
And rampant shakes his brinded mane; the ounce,
The libbard and the tiger, as the mole
Rising, the crumbled earth above them threw
In hillocks; the swift stag from underground
Bore up his branching head; scarce from his mould
Behemoth, biggest born of earth, upheav'd
His vastness; fleec'd the flocks and bleating rose
As plants; ambiguous between sea and land
The river-horse and scaly crocodile.
At once came forth whatever creeps the ground,
Insect or worm; those wav'd their limber fans
For wings, and smallest lineaments exact
In all the liveries deck'd of summer's pride
With spots of gold and purple, azure and green;
These as a line their long dimension drew,
Streaking the ground with sinuous trace, not all

Minims of nature: some of serpent kind
Wondrous in length and corpulence involv'd
Their snaky folds and added wings. First crept
The parsimonious emmet, provident
Of future, in small room large heart enclos'd,
Pattern of just equality perhaps
Hereafter, join'd in her popular tribes
Of commonalty; swarming next appear'd
The female bee that feeds her husband drone
Deliciously and builds her waxen cells
With honey stor'd; the rest are numberless,
And thou their natures know'st and gav'st them names,
Needless to thee repeated; nor unknown
The serpent, subtlest beast of all the field,
Of huge extent sometimes, with brazen eyes
And hairy mane terrific, though to thee
Not noxious but obedient at thy call.
Now heaven in all her glory shone, and roll'd
Her motions as the great first mover's hand
First wheel'd their course; earth in her rich attire
Consummate lovely smil'd; air, water, earth
By fowl, fish, beast was flown, was swum, was walk'd
Frequent, and of the sixth day yet remain'd.
There wanted yet the master work, the end
Of all yet done: a creature who, not prone
And brute as other creatures, but endu'd
With sanctity of reason, might erect
His stature and upright with front serene
Govern the rest, self-knowing and from thence
Magnanimous to correspond with heaven,
But grateful to acknowledge whence his good
Descends, thither with heart and voice and eyes
Directed in devotion, to adore
And worship God supreme who made him chief
Of all his works. Therefore th' omnipotent
Eternal Father (for where is not he
Present?) thus to the Son audibly spake.
Let us make now man in our image, man
In our similitude, and let them rule

Over the fish and fowl of sea and air,
Beast of the field, and over all the earth
And every creeping thing that creeps the ground.
This said, he form'd thee, Adam, thee, O man,
Dust of the ground, and in thy nostrils breath'd
The breath of life; in his own image he
Created thee, in th' image of a God
Express, and thou becam'st a living soul.
Male he created thee, but thy consort
Female for race, then bless'd mankind and said,
Be fruitful, multiply, and fill the earth,
Subdue it and throughout dominion hold
Over fish of the sea and fowl of the air
And every living thing that moves on th' earth.
Wherever thus created, for no place
Is yet distinct by name, thence, as thou know'st,
He brought thee into this delicious grove,
This garden planted with the trees of God,
Delectable both to behold and taste,
And freely all their pleasant fruit for food
Gave thee, all sorts are here that all th' earth yields,
Variety without end. But of the tree
Which tasted works knowledge of good and evil
Thou mayst not; in the day thou eat'st, thou diest;
Death is the penalty impos'd. Beware,
And govern well thy appetite, lest Sin
Surprise thee and her black attendant Death.
Here finish'd he, and all that he had made
View'd, and behold all was entirely good.
So ev'n and morn accomplish'd the sixth day,
Yet not till the creator from his work
Desisting, though unweari'd, up return'd
Up to the heaven of heavens his high abode,
Thence to behold this new-created world,
Th' addition to his empire, how it show'd
In prospect from his throne, how good, how fair,
Answering his great idea. Up he rode
Follow'd with acclamation and the sound

Symphonious of ten thousand harps that tun'd
Angelic harmonies; the earth, the air
Resounded (thou remember'st, for thou heard'st),
The heavens and all the constellations rung,
The planets in their stations list'ning stood
While the bright pomp ascended jubilant.
Open ye everlasting gates, they sung,
Open ye heavens your living doors, let in
The great creator from his work return'd
Magnificent, his six days' work, a world;
Open, and henceforth oft, for God will deign
To visit oft the dwellings of just men
Delighted, and with frequent intercourse
Thither will send his winged messengers
On errands of supernal grace. So sung
The glorious train ascending; he through heaven
That open'd wide her blazing portals led
To God's eternal house direct the way,
A broad and ample road, whose dust is gold
And pavement stars, as stars to thee appear
Seen in the galaxy, that milky way
Which nightly as a circling zone thou see'st
Powder'd with stars. And now on earth the seventh
Ev'ning arose in Eden, for the sun
Was set, and twilight from the east came on
Forerunning night, when at the holy mount
Of heaven's high-seated top, th' imperial throne
Of Godhead fix'd for ever firm and sure,
The filial power arriv'd and sat him down
With his great Father; for he also went
Invisible, yet stay'd (such privilege
Hath omnipresence), and the work ordain'd,
Author and end of all things, and from work
Now resting bless'd and hallow'd the seventh day,
As resting on that day from all his work,
But not in silence holy kept. The harp
Had work and rested not, the solemn pipe
And dulcimer, all organs of sweet stop,
All sounds on fret by string or golden wire

Temper'd soft tunings, intermix'd with voice
Choral or unison; of incense clouds
Fuming from golden censers hid the mount.
Creation and the six days' acts they sung:
Great are thy works, Jehovah, infinite
Thy power; what thought can measure thee or tongue
Relate thee, greater now in thy return
Than from the giant angels. Thee that day
Thy thunders magnifi'd, but to create
Is greater than created to destroy.
Who can impair thee, mighty king, or bound
Thy empire? Easily the proud attempt
Of spirits apostate and their counsels vain
Thou hast repell'd, while impiously they thought
Thee to diminish and from thee withdraw
The number of thy worshippers. Who seeks
To lessen thee, against his purpose serves
To manifest the more thy might. His evil
Thou usest and from thence creat'st more good,
Witness this new-made world, another heaven
From heaven gate not far, founded in view
On the clear hyaline, the glassy sea
Of amplitude almost immense, with stars
Numerous, and every star perhaps a world
Of destin'd habitation; but thou know'st
Their seasons, among these the seat of men,
Earth with her nether ocean circumfus'd,
Their pleasant dwelling place. Thrice happy men,
And sons of men, whom God hath thus advanc'd,
Created in his image, there to dwell
And worship him, and in reward to rule
Over his works on earth, in sea or air,
And multiply a race of worshippers
Holy and just; thrice happy if they know
Their happiness and persevere upright.
So sung they, and the empyrean rung
With halleluiahs; thus was sabbath kept.
And thy request think now fulfill'd, that ask'd
How first this world and face of things began,

And what before thy memory was done
From the beginning, that posterity
Inform'd by thee might know. If else thou seek'st
Aught not surpassing human measure, say.

BOOK IX

No more of talk where God or angel guest
With man, as with his friend, familiar us'd
To sit indulgent and with him partake
Rural repast, permitting him the while
Venial discourse unblam'd; I now must change
These notes to tragic: foul distrust and breach
Disloyal on the part of man, revolt
And disobedience, on the part of heaven
Now alienated, distance and distaste,
Anger and just rebuke and judgement giv'n
That brought into this world a world of woe,
Sin and her shadow Death, and misery,
Death's harbinger; sad task, yet argument
Not less but more heroic than the wrath
Of stern Achilles on his foe pursu'd
Thrice fugitive about Troy wall, or rage
Of Turnus for Lavinia disespous'd,
Or Neptune's ire or Juno's, that so long
Perplex'd the Greek and Cytherea's son,
If answerable style I can obtain
Of my celestial patroness, who deigns
Her nightly visitation unimplor'd,
And dictates to me slumbering, or inspires
Easy my unpremeditated verse,
Since first this subject for heroic song
Pleas'd me, long choosing and beginning late;
Not sedulous by nature to indite
Wars, hitherto the only argument
Heroic deem'd, chief mastery to dissect
With long and tedious havoc fabled knights
In battles feign'd, the better fortitude

Of patience and heroic martyrdom
Unsung, or to describe races and games,
Or tilting furniture, emblazon'd shields,
Impreses quaint, caparisons and steeds,
Bases and tinsel trappings, gorgeous knights
At joust and tournament; then marshall'd feast
Serv'd up in hall with sewers and seneschals;
The skill of artifice or office mean,
Not that which justly gives heroic name
To person or to poem. Me of these
Not skill'd nor studious higher argument
Remains, sufficient of itself to raise
That name, unless an age too late, or cold
Climate, or years damp my intended wing
Depress'd; and much they may, if all be mine,
Not hers who brings it nightly to my ear.
  The sun was sunk, and after him the star
Of Hesperus whose office is to bring
Twilight upon the earth, short arbiter
Twixt day and night, and now from end to end
Night's hemisphere had veil'd th' horizon round,
When Satan, who late fled before the threats
Of Gabriel out of Eden, now improv'd
In meditated fraud and malice bent
On man's destruction, maugre what might hap
Of heavier on himself, fearless return'd.
By night he fled, and at midnight return'd
From compassing the earth, cautious of day
Since Uriel regent of the sun descri'd
His entrance and forewarn'd the cherubim
That kept their watch. Thence full of anguish driven
The space of seven continu'd nights he rode
With darkness; thrice the equinoctial line
He circled, four times cross'd the car of night
From pole to pole, traversing each colure,
On th' eighth return'd, and on the coast averse
From entrance or cherubic watch by stealth
Found unsuspected way. There was a place,

Now not, though sin not time first wrought the change,
Where Tigris at the foot of Paradise
Into a gulf shot under ground, till part
Rose up a fountain by the tree of life;
In with the river sunk and with it rose
Satan involv'd in rising mist, then sought
Where to lie hid. Sea he had search'd and land
From Eden over Pontus and the pool
Maeotis, up beyond the river Ob,
Downward as far antarctic, and in length
West from Orontes to the ocean barr'd
At Darien, thence to the land where flows
Ganges and Indus; thus the orb he roam'd
With narrow search, and with inspection deep
Consider'd every creature, which of all
Most opportune might serve his wiles, and found
The serpent, subtlest beast of all the field.
Him after long debate, irresolute
Of thoughts revolv'd, his final sentence chose
Fit vessel, fittest imp of fraud, in whom
To enter and his dark suggestions hide
From sharpest sight; for in the wily snake
Whatever sleights none would suspicious mark,
As from his wit and native subtlety
Proceeding, which in other beasts observ'd
Doubt might beget of diabolic power
Active within, beyond the sense of brute.
Thus he resolv'd, but first from inward grief
His bursting passion into plaints thus pour'd.
  O earth, how like to heaven, if not preferr'd
More justly, seat worthier of gods, as built
With second thoughts, reforming what was old!
For what god after better worse would build?
Terrestrial heaven, danc'd round by other heavens
That shine, yet bear their bright officious lamps,
Light above light, for thee alone, as seems,
In thee concentring all their precious beams
Of sacred influence. As God in heaven

Is centre yet extends to all, so thou
Centring receiv'st from all those orbs; in thee,
Not in themselves, all their known virtue appears
Productive in herb, plant and nobler birth
Of creatures animate with gradual life
Of growth, sense, reason, all summ'd up in man.
With what delight could I have walk'd thee round,
If I could joy in aught, sweet interchange
Of hill and valley, rivers, woods and plains,
Now land, now sea, and shores with forest crown'd,
Rocks, dens and caves. But I in none of these
Find place or refuge, and the more I see
Pleasures about me, so much more I feel
Torment within me, as from the hateful siege
Of contraries; all good to me becomes
Bane, and in heaven much worse would be my state.
But neither here seek I, no, nor in heaven
To dwell, unless by mast'ring heaven's supreme,
Nor hope to be myself less miserable
By what I seek, but others to make such
As I, though thereby worse to me redound;
For only in destroying I find ease
To my relentless thoughts, and him destroy'd
Or won to what may work his utter loss
For whom all this was made, all this will soon
Follow, as to him link'd in weal or woe.
In woe, then, that destruction wide may range;
To me shall be the glory sole among
Th'infernal powers, in one day to have marr'd
What he almighty styl'd six nights and days
Continu'd making, and who knows how long
Before had been contriving, though perhaps
Not longer than since I in one night freed
From servitude inglorious well-nigh half
Th'angelic name, and thinner left the throng
Of his adorers. He to be aveng'd
And to repair his numbers thus impair'd,
Whether such virtue spent of old now fail'd
More angels to create, if they at least

Are his created, or to spite us more,
Determin'd to advance into our room
A creature form'd of earth and him endow,
Exalted from so base original,
With heavenly spoils, our spoils. What he decreed
He effected; man he made, and for him built
Magnificent this world, and earth his seat,
Him lord pronounc'd and, O indignity!
Subjected to his service angel wings
And flaming ministers to watch and tend
Their earthly charge. Of these the vigilance
I dread, and to elude thus wrapp'd in mist
Of midnight vapour glide obscure, and pry
In every bush and brake where hap may find
The serpent sleeping, in whose mazy folds
To hide me and the dark intent I bring.
O foul descent! that I who erst contended
With gods to sit the highest am now constrain'd
Into a beast and mix'd with bestial slime,
This essence to incarnate and imbrute
That to the height of deity aspir'd.
But what will not ambition and revenge
Descend to? Who aspires must down as low
As high he soar'd, obnoxious first or last
To basest things. Revenge, at first though sweet,
Bitter ere long back on itself recoils.
Let it; I reck not, so it light well aim'd,
Since higher I fall short, on him who next
Provokes my envy, this new favourite
Of heaven, this man of clay, son of despite,
Whom us the more to spite his maker rais'd
From dust. Spite then with spite is best repaid.
  So saying, through each thicket dank or dry
Like a black mist low creeping he held on
His midnight search, where soonest he might find
The serpent. Him fast sleeping soon he found
In labyrinth of many a round self-roll'd,
His head the midst, well stor'd with subtle wiles;
Not yet in horrid shade or dismal den,

Nor nocent yet, but on the grassy herb
Fearless unfear'd he slept. In at his mouth
The devil enter'd, and his brutal sense
In heart or head possessing soon inspir'd
With act intelligential, but his sleep
Disturb'd not, waiting close th' approach of morn.
Now whenas sacred light began to dawn
In Eden on the humid flowers that breath'd
Their morning incense, when all things that breathe
From th' earth's great altar send up silent praise
To the creator and his nostrils fill
With grateful smell, forth came the human pair
And join'd their vocal worship to the choir
Of creatures wanting voice; that done, partake
The season, prime for sweetest scents and airs;
Then commune how that day they best may ply
Their growing work, for much their work outgrew
The hands' dispatch of two, gardening so wide,
And Eve first to her husband thus began.
  Adam, well may we labour still to dress
This garden, still to tend plant, herb and flower,
Our pleasant task enjoin'd, but till more hands
Aid us the work under our labour grows,
Luxurious by restraint; what we by day
Lop overgrown or prune or prop or bind
One night or two with wanton growth derides
Tending to wild. Thou therefore now advise
Or hear what to my mind first thoughts present.
Let us divide our labours, thou where choice
Leads thee, or where most needs, whether to wind
The woodbine round this arbour or direct
The clasping ivy where to climb, while I
In yonder spring of roses intermix'd
With myrtle find what to redress till noon;
For while so near each other thus all day
Our task we choose, what wonder if so near
Looks intervene and smiles, or object new
Casual discourse draw on, which intermits

Our day's work brought to little, though begun
Early, and th' hour of supper comes unearn'd.
To whom mild answer Adam thus return'd.
Sole Eve, associate sole, to me beyond
Compare above all living creatures dear,
Well hast thou motion'd, well thy thoughts employ'd
How we might best fulfil the work which here
God hath assign'd us, nor of me shalt pass
Unprais'd; for nothing lovelier can be found
In woman than to study household good
And good works in her husband to promote.
Yet not so strictly hath our lord impos'd
Labour as to debar us when we need
Refreshment, whether food or talk between,
Food of the mind, or this sweet intercourse
Of looks and smiles, for smiles from reason flow
To brute deni'd, and are of love the food,
Love not the lowest end of human life;
For not to irksome toil but to delight
He made us, and delight to reason join'd.
These paths and bowers doubt not but our joint hands
Will keep from wilderness with ease as wide
As we need walk, till younger hands ere long
Assist us. But if much converse perhaps
Thee satiate, to short absence I could yield;
For solitude sometimes is best society,
And short retirement urges sweet return.
But other doubt possesses me, lest harm
Befall thee sever'd from me, for thou know'st
What hath been warn'd us, what malicious foe
Envying our happiness and of his own
Despairing seeks to work us woe and shame
By sly assault, and somewhere nigh at hand
Watches no doubt with greedy hope to find
His wish and best advantage, us asunder,
Hopeless to circumvent us join'd, where each
To other speedy aid might lend at need;
Whether his first design be to withdraw
Our fealty from God or to disturb

Conjugal love, than which perhaps no bliss
Enjoy'd by us excites his envy more.
Or this or worse, leave not the faithful side
That gave thee being, still shades thee and protects.
The wife, where danger or dishonour lurks,
Safest and seemliest by her husband stays,
Who guards her, or with her the worst endures.
  To whom the virgin majesty of Eve,
As one who loves and some unkindness meets,
With sweet austere composure thus repli'd.
  Offspring of heaven and earth and all earth's lord,
That such an enemy we have, who seeks
Our ruin, both by thee inform'd I learn
And from the parting angel overheard
As in a shady nook I stood behind,
Just then return'd at shut of ev'ning flowers.
But that thou should'st my firmness therefore doubt
To God or thee because we have a foe
May tempt it, I expected not to hear.
His violence thou fear'st not, being such
As we, not capable of death or pain,
Can either not receive or can repel.
His fraud is then thy fear, which plain infers
Thy equal fear that my firm faith and love
Can by his fraud be shaken or seduc'd;
Thoughts which how found they harbour in thy breast,
Adam, misthought of her to thee so dear?
  To whom with healing words Adam repli'd.
Daughter of God and man, immortal Eve,
For such thou art, from sin and blame entire,
Not diffident of thee do I dissuade
Thy absence from my sight, but to avoid
Th' attempt itself intended by our foe.
For he who tempts, though in vain, at least asperses
The tempted with dishonour foul, suppos'd
Not incorruptible of faith, not proof
Against temptation. Thou thyself with scorn
And anger would'st resent the offer'd wrong,
Though ineffectual found. Misdeem not then

If such affront I labour to avert
From thee alone, which on us both at once
The enemy though bold will hardly dare,
Or daring, first on me th'assault shall light.
Nor thou his malice and false guile contemn;
Subtle he needs must be who could seduce
Angels. Nor think superfluous others' aid;
I from the influence of thy looks receive
Access in every virtue, in thy sight
More wise, more watchful, stronger, if need were
Of outward strength, while shame, thou looking on,
Shame to be overcome or overreach'd
Would utmost vigour raise, and rais'd unite.
Why should'st not thou like sense within thee feel
When I am present, and thy trial choose
With me, best witness of thy virtue tri'd?
So spake domestic Adam in his care
And matrimonial love; but Eve, who thought
Less attributed to her faith sincere,
Thus her reply with accent sweet renew'd.
If this be our condition, thus to dwell
In narrow circuit straiten'd by a foe
Subtle or violent, we not endu'd
Single with like defence wherever met,
How are we happy, still in fear of harm?
But harm precedes not sin. Only our foe
Tempting affronts us with his foul esteem
Of our integrity; his foul esteem
Sticks no dishonour on our front, but turns
Foul on himself. Then wherefore shunn'd or fear'd
By us? who rather double honour gain
From his surmise prov'd false, find peace within,
Favour from heaven our witness from the event.
And what is faith, love, virtue unassay'd
Alone, without exterior help sustain'd?
Let us not then suspect our happy state
Left so imperfect by the maker wise
As not secure to single or combined.
Frail is our happiness if this be so,

And Eden were no Eden thus expos'd.
  To whom thus Adam fervently repli'd.
O woman, best are all things as the will
Of God ordain'd them; his creating hand
Nothing imperfect or deficient left
Of all that he created, much less man
Or aught that might his happy state secure,
Secure from outward force; within himself
The danger lies, yet lies within his power,
Against his will he can receive no harm.
But God left free the will, for what obeys
Reason is free, and reason he made right,
But bid her well beware and still erect
Lest by some fair appearing good surpris'd
She dictate false, and misinform the will
To do what God expressly hath forbid.
Not then mistrust but tender love enjoins
That I should mind thee oft, and mind thou me.
Firm we subsist, yet possible to swerve,
Since reason not impossibly may meet
Some specious object by the foe suborn'd,
And fall into deception unaware,
Not keeping strictest watch as she was warn'd.
Seek not temptation then, which to avoid
Were better, and most likely if from me
Thou sever not; trial will come unsought.
Would'st thou approve thy constancy, approve
First thy obedience; th' other who can know
Not seeing thee attempted, who attest?
But if thou think trial unsought may find
Us both securer than thus warn'd thou seem'st,
Go; for thy stay, not free, absents thee more.
Go in thy native innocence, rely
On what thou hast of virtue, summon all;
For God towards thee hath done his part; do thine.
  So spake the patriarch of mankind, but Eve
Persisted, yet submiss though last repli'd.
  With thy permission then and thus forewarn'd

Chiefly by what thy own last reasoning words
Touch'd only, that our trial when least sought
May find us both perhaps far less prepar'd,
The willinger I go, nor much expect
A foe so proud will first the weaker seek;
So bent, the more shall shame him his repulse.
Thus saying from her husband's hand her hand
Soft she withdrew, and like a wood-nymph light,
Oread or dryad, or of Delia's train,
Betook her to the groves; but Delia's self
In gait surpass'd and goddess-like deport,
Though not as she with bow and quiver arm'd
But with such gardening tools as art yet rude
Guiltless of fire had form'd, or angels brought.
To Pales or Pomona thus adorn'd
Likeliest she seem'd, Pomona when she fled
Vertumnus, or to Ceres in her prime,
Yet virgin of Proserpina from Jove.
Her long with ardent look his eye pursu'd
Delighted, but desiring more her stay.
Oft he to her his charge of quick return
Repeated, she to him as oft engag'd
To be return'd by noon amid the bower,
And all things in best order to invite
Noontide repast or afternoon's repose.
O much deceiv'd, much failing, hapless Eve,
Of thy presum'd return! Event perverse!
Thou never from that hour in Paradise
Found'st either sweet repast or sound repose,
Such ambush hid among sweet flowers and shades
Waited with hellish rancour imminent
To intercept thy way, or send thee back
Despoil'd of innocence, of faith, of bliss.
For now and since first break of dawn the fiend,
Mere serpent in appearance, forth was come
And on his quest where likeliest he might find
The only two of mankind, but in them
The whole included race, his purpos'd prey.
In bower and field he sought, where any tuft

Of grove or garden-plot more pleasant lay,
Their tendance or plantation for delight;
By fountain or by shady rivulet
He sought them both, but wish'd his hap might find
Eve separate; he wish'd, but not with hope
Of what so seldom chanc'd, when to his wish,
Beyond his hope, Eve separate he spies,
Veil'd in a cloud of fragrance where she stood,
Half-spi'd, so thick the roses bushing round
About her glow'd, oft stooping to support
Each flower of slender stalk whose head though gay
Carnation, purple, azure or speck'd with gold
Hung drooping unsustain'd; them she upstays
Gently with myrtle band, mindless the while
Her self, though fairest unsupported flower,
From her best prop so far, and storm so nigh.
Nearer he drew, and many a walk travers'd
Of stateliest covert, cedar, pine or palm,
Then voluble and bold, now hid, now seen
Among thick-woven arborets and flowers
Emborder'd on each bank, the hand of Eve;
Spot more delicious than those gardens feign'd
Or of reviv'd Adonis or renown'd
Alcinous, host of old Laertes' son,
Or that not mystic where the sapient king
Held dalliance with his fair Egyptian spouse.
Much he the place admir'd, the person more,
As one who long in populous city pent,
Where houses thick and sewers annoy the air,
Forth issuing on a summer's morn to breathe
Among the pleasant villages and farms
Adjoin'd, from each thing met conceives delight,
The smell of grain, or tedded grass, or kine,
Or dairy, each rural sight, each rural sound,
If chance with nymph-like step fair virgin pass,
What pleasing seem'd, for her now pleases more,
She most, and in her look sums all delight;
Such pleasure took the serpent to behold
This flowery plat, the sweet recess of Eve

Thus early, thus alone. Her heavenly form
Angelic, but more soft and feminine,
Her graceful innocence, her every air
Of gesture or least action overaw'd
His malice and with rapine sweet bereav'd
His fierceness of the fierce intent it brought.
That space the evil one abstracted stood
From his own evil, and for the time remain'd
Stupidly good, of enmity disarm'd,
Of guile, of hate, of envy, of revenge.
But the hot hell that always in him burns,
Though in mid-heaven, soon ended his delight,
And tortures him now more the more he sees
Of pleasure not for him ordain'd; then soon
Fierce hate he recollects, and all his thoughts
Of mischief gratulating thus excites.
  Thoughts, whither have ye led me? With what sweet
Compulsion thus transported, to forget
What hither brought us, hate, not love, nor hope
Of Paradise for hell; hope here to taste
Of pleasure, but all pleasure to destroy,
Save what is in destroying, other joy
To me is lost. Then let me not let pass
Occasion which now smiles. Behold alone
The woman, opportune to all attempts,
Her husband, for I view far round, not nigh,
Whose higher intellectual more I shun
And strength, of courage haughty and of limb
Heroic built, though of terrestrial mould,
Foe not informidable, exempt from wound,
I not; so much hath hell debas'd and pain
Enfeebled me to what I was in heaven;
She fair, divinely fair, fit love for gods,
Not terrible, though terror be in love
And beauty not approach'd by stronger hate,
Hate stronger under show of love well feign'd,
The way which to her ruin now I tend.
  So spake the enemy of mankind, enclos'd
In serpent, inmate bad, and toward Eve

Address'd his way, not with indented wave
Prone on the ground, as since, but on his rear,
Circular base of rising folds that tower'd
Fold above fold a surging maze, his head
Crested aloft and carbuncle his eyes,
With burnish'd neck of verdant gold erect
Amidst his circling spires that on the grass
Floated redundant. Pleasing was his shape
And lovely, never since of serpent kind
Lovelier; not those that in Illyria chang'd
Hermione and Cadmus, or the god
In Epidaurus; nor to which transform'd
Ammonian Jove or Capitoline was seen,
He with Olympias, this with her who bore
Scipio, the height of Rome. With tract oblique
At first, as one who sought access but fear'd
To interrupt, sidelong he works his way;
As when a ship by skilful steersman wrought
Nigh river's mouth or foreland, where the wind
Veers oft, as oft so steers and shifts her sail,
So varied he, and of his tortuous train
Curl'd many a wanton wreath in sight of Eve
To lure her eye. She busi'd heard the sound
Of rustling leaves, but minded not, as us'd
To such disport before her through the field
From every beast, more duteous at her call
Than at Circean call the herd disguis'd.
He bolder now uncall'd before her stood,
But as in gaze admiring; oft he bow'd
His turret crest and sleek enamel neck,
Fawning, and lick'd the ground whereon she trod.
His gentle dumb expression turn'd at length
The eye of Eve to mark his play. He, glad
Of her attention gain'd, with serpent tongue
Organic or impulse of vocal air
His fraudulent temptation thus began.
  Wonder not, sovereign mistress, if perhaps
Thou canst who art sole wonder, much less arm

Thy looks, the heaven of mildness, with disdain,
Displeas'd that I approach thee thus and gaze
Insatiate, I thus single, nor have fear'd
Thy awful brow, more awful thus retir'd.
Fairest resemblance of thy maker fair,
Thee all things living gaze on, all things thine
By gift, and thy celestial beauty adore
With ravishment beheld, there best beheld
Where universally admir'd, but here
In this enclosure wild, these beasts among,
Beholders rude and shallow to discern
Half what in thee is fair, one man except,
Who sees thee? and what is one? who should'st be seen
A goddess among gods, ador'd and serv'd
By angels numberless thy daily train.
  So gloz'd the tempter, and his proem tun'd.
Into the heart of Eve his words made way,
Though at the voice much marvelling; at length
Not unamaz'd she thus in answer spake.
  What may this mean? Language of man pronounc'd
By tongue of brute, and human sense express'd?
The first at least of these I thought deni'd
To beasts, whom God on their creation day
Created mute to all articulate sound;
The latter I demur, for in their looks
Much reason and in their actions oft appears.
Thee, serpent, subtlest beast of all the field
I knew, but not with human voice endu'd.
Redouble then this miracle, and say
How cam'st thou speakable of mute, and how
To me so friendly grown above the rest
Of brutal kind that daily are in sight?
Say, for such wonder claims attention due.
  To whom the guileful tempter thus repli'd.
Empress of this fair world, resplendent Eve,
Easy to me it is to tell thee all
What thou command'st, and right thou should'st be obey'd.
I was at first as other beasts that graze

The trodden herb, of abject thoughts and low
As was my food, nor aught but food discern'd
Or sex, and apprehended nothing high,
Till on a day roving the field I chanc'd
A goodly tree far distant to behold
Loaden with fruit of fairest colours mix'd,
Ruddy and gold. I nearer drew to gaze,
When from the boughs a savoury odour blown
Grateful to appetite more pleas'd my sense
Than smell of sweetest fennel or the teats
Of ewe or goat dropping with milk at even,
Unsuck'd of lamb or kid that tend their play.
To satisfy the sharp desire I had
Of tasting those fair apples I resolv'd
Not to defer; hunger and thirst at once,
Powerful persuaders, quicken'd at the scent
Of that alluring fruit, urg'd me so keen.
About the mossy trunk I wound me soon,
For high from ground the branches would require
Thy utmost reach or Adam's; round the tree
All other beasts that saw with like desire
Longing and envying stood, but could not reach.
Amid the tree now got, where plenty hung
Tempting so nigh, to pluck and eat my fill
I spar'd not, for such pleasure till that hour
At feed or fountain never had I found.
Sated at length, ere long I might perceive
Strange alteration in me, to degree
Of reason in my inward powers, and speech
Wanted not long, though to this shape retain'd.
Thenceforth to speculations high or deep
I turn'd my thoughts and with capacious mind
Consider'd all things visible in heaven
Or earth or middle, all things fair and good;
But all that fair and good in thy divine
Semblance and in thy beauty's heavenly ray
United I beheld, no fair to thine
Equivalent or second, which compell'd
Me thus, though importune perhaps, to come

And gaze, and worship thee of right declar'd
Sovereign of creatures, universal dame.
So talk'd the spirited sly snake; and Eve
Yet more amaz'd unwary thus repli'd.
Serpent, thy overpraising leaves in doubt
The virtue of that fruit, in thee first prov'd.
But say, where grows the tree, from hence how far?
For many are the trees of God that grow
In Paradise and various, yet unknown
To us; in such abundance lies our choice
As leaves a greater store of fruit untouch'd,
Still hanging incorruptible till men
Grow up to their provision and more hands
Help to disburden nature of her birth.
To whom the wily adder, blithe and glad,
Empress, the way is ready and not long,
Beyond a row of myrtles, on a flat
Fast by a fountain, one small thicket past
Of blowing myrrh and balm. If thou accept
My conduct, I can bring thee thither soon.
Lead then, said Eve. He leading swiftly roll'd
In tangles and made intricate seem straight,
To mischief swift. Hope elevates and joy
Brightens his crest, as when a wandering fire,
Compact of unctuous vapour which the night
Condenses and the cold environs round,
Kindled through agitation to a flame
Which oft, they say, some evil spirit attends
Hovering and blazing with delusive light,
Misleads th'amaz'd night-wanderer from his way
To bogs and mires, and oft through pond or pool,
There swallow'd up and lost, from succour far.
So glister'd the dire snake, and into fraud
Led Eve our credulous mother to the tree
Of prohibition, root of all our woe;
Which when she saw, thus to her guide she spake.
Serpent, we might have spar'd our coming hither,
Fruitless to me, though fruit be here to excess,

The credit of whose virtue rest with thee,
Wondrous indeed if cause of such effects.
But of this tree we may not taste or touch;
God so commanded, and left that command
Sole daughter of his voice; the rest, we live
Law to our selves, our reason is our law.
  To whom the tempter guilefully repli'd.
Indeed? Hath God then said that of the fruit
Of all these garden trees ye shall not eat,
Yet lords declar'd of all in earth or air?
  To whom thus Eve yet sinless, Of the fruit
Of each tree in the garden we may eat,
But of the fruit of this fair tree amidst
The garden God hath said, Ye shall not eat
Thereof, nor shall ye touch it, lest ye die.
  She scarce had said, though brief, when now more bold
The tempter, but with show of zeal and love
To man and indignation at his wrong,
New part puts on, and as to passion mov'd
Fluctuates disturb'd, yet comely and in act
Rais'd, as of some great matter to begin,
As when of old some orator renown'd
In Athens or free Rome, where eloquence
Flourish'd, since mute, to some great cause address'd,
Stood in himself collected while each part,
Motion, each act won audience ere the tongue,
Sometimes in height began, as no delay
Of preface brooking through his zeal of right;
So standing, moving or to height upgrown
The tempter all impassion'd thus began.
  O sacred, wise and wisdom-giving plant,
Mother of science, now I feel thy power
Within me clear, not only to discern
Things in their causes but to trace the ways
Of highest agents, deem'd however wise.
Queen of this universe, do not believe
Those rigid threats of death: ye shall not die.
How should ye? By the fruit? It gives you life
To knowledge. By the threatener? Look on me,

Me who have touch'd and tasted, yet both live
And life more perfect have attain'd than fate
Meant me, by venturing higher then my lot.
Shall that be shut to man which to the beast
Is open? Or will God incense his ire
For such a petty trespass, and not praise
Rather your dauntless virtue whom the pain
Of death denounc'd, whatever thing death be,
Deterr'd not from achieving what might lead
To happier life, knowledge of good and evil;
Of good, how just? Of evil, if what is evil
Be real, why not known, since easier shunn'd?
God therefore cannot hurt ye and be just;
Not just, not God; not fear'd then, nor obey'd;
Your fear itself of death removes the fear.
Why then was this forbid? Why but to awe,
Why but to keep ye low and ignorant,
His worshippers? He knows that in the day
Ye eat thereof your eyes, that seem so clear
Yet are but dim, shall perfectly be then
Open'd and clear'd, and ye shall be as gods,
Knowing both good and evil as they know.
That ye should be as gods since I as man,
Internal man, is but proportion meet:
I of brute human, ye of human gods.
So ye shall die perhaps, by putting off
Human to put on gods; death to be wish'd,
Though threaten'd, which no worse than this can bring.
And what are gods that man may not become
As they, participating godlike food?
The gods are first, and that advantage use
On our belief that all from them proceeds.
I question it, for this fair earth I see,
Warm'd by the sun, producing every kind,
Them nothing; if they all things, who enclos'd
Knowledge of good and evil in this tree,
That whoso eats thereof forthwith attains
Wisdom without their leave? And wherein lies

Th'offence that man should thus attain to know?
What can your knowledge hurt him, or this tree
Impart against his will, if all be his?
Or is it envy, and can envy dwell
In heavenly breasts? These, these and many more
Causes import your need of this fair fruit.
Goddess humane, reach then and freely taste.
  He ended, and his words, replete with guile,
Into her heart too easy entrance won.
Fix'd on the fruit she gaz'd, which to behold
Might tempt alone, and in her ears the sound
Yet rung of his persuasive words impregn'd
With reason, to her seeming, and with truth.
Meanwhile the hour of noon drew on, and wak'd
An eager appetite, rais'd by the smell
So savoury of that fruit, which with desire
Inclinable now grown to touch or taste
Solicited her longing eye; yet first
Pausing a while thus to herself she mus'd.
  Great are thy virtues, doubtless, best of fruits,
Though kept from man, and worthy to be admir'd,
Whose taste too long forborne at first assay
Gave elocution to the mute and taught
The tongue not made for speech to speak thy praise.
Thy praise he also who forbids thy use
Conceals not from us, naming thee the tree
Of knowledge, knowledge both of good and evil;
Forbids us then to taste, but his forbidding
Commends thee more while it infers the good
By thee communicated, and our want;
For good unknown sure is not had, or had
And yet unknown is as not had at all.
In plain, then, what forbids he but to know,
Forbids us good, forbids us to be wise?
Such prohibitions bind not; but if death
Bind us with after-bands, what profits then
Our inward freedom? In the day we eat
Of this fair fruit, our doom is, we shall die.

How dies the serpent? He hath eaten, and lives,
And knows, and speaks, and reasons, and discerns,
Irrational till then. For us alone
Was death invented? Or to us deni'd
This intellectual food, for beasts reserv'd?
For beasts it seems; yet that one beast which first
Hath tasted envies not, but brings with joy
The good befall'n him, author unsuspect,
Friendly to man, far from deceit or guile.
What fear I then, rather what know to fear
Under this ignorance of good and evil,
Of God or death, of law or penalty?
Here grows the cure of all, this fruit divine,
Fair to the eye, inviting to the taste,
Of virtue to make wise. What hinders then
To reach and feed at once both body and mind?
  So saying, her rash hand in evil hour
Forth reaching to the fruit she pluck'd, she ate.
Earth felt the wound, and nature from her seat
Sighing through all her works gave signs of woe
That all was lost. Back to the thicket slunk
The guilty serpent, and well might, for Eve,
Intent now wholly on her taste, naught else
Regarded; such delight till then, as seem'd,
In fruit she never tasted, whether true
Or fanci'd so through expectation high
Of knowledge, nor was godhead from her thought.
Greedily she engorg'd without restraint,
And knew not eating death. Satiate at length,
And heighten'd as with wine, jocund and boon,
Thus to herself she pleasingly began.
  O sovereign, virtuous, precious of all trees
In Paradise, of operation bless'd
To sapience hitherto obscur'd, infam'd,
And thy fair fruit let hang as to no end
Created; but henceforth my early care
Not without song each morning and due praise
Shall tend thee and the fertile burden ease
Of thy full branches offer'd free to all,

Till dieted by thee I grow mature
In knowledge as the gods, who all things know,
Though others envy what they cannot give,
For had the gift been theirs, it had not here
Thus grown. Experience, next to thee I owe,
Best guide; not following thee, I had remain'd
In ignorance; thou open'st wisdom's way
And giv'st access, though secret she retire.
And I perhaps am secret; heaven is high,
High and remote to see from thence distinct
Each thing on earth, and other care perhaps
May have diverted from continual watch
Our great forbidder, safe with all his spies
About him. But to Adam in what sort
Shall I appear? Shall I to him make known
As yet my change and give him to partake
Full happiness with me, or rather not,
But keep the odds of knowledge in my power
Without co-partner, so to add what wants
In female sex, the more to draw his love
And render me more equal, and perhaps,
A thing not undesirable, sometime
Superior? For inferior who is free?
This may be well; but what if God hath seen
And death ensue? Then I shall be no more,
And Adam wedded to another Eve
Shall live with her enjoying, I extinct,
A death to think. Confirm'd then I resolve,
Adam shall share with me in bliss or woe.
So dear I love him that with him all deaths
I could endure, without him live no life.
  So saying from the tree her step she turn'd,
But first low reverence done, as to the power
That dwelt within, whose presence had infus'd
Into the plant sciential sap deriv'd
From nectar, drink of gods. Adam the while
Waiting desirous her return had wove
Of choicest flowers a garland to adorn
Her tresses and her rural labours crown,

As reapers oft are wont their harvest queen.
Great joy he promis'd to his thoughts, and new
Solace in her return so long delay'd;
Yet oft his heart, divine of something ill,
Misgave him, he the falt'ring measure felt,
And forth to meet her went the way she took
That morn when first they parted. By the tree
Of knowledge he must pass; there he her met
Scarce from the tree returning, in her hand
A bough of fairest fruit that downy smil'd
New-gather'd and ambrosial smell diffus'd.
To him she hasted; in her face excuse
Came prologue and apology to prompt,
Which with bland words at will she thus address'd.
  Hast thou not wonder'd, Adam, at my stay?
Thee I have miss'd, and thought it long, depriv'd
Thy presence, agony of love till now
Not felt, nor shall be twice, for never more
Mean I to try what rash untri'd I sought,
The pain of absence from thy sight. But strange
Hath been the cause and wonderful to hear.
This tree is not as we were told, a tree
Of danger tasted, nor to evil unknown
Op'ning the way, but of divine effect
To open eyes and make them gods who taste,
And hath been tasted such: the serpent wise,
Or not restrain'd as we or nor obeying,
Hath eaten of the fruit, and is become
Not dead, as we are threaten'd, but thenceforth
Endu'd with human voice and human sense,
Reasoning to admiration, and with me
Persuasively hath so prevail'd that I
Have also tasted and have also found
Th' effects to correspond, opener mine eyes
Dim erst, dilated spirits, ampler heart,
And growing up to godhead, which for thee
Chiefly I sought, without thee can despise;
For bliss, as thou hast part, to me is bliss,
Tedious unshar'd with thee, and odious soon.

Thou therefore also taste, that equal lot
May join us, equal joy as equal love,
Lest thou not tasting, different degree
Disjoin us, and I then too late renounce
Deity for thee when fate will not permit.
  Thus Eve with count'nance blithe her story told,
But in her cheek distemper blushing glow'd.
On th'other side Adam, soon as he heard
The fatal trespass done by Eve, amaz'd,
Astoni'd stood and blank, while horror chill
Ran through his veins and all his joints relax'd.
From his slack hand the garland wreath'd for Eve
Down dropp'd and all the faded roses shed.
Speechless he stood and pale, till thus at length
First to himself he inward silence broke.
  O fairest of creation, last and best
Of all God's works, creature in whom excell'd
Whatever can to sight or thought be form'd
Holy, divine, good, amiable or sweet!
How art thou lost, how on a sudden lost,
Defac'd, deflower'd and now to death devote?
Rather how hast thou yielded to transgress
The strict forbiddance, how to violate
The sacred fruit forbidden? Some cursed fraud
Of enemy hath beguil'd thee, yet unknown,
And me with thee hath ruin'd, for with thee
Certain my resolution is to die;
How can I live without thee? How forgo
Thy sweet converse and love so dearly join'd
To live again in these wild woods forlorn?
Should God create another Eve, and I
Another rib afford, yet loss of thee
Would never from my heart; no, no, I feel
The link of nature draw me, flesh of flesh,
Bone of my bone thou art, and from thy state
Mine never shall be parted, bliss or woe.
  So having said, as one from sad dismay
Recomforted, and after thoughts disturb'd

Submitting to what seem'd remediless,
Thus in calm mood his words to Eve he turn'd.
  Bold deed thou hast presum'd, advent'rous Eve,
And peril great provok'd, who thus hast dar'd
Had it been only coveting to eye
That sacred fruit, sacred to abstinence,
Much more to taste it under ban to touch.
But past who can recall or done undo?
Not God omnipotent, nor fate; yet so
Perhaps thou shalt not die, perhaps the fact
Is not so heinous now, foretasted fruit,
Profan'd first by the serpent, by him first
Made common and unhallow'd ere our taste,
Nor yet on him found deadly; he yet lives,
Lives, as thou saidst, and gains to live as man
Higher degree of life, inducement strong
To us as likely tasting to attain
Proportional ascent, which cannot be
But to be gods, or angels, demi-gods.
Nor can I think that God, creator wise,
Though threat'ning, will in earnest so destroy
Us his prime creatures, dignifi'd so high,
Set over all his works, which in our fall
For us created needs with us must fail,
Dependent made; so God shall uncreate,
Be frustrate, do, undo and labour loose,
Not well conceiv'd of God, who though his power
Creation could repeat yet would be loth
Us to abolish, lest the adversary
Triumph and say, Fickle their state whom God
Most favours; who can please him long? Me first
He ruin'd, now mankind. Whom will he next?
Matter of scorn, not to be giv'n the foe.
However I with thee have fix'd my lot,
Certain to undergo like doom; if death
Consort with thee, death is to me as life,
So forcible within my heart I feel
The bond of nature draw me to my own,
My own in thee, for what thou art is mine.

Our state cannot be sever'd, we are one,
One flesh; to lose thee were to lose myself.
  So Adam; and thus Eve to him repli'd.
O glorious trial of exceeding love,
Illustrious evidence, example high,
Engaging me to emulate, but short
Of thy perfection how shall I attain,
Adam, from whose dear side I boast me sprung
And gladly of our union hear thee speak,
One heart, one soul in both, whereof good proof
This day affords, declaring thee resolv'd,
Rather than death or aught than death more dread
Shall separate us link'd in love so dear,
To undergo with me one guilt, one crime,
If any be of tasting this fair fruit
Whose virtue, for of good still good proceeds,
Direct or by occasion hath presented
This happy trial of thy love, which else
So eminently never had been known.
Were it I thought death menac'd would ensue
This my attempt, I would sustain alone
The worst and not persuade thee, rather die
Deserted than oblige thee with a fact
Pernicious to thy peace, chiefly assur'd
Remarkably so late of thy so true,
So faithful love unequall'd; but I feel
Far otherwise th' event, not death but life
Augmented, open'd eyes, new hopes, new joys,
Taste so divine that what of sweet before
Hath touch'd my sense flat seems to this and harsh.
On my experience, Adam, freely taste,
And fear of death deliver to the winds.
  So saying she embrac'd him and for joy
Tenderly wept, much won that he his love
Had so ennobled as of choice to incur
Divine displeasure for her sake and death.
In recompense (for such compliance bad
Such recompense best merits) from the bough
She gave him of that fair enticing fruit

With liberal hand; he scrupl'd not to eat
Against his better knowledge, not deceiv'd
But fondly overcome with female charm.
Earth trembl'd from her entrails as again
In pangs, and nature gave a second groan,
Sky lour'd and muttering thunder some sad drops
Wept at completing of the mortal sin
Original, while Adam took no thought,
Eating his fill, nor Eve to iterate
Her former trespass fear'd, the more to soothe
Him with her lov'd society, that now
As with new wine intoxicated both
They swim in mirth and fancy that they feel
Divinity within them breeding wings
Wherewith to scorn the earth. But that false fruit
Far other operation first display'd,
Carnal desire inflaming; he on Eve
Began to cast lascivious eyes, she him
As wantonly repaid. In lust they burn,
Till Adam thus gan Eve to dalliance move.
  Eve, now I see thou art exact of taste
And elegant, of sapience no small part,
Since to each meaning savour we apply
And palate call judicious. I the praise
Yield thee, so well this day thou hast purvey'd.
Much pleasure we have lost while we abstain'd
From this delightful fruit, nor known till now
True relish, tasting. If such pleasure be
In things to us forbidden, it might be wish'd
For this one tree had been forbidden ten.
But come, so well refresh'd now let us play,
As meet is after such delicious fare,
For never did thy beauty since the day
I saw thee first and wedded thee, adorn'd
With all perfections, so inflame my sense
With ardour to enjoy thee, fairer now
Than ever, bounty of this virtuous tree.
  So said he, and forbore not glance or toy
Of amorous intent, well understood

Of Eve, whose eye darted contagious fire.
Her hand he seiz'd and to a shady bank
Thick overhead with verdant roof embower'd
He led her nothing loth. Flowers were the couch,
Pansies and violets and asphodel
And hyacinth, earth's freshest softest lap.
There they their fill of love and love's disport
Took largely, of their mutual guilt the seal,
The solace of their sin, till dewy sleep
Oppress'd them, weari'd with their amorous play.
Soon as the force of that fallacious fruit
That with exhilarating vapour bland
About their spirits had play'd and inmost powers
Made err was now exhal'd, and grosser sleep
Bred of unkindly fumes, with conscious dreams
Encumber'd, now had left them, up they rose
As from unrest, and each the other viewing
Soon found their eyes how open'd, and their minds
How darken'd. Innocence, that as a veil
Had shadow'd them from knowing ill, was gone,
Just confidence and native righteousness
And honour from about them; naked left
To guilty shame he cover'd, but his robe
Uncover'd more. So rose the Danite strong,
Herculean Samson, from the harlot lap
Of Philistean Dalilah, and wak'd
Shorn of his strength, they destitute and bare
Of all their virtue. Silent and in face
Confounded long they sat, as strucken mute,
Till Adam, though not less than Eve abash'd,
At length gave utterance to these words constrain'd.
  O Eve, in evil hour thou didst give ear
To that false worm, of whomsoever taught
To counterfeit man's voice, true in our fall,
False in our promis'd rising, since our eyes
Open'd we find indeed, and find we know
Both good and evil, good lost and evil got,
Bad fruit of knowledge if this be to know

Which leaves us naked thus, of honour void,
Of innocence, of faith, of purity,
Our wonted ornaments now soil'd and stain'd,
And in our faces evident the signs
Of foul concupiscence, whence evil store,
Even shame, the last of evils; of the first
Be sure then. How shall I behold the face
Henceforth of God or angel, erst with joy
And rapture so oft beheld? Those heavenly shapes
Will dazzle now this earthly with their blaze
Insufferably bright. O might I here
In solitude live savage, in some glade
Obscur'd, where highest woods impenetrable
To star or sunlight spread their umbrage broad
And brown as evening; cover me ye pines,
Ye cedars, with innumerable boughs
Hide me where I may never see them more.
But let us now, as in bad plight, devise
What best may for the present serve to hide
The parts of each from other that seem most
To shame obnoxious and unseemliest seen,
Some tree whose broad smooth leaves together sew'd
And girded on our loins may cover round
Those middle parts, that this newcomer, shame,
There sit not and reproach us as unclean.
  So counsell'd he, and both together went
Into the thickest wood; there soon they chose
The fig-tree, not that kind for fruit renown'd,
But such as at this day to Indians known
In Malabar or Deccan spreads her arms
Branching so broad and long that in the ground
The bended twigs take root and daughters grow
About the mother tree, a pillar'd shade
High overarch'd, and echoing walks between;
There oft the Indian herdsman shunning heat
Shelters in cool, and tends his pasturing herds
At loopholes cut through thickest shade. Those leaves
They gather'd, broad as Amazonian targe,
And with what skill they had together sew'd

To gird their waist, vain covering if to hide
Their guilt and dreaded shame; O how unlike
To that first naked glory. Such of late
Columbus found th' American so girt
With feather'd cincture, naked else and wild
Among the trees on isles and woody shores.
Thus fenc'd and, as they thought, their shame in part
Cover'd, but not at rest or ease of mind,
They sat them down to weep, nor only tears
Rain'd at their eyes, but high winds worse within
Began to rise, high passions, anger, hate,
Mistrust, suspicion, discord, and shook sore
Their inward state of mind, calm region once
And full of peace, now toss'd and turbulent;
For understanding rul'd not and the will
Heard not her lore, both in subjection now
To sensual appetite who from beneath
Usurping over sovereign reason claim'd
Superior sway. From thus distemper'd breast
Adam, estrang'd in look and alter'd style,
Speech intermitted thus to Eve renew'd.
  Would thou hadst hearken'd to my words, and stay'd
With me as I besought thee, when that strange
Desire of wand'ring this unhappy morn
I know not whence possess'd thee; we had then
Remain'd still happy, not as now despoil'd
Of all our good, sham'd, naked, miserable.
Let none henceforth seek needless cause to approve
The faith they owe; when earnestly they seek
Such proof, conclude, they then begin to fall.
  To whom soon mov'd with touch of blame thus Eve.
What words have pass'd thy lips, Adam severe?
Imput'st thou that to my default or will
Of wand'ring, as thou call'st it, which who knows
But might as ill have happen'd thou being by,
Or to thyself perhaps? Hadst thou been there,
Or here th'attempt, thou could'st not have discern'd
Fraud in the serpent, speaking as he spake.
No ground of enmity between us known,

Why should he mean me ill or seek to harm?
Was I t' have never parted from thy side?
As good have grown there still a lifeless rib.
Being as I am, why didst not thou the head
Command me absolutely not to go,
Coming into such danger as thou said'st?
Too facile then thou didst not much gainsay,
Nay, didst permit, approve and fair dismiss.
Hadst thou been firm and fix'd in thy dissent,
Neither had I transgress'd nor thou with me.
To whom then first incens'd Adam repli'd.
Is this thy love, is this the recompense
Of mine to thee, ingrateful Eve, express'd
Immutable when thou wert lost, not I,
Who might have liv'd and joy'd immortal bliss,
Yet willingly chose rather death with thee?
And am I now upbraided as the cause
Of thy transgressing? Not enough severe,
It seems, in thy restraint; what could I more?
I warn'd thee, I admonish'd thee, foretold
The danger and the lurking enemy
That lay in wait; beyond this had been force,
And force upon free will hath here no place.
But confidence then bore thee on secure
Either to meet no danger or to find
Matter of glorious trial; and perhaps
I also err'd in overmuch admiring
What seem'd in thee so perfect that I thought
No evil durst attempt thee, but I rue
That error now, which is become my crime,
And thou th' accuser. Thus it shall befall
Him who to worth in women overtrusting
Lets her will rule; restraint she will not brook,
And left to herself, if evil thence ensue,
She first his weak indulgence will accuse.
Thus they in mutual accusation spent
The fruitless hours, but neither self-condemning,
And of their vain contest appear'd no end.

BOOK XII

As one who in his journey baits at noon
Though bent on speed, so here th' archangel paus'd
Betwixt the world destroy'd and world restor'd,
If Adam aught perhaps might interpose,
Then with transition sweet new speech resumes.
Thus thou hast seen one world begin and end,
And man as from a second stock proceed.
Much thou hast yet to see, but I perceive
Thy mortal sight to fail; objects divine
Must needs impair and weary human sense.
Henceforth what is to come I will relate;
Thou therefore give due audience, and attend.
This second source of men, while yet but few,
And while the dread of judgement past remains
Fresh in their minds fearing the Deity,
With some regard to what is just and right
Shall lead their lives, and multiply apace,
Labouring the soil and reaping plenteous crop,
Corn, wine and oil, and from the herd or flock
Oft sacrificing bullock, lamb or kid
With large wine-offerings pour'd and sacred feast,
Shall spend their days in joy unblam'd, and dwell
Long time in peace by families and tribes
Under paternal rule; till one shall rise
Of proud ambitious heart, who not content
With fair equality, fraternal state,
Will arrogate dominion undeserv'd
Over his brethren and quite dispossess
Concord and law of nature from the earth,
Hunting (and men, not beasts shall be his game)
With war and hostile snare such as refuse
Subjection to his empire tyrannous.
A mighty hunter thence he shall be styl'd
Before the Lord, as in despite of heaven
Or from heav'n claiming second sovereignty,
And from rebellion shall derive his name,
Though of rebellion others he accuse.

He, with a crew whom like ambition joins
With him or under him to tyrannise,
Marching from Eden towards the west shall find
The plain wherein a black bituminous gurge
Boils out from under ground, the mouth of hell;
Of brick and of that stuff they cast to build
A city and tower whose top may reach to heaven,
And get themselves a name, lest far-dispers'd
In foreign lands their memory be lost,
Regardless whether good or evil fame.
But God, who oft descends to visit men
Unseen and through their habitations walks
To mark their doings, them beholding soon
Comes down to see their city ere the tower
Obstruct heav'n towers, and in derision sets
Upon their tongues a various spirit to raze
Quite out their native language and instead
To sow a jangling noise of words unknown.
Forthwith a hideous gabble rises loud
Among the builders; each to other calls
Not understood, till hoarse and all in rage
As mock'd they storm. Great laughter was in heaven
And looking down, to see the hubbub strange
And hear the din. Thus was the building left
Ridiculous, and the the work confusion nam'd.
  Whereto thus Adam, fatherly displeas'd.
O execrable son thus to aspire
Above his brethren, to himself assuming
Authority usurp'd, from God not given.
He gave us only over beast, fish, fowl
Dominion absolute; that right we hold
By his donation. But man over men
He made not lord, such title to himself
Reserving, human left from human free.
But this usurper his encroachment proud
Stays not on man; to God his tower intends
Siege and defiance. Wretched man! What food
Will he convey up thither to sustain
Himself and his rash army, where thin air

Above the clouds will pine his entrails gross
And famish him of breath, if not of bread?
  To whom thus Michael, Justly thou abhorr'st
That son, who on the quiet state of men
Such trouble brought, affecting to subdue
Rational liberty. Yet know withal,
Since thy original lapse true liberty
Is lost, which always with right reason dwells
Twinn'd and from her hath no dividual being.
Reason in man obscur'd, or not obey'd,
Immediately inordinate desires
And upstart passions catch the government
From reason and to servitude reduce
Man till then free. Therefore since he permits
Within himself unworthy powers to reign
Over free reason, God in judgement just
Subjects him from without to violent lords,
Who oft as undeservedly enthrall
His outward freedom. Tyranny must be,
Though to the tyrant thereby no excuse.
Yet sometimes nations will decline so low
From virtue, which is reason, that no wrong
But justice, and some fatal curse annex'd,
Deprives them of their outward liberty,
Their inward lost; witness th' irreverent son
Of him that built the ark, who for the shame
Done to his father heard this heavy curse,
Servant of servants, on his vicious race.
Thus will this latter as the former world
Still tend from bad to worse, till God at last
Weari'd with their iniquities withdraw
His presence from among them and avert
His holy eyes, resolving from thenceforth
To leave them to their own polluted ways,
And one peculiar nation to select
From all the rest of whom to be invok'd,
A nation from one faithful man to spring,
Him on this side Euphrates yet residing,
Bred up in idol-worship. O that men

(Canst thou believe?) should be so stupid grown,
While yet the patriarch liv'd who scap'd the flood,
As to forsake the living God and fall
To worship their own work in wood or stone
For gods! Yet him God the most high vouchsafes
To call by vision from his father's house,
His kindred and false gods, into a land
Which he will show him, and from him will raise
A mighty nation and upon him shower
His benediction so, that in his seed
All nations shall be bless'd. He straight obeys,
Not knowing to what land, yet firm believes;
I see him, but thou canst not, with what faith
He leaves his gods, his friends and native soil,
Ur of Chaldea, passing now the ford
To Haran, after him a cumbrous train
Of herds and flocks and numerous servitude,
Not wandering poor, but trusting all his wealth
With God who call'd him in a land unknown.
Canaan he now attains, I see his tents
Pitch'd about Sechem and the neighbouring plain
Of Moreh. There by promise he receives
Gift to his progeny of all that land:
From Hamath northward to the desert south
(Things by their names I call, though yet unnam'd)
From Hermon east to the great western sea;
Mount Hermon, yonder sea, each place behold
In prospect as I point them; on the shore
Mount Carmel; here the double-founted stream
Jordan, true limit eastward; but his sons
Shall dwell to Senir, that long ridge of hills.
This ponder, that all nations of the earth
Shall in his seed be blessed; by that seed
Is meant thy great deliverer, who shall bruise
The serpent's head, whereof to thee anon
Plainlier shall be reveal'd. This patriarch bless'd,
Whom faithful Abraham due time shall call,
A son, and of his son a grandchild leaves,

Like him in faith, in wisdom and renown.
The grandchild with twelve sons increas'd departs
From Canaan to a land hereafter call'd
Egypt, divided by the river Nile;
See where it flows, disgorging at seven mouths
Into the sea. To sojourn in that land
He comes invited by a younger son
In time of dearth, a son whose worthy deeds
Raise him to be the second in that realm
To Pharaoh. There he dies, and leaves his race
Growing into a nation, and now grown
Suspected to a sequent king, who seeks
To stop their overgrowth, as inmate guests
Too numerous; whence of guests he makes them slaves
Inhospitably and kills their infant males,
Till by two brethren (those two brethren call
Moses and Aaron) sent from God to claim
His people from enthralment they return
With glory and spoil back to their promis'd land.
But first the lawless tyrant, who denies
To know their God or message to regard,
Must be compell'd by signs and judgements dire;
To blood unshed the rivers must be turn'd,
Frogs, lice and flies must all his palace fill
With loath'd intrusion, and fill all the land;
His cattle must of rot and murrain die,
Botches and blains must all his flesh emboss
And all his people; thunder mix'd with hail,
Hail mix'd with fire must rend th' Egyptian sky
And wheel on th'earth, devouring where it rolls;
What it devours not, herb, or fruit, or grain,
A darksome cloud of locusts swarming down
Must eat, and on the ground leave nothing green;
Darkness must overshadow all his bounds,
Palpable darkness, and blot out three days;
Last, with one midnight stroke all the first-born
Of Egypt must lie dead. Thus with ten wounds
The river-dragon tam'd at length submits
To let his sojourners depart, and oft

Humbles his stubborn heart, but still as ice
More harden'd after thaw, till in his rage
Pursuing whom he late dismiss'd, the sea
Swallows him with his host, but lets them pass
As on dry land between two crystal walls
Aw'd by the rod of Moses so to stand
Divided till his rescu'd gain their shore.
Such wondrous power God to his saint will lend,
Though present in his angel, who shall go
Before them in a cloud and pillar of fire,
By day a cloud, by night a pillar of fire
To guide them in their journey, and remove
Behind them while th'obdurate king pursues.
All night he will pursue, but his approach
Darkness defends between till morning watch;
Then through the fiery pillar and the cloud
God looking forth will trouble all his host
And craze their chariot wheels, when by command
Moses once more his potent rod extends
Over the sea. The sea his rod obeys;
On their embattl'd ranks the waves return
And overwhelm their war. The race elect
Safe towards Canaan from the shore advance
Through the wild desert, not the readiest way,
Lest entering on the Canaanite alarm'd
War terrify them inexpert, and fear
Return them back to Egypt, choosing rather
Inglorious life with servitude; for life
To noble and ignoble is more sweet
Untrain'd in arms, where rashness leads not on.
This also shall they gain by their delay
In the wide wilderness: there they shall found
Their government and their great senate choose
Through the twelve tribes to rule by laws ordain'd.
God from the mount of Sinai, whose grey top
Shall tremble, he descending, will himself
In thunder, lightning and loud trumpet's sound
Ordain them laws, part such as appertain
To civil justice, part religious rites

Of sacrifice, informing them, by types
And shadows of that destin'd seed to bruise
The serpent, by what means he shall achieve
Mankind's deliverance. But the voice of God
To mortal ear is dreadful; they beseech
That Moses might report to them his will,
And terror cease. He grants what they besought,
Instructed that to God is no access
Without mediator, whose high office now
Moses in figure bears, to introduce
One greater of whose day he shall foretell,
And all the prophets in their age the times
Of great Messiah shall sing. Thus laws and rites
Establish'd, such delight hath God in men
Obedient to his will that he vouchsafes
Among them to set up his tabernacle,
The holy one with mortal men to dwell.
By his prescript a sanctuary is fram'd
Of cedar overlaid with gold, therein
An ark, and in the ark his testimony,
The records of his cov'nant, over these
A mercy-seat of gold between the wings
Of two bright cherubim; before him burn
Seven lamps as in a zodiac representing
The heavenly fires; over the tent a cloud
Shall rest by day, a fiery gleam by night,
Save when they journey; and at length they come
Conducted by the angel to the land
Promis'd to Abraham and his seed. The rest
Were long to tell, how many battles fought,
How many kings destroy'd and kingdoms won,
Or how the sun shall in mid-heav'n stand still
A day entire and night's due course adjourn,
Man's voice commanding, sun in Gibeon stand,
And thou moon in the vale of Aialon,
Till Israel overcome: so call the third
From Abraham, son of Isaac, and from him
His whole descent, who thus shall Canaan win.
　Here Adam interpos'd. O sent from heaven

Enlight'ner of my darkness, gracious things
Thou hast reveal'd, those chiefly which concern
Just Abraham and his seed. Now first I find
Mine eyes true opening and my heart much eas'd,
Erewhile perplex'd with thoughts what would become
Of me and all mankind; but now I see
His day, in whom all nations shall be bless'd,
Favour unmerited by me who sought
Forbidden knowledge by forbidden means.
This yet I apprehend not, why to those
Amongst whom God will deign to dwell on earth
So many and so various laws are giv'n.
So many laws argue so many sins
Among them; how can God with such reside?
  To whom thus Michael, Doubt not but that sin
Will reign among them, as of thee begot;
And therefore was law given them, to evince
Their natural pravity by stirring up
Sin against law to fight, that when they see
Law can discover sin but not remove
Save by those shadowy expiations weak,
The blood of bulls and goats, they may conclude
Some blood more precious must be paid for man,
Just for unjust, that in such righteousness
To them by faith imputed they may find
Justification towards God and peace
Of conscience, which the law by ceremonies
Cannot appease nor man the moral part
Perform, and not performing cannot live.
So law appears imperfect, and but given
With purpose to resign them in full time
Up to a better cov'nant, disciplin'd
From shadowy types to truth, from flesh to spirit,
From imposition of strict laws to free
Acceptance of large grace, from servile fear
To filial, works of law to works of faith.
And therefore shall not Moses, though of God
Highly belov'd, being but the minister

Of law, his people into Canaan lead,
But Joshua, whom the gentiles Jesus call,
His name and office bearing, who shall quell
The adversary serpent and bring back
Through the world's wilderness long-wander'd man
Safe to eternal paradise of rest.
Meanwhile they in their earthly Canaan plac'd
Long time shall dwell and prosper, but when sins
National interrupt their public peace,
Provoking God to raise them enemies,
From whom as oft he saves them penitent
By judges first, then under kings, of whom
The second, both for piety renown'd
And puissant deeds, a promise shall receive
Irrevocable that his regal throne
For ever shall endure. The like shall sing
All prophecy that of the royal stock
Of David (so I name this king) shall rise
A son, the woman's seed to thee foretold,
Foretold to Abraham, as in whom shall trust
All nations, and to kings foretold, of kings
The last, for of his reign shall be no end.
But first a long succession must ensue,
And his next son, for wealth and wisdom fam'd,
The clouded ark of God, till then in tents
Wand'ring, shall in a glorious temple enshrine.
Such follow him as shall be register'd
Part good, part bad, of bad the longer scroll,
Whose foul idolatries and other faults,
Heap'd to the popular sum, will so incense
God as to leave them and expose their land,
Their city, his temple and his holy ark
With all his sacred things a scorn and prey
To that proud city whose high walls thou saw'st
Left in confusion, Babylon thence call'd.
There in captivity he lets them dwell
The space of seventy years, then brings them back,
Rememb'ring mercy and his cov'nant sworn
To David, stablish'd as the days of heaven.

Return'd from Babylon by leave of kings
Their lords, whom God dispos'd, the house of God
They first re-edify, and for a while
In mean estate live moderate, till grown
In wealth and multitude factious they grow;
But first among the priests dissension springs,
Men who attend the altar and should most
Endeavour peace. Their strife pollution brings
Upon the temple itself; at last they seize
The sceptre and regard not David's sons,
Then lose it to a stranger, that the true
Anointed king Messiah might be born
Barr'd of his right. Yet at his birth a star
Unseen before in heaven proclaims him come,
And guides the eastern sages, who enquire
His place to offer incense, myrrh and gold.
His place of birth a solemn angel tells
To simple shepherds keeping watch by night;
They gladly thither haste, and by a choir
Of squadron'd angels hear his carol sung.
A virgin is his mother, but his sire
The power of the most high. He shall ascend
The throne hereditary and bound his reign
With earth's wide bounds, his glory with the heavens.
  He ceas'd, discerning Adam with such joy
Surcharg'd as had like grief been dew'd in tears
Without the vent of words, which these he breath'd.
  O prophet of glad tidings, finisher
Of utmost hope! Now clear I understand
What oft my steadiest thoughts have search'd in vain,
Why our great expectation should be call'd
The seed of woman. Virgin mother, hail,
High in the love of heaven, yet from my loins
Thou shalt proceed, and from thy womb the son
Of God most high; so God with man unites.
Needs must the serpent now his capital bruise
Expect with mortal pain; say where and when
Their fight, what stroke shall bruise the victor's heel.
  To whom thus Michael, Dream not of their fight

As of a duel, or the local wounds
Of head or heel; not therefore joins the Son
Manhood to godhead, with more strength to foil
Thy enemy, nor so is overcome
Satan, whose fall from heaven, a deadlier bruise,
Disabled not to give thee thy death's wound,
Which he who comes thy saviour shall recure
Not by destroying Satan but his works
In thee and in thy seed; nor can this be
But by fulfilling that which thou didst want,
Obedience to the law of God impos'd
On penalty of death, and suffering death,
The penalty of thy transgression due,
And due to theirs which out of thine will grow;
So only can high justice rest apaid.
The law of God exact he shall fulfil
Both by obedience and by love, though love
Alone fulfil the law; thy punishment
He shall endure by coming in the flesh
To a reproachful life and cursed death,
Proclaiming life to all who shall believe
In his redemption, and that his obedience
Imputed becomes theirs by faith, his merits
To save them, not their own, though legal works.
For this he shall live hated, be blasphem'd,
Seiz'd on by force, judg'd, and to death condemn'd
A shameful and accurs'd, nail'd to the cross
By his own nation, slain for bringing life;
But to the cross he nails thy enemies,
The law that is against thee and the sins
Of all mankind with him there crucifi'd,
Never to hurt them more who rightly trust
In this his satisfaction. So he dies,
But soon revives; death over him no power
Shall long usurp. Ere the third dawning light
Return, the stars of morn shall see him rise
Out of his grave, fresh as the dawning light,
Thy ransom paid which man from death redeems,
His death for man, as many as offer'd life

Neglect not and the benefit embrace
By faith not void of works. This godlike act
Annuls thy doom, the death thou should'st have died,
In sin forever lost from life; this act
Shall bruise the head of Satan, crush his strength,
Defeating sin and death, his two main arms,
And fix far deeper in his head their stings
Than temporal death shall bruise the victor's heel
Or theirs whom he redeems, a death-like sleep,
A gentle wafting to immortal life.
Nor after resurrection shall he stay
Longer on earth than certain times to appear
To his disciples, men who in his life
Still follow'd him; to them shall leave in charge
To teach all nations what of him they learn'd
And his salvation, them who shall believe
Baptising in the profluent stream, the sign
Of washing them from guilt of sin to life
Pure, and in mind prepar'd, if so befall,
For death like that which the redeemer died.
All nations they shall teach, for from that day
Not only to the sons of Abraham's loins
Salvation shall be preach'd but to the sons
Of Abraham's faith wherever through the world,
So in his seed all nations shall be bless'd.
Then to the heaven of heavens he shall ascend
With victory, triumphing through the air
Over his foes and thine; there shall surprise
The serpent, prince of air, and drag in chains
Through all his realm, and there confounded leave;
Then enter into glory and resume
His seat at God's right hand, exalted high
Above all names in heaven, and thence shall come
When this world's dissolution shall be ripe
With glory and power to judge both quick and dead,
To judge th' unfaithful dead, but to reward
His faithful and receive them into bliss,
Whether in heaven or earth; for then the earth

Shall all be paradise, far happier place
Than this of Eden, and far happier days.
  So spake th' archangel Michael, then paus'd,
As at the world's great period, and our sire
Replete with joy and wonder thus repli'd.
  O goodness infinite, goodness immense!
That all this good of evil shall produce
And evil turn to good, more wonderful
Than that which by creation first brought forth
Light out of darkness! Full of doubt I stand
Whether I should repent me now of sin
By me done and occasion'd, or rejoice
Much more that much more good thereof shall spring,
To God more glory, more goodwill to men
From God, and over wrath grace shall abound.
But say, if our deliverer up to heaven
Must reascend, what will betide the few
His faithful, left among th' unfaithful herd,
The enemies of truth? Who then shall guide
His people, who defend? Will they not deal
Worse with his followers than with him they dealt?
  Be sure they will, said th' angel; but from heaven
He to his own a comforter will send,
The promise of the Father, who shall dwell
His spirit within them, and the law of faith
Working through love upon their hearts shall write,
To guide them in all truth, and also arm
With spiritual armour able to resist
Satan's assaults and quench his fiery darts,
What man can do against them not afraid
Though to the death, against such cruelties
With inward consolations recompens'd
And oft supported so as shall amaze
Their proudest persecutors; for the spirit
Pour'd first on his apostles, whom he sends
T' evangelize the nations, then on all
Baptiz'd, shall them with wondrous gifts endue
To speak all tongues and do all miracles,
As did their Lord before them. Thus they win

Great numbers of each nation to receive
With joy the tidings brought from heaven; at length,
Their ministry perform'd and race well run,
Their doctrine and their story written left,
They die, but in their room, as they forewarn,
Wolves shall succeed for teachers, grievous wolves,
Who all the sacred mysteries of heaven
To their own vile advantages shall turn
Of lucre and ambition, and the truth
With superstitions and traditions taint,
Left only in those written records pure
Though not but by the spirit understood.
Then they shall seek to avail themselves of names,
Places and titles, and with these to join
Secular power, though feigning still to act
By spiritual, to themselves appropriating
The spirit of God promis'd alike and giv'n
To all believers, and from that pretence
Spiritual laws by carnal power shall force
On every conscience, laws which none shall find
Left them enroll'd, or what the spirit within
Shall on the heart engrave. What will they then
But force the spirit of grace itself, and bind
His consort liberty? What, but unbuild
His living temples, built by faith to stand,
Their own faith not another's? For on earth
Who against faith and conscience can be heard
Infallible? Yet many will presume,
Whence heavy persecution shall arise
Of all who in the worship persevere
Of spirit and truth; the rest, far greater part,
Well deem in outward rites and specious forms
Religion satisfi'd. Truth shall retire
Bestuck with sland'rous darts, and works of faith
Rarely be found; so shall the world go on,
To good malignant, to bad men benign,
Under her own weight groaning till the day
Appear of respiration to the just
And vengeance to the wicked at return

Of him so lately promis'd to thy aid,
The woman's seed, obscurely then foretold,
Now amplier known thy saviour and thy Lord,
Last in the clouds from heaven to be reveal'd
In glory of the Father, to dissolve
Satan with his perverted world, then raise
From the conflagrant mass, purg'd and refin'd,
New heavens, new earth, ages of endless date
Founded in righteousness and peace and love
To bring forth fruits, joy and eternal bliss.
He ended, and thus Adam last repli'd.
How soon hath thy prediction, seer bless'd,
Measur'd this transient world, the race of time,
Till time stand fix'd; beyond is all abyss,
Eternity, whose end no eye can reach.
Greatly instructed I shall hence depart,
Greatly in peace of thought, and have my fill
Of knowledge what this vessel can contain,
Beyond which was my folly to aspire.
Henceforth I learn that to obey is best,
And love with fear the only God, to walk
As in his presence, ever to observe
His providence and on him sole depend,
Merciful over all his works, with good
Still overcoming evil and by small
Accomplishing great things, by things deem'd weak
Subverting worldly strong and worldly wise
By simply meek; that suffering for truth's sake
Is fortitude to highest victory,
And to the faithful, death the gate of life;
Taught this by his example whom I now
Acknowledge my redeemer ever bless'd.
To whom thus also th'angel last repli'd.
This having learn'd, thou hast attain'd the sum
Of wisdom. Hope no higher, though all the stars
Thou knew'st by name and all th' ethereal powers,
All secrets of the deep, all nature's works
Or works of God in heaven, air, earth or sea,
And all the riches of this world enjoy'st,

And all the rule, one empire. Only add
Deeds to thy knowledge answerable, add faith,
Add virtue, patience, temperance, add love
By name to come call'd charity, the soul
Of all the rest; then wilt thou not be loth
To leave this Paradise, but shalt possess
A paradise within thee, happier far.
Let us descend now therefore from this top
Of speculation, for the hour precise
Exacts our parting hence; and see, the guards
Encamp'd by me on yonder hill expect
Their motion, at whose front a flaming sword
In signal of remove waves fiercely round.
We may no longer stay; go, waken Eve.
Her also I with gentle dreams have calm'd
Portending good, and all her spirits compos'd
To meek submission. Thou at season fit
Let her with thee partake what thou hast heard,
Chiefly what may concern her faith to know,
The great deliverance by her seed to come
(For by the woman's seed) on all mankind,
That ye may live, which will be many days,
Both in one faith unanimous, though sad
With cause for evils past, yet much more cheer'd
With meditation on the happy end.
He ended, and they both descend the hill.
Descended, Adam to the bower where Eve
Lay sleeping ran before, but found her wak'd;
And thus with words not sad she him receiv'd.
Whence thou return'st and whither went'st I know,
For God is also in sleep, and dreams advise,
Which he hath sent propitious, some great good
Presaging, since with sorrow and heart's distress
Weari'd I fell asleep. But now lead on;
In me is no delay. With thee to go
Is to stay here, without thee here to stay
Is to go hence unwilling; thou to me
Art all things under heaven, all places thou,

Who for my wilful crime art banish'd hence.
This further consolation yet secure
I carry hence: though all by me is lost,
Such favour I unworthy am vouchsaf'd,
By me the promis'd seed shall all restore.
  So spake our mother Eve, and Adam heard
Well pleas'd but answer'd not; for now too nigh
Th' archangel stood, and from the other hill
To their fix'd station all in bright array
The cherubim descended, on the ground
Gliding meteorous, as evening mist
Ris'n from a river o'er the marish glides
And gathers ground fast at the labourer's heel
Homeward returning. High in front advanc'd
The brandish'd sword of God before them blaz'd
Fierce as a comet, which with torrid heat
And vapour as the Lybian air adust
Began to parch that temperate clime; whereat
In either hand the hast'ning angel caught
Our lingering parents and to th' eastern gate
Led them direct, and down the cliff as fast
To the subjected plain, then disappear'd.
They looking back all th' eastern side beheld
Of Paradise, so late their happy seat,
Wav'd over by that flaming sword, the gate
With dreadful faces throng'd and fiery arms.
Some natural tears they dropp'd, but wip'd them soon;
The world was all before them, where to choose
Their place of rest, and providence their guide.
They hand in hand with wand'ring steps and slow
Through Eden took their solitary way.

The History of Britain

From Book 1

The beginning of nations, those excepted of whom sacred books have spoken, is to this day unknown. Nor only the beginning, but the deeds also of many succeeding ages, yea periods of ages, either wholly unknown, or obscured and blemished with fables; whether it were that the use of letters came in long after, or were it the violence of barbarous inundations, or they themselves at certain revolutions of time fatally decaying and degenerating into sloth and ignorance, whereby the monuments of more ancient civility have been some destroyed, some lost. Perhaps disesteem and contempt of the public affairs then present, as not worth recording, might partly be the cause. Certainly oft-times we see that wise men and of best ability have forborne to write the acts of their own days, while they beheld with a just loathing and disdain not only how unworthy, how perverse, how corrupt, but often how ignoble, how petty, how below all history the persons and their actions were who either by fortune or some rude election had attained, as a sore judgement and ignominy upon the land, to have chief sway in managing the commonwealth. But that any law or superstition of our old philosophers the Druids forbade the Britons to write their memorable deeds, I know not why any out of Caesar should allege. He indeed saith that their doctrine they thought not lawful to commit to letters, but in most matters else, both private and public, among which well may history be reckoned, they used the Greek tongue; and that the

British Druids who taught those in Gaul would be ignorant of any language known and used by their disciples or, so frequently writing other things and so inquisitive into highest, would for want of recording be ever children in the knowledge of times and ages is not likely. Whatever might be the reason, this we find, that of British affairs from the first peopling of the island to the coming of Julius Caesar nothing certain, either by tradition, history or ancient fame, hath hitherto been left us. That which we have of oldest seeming hath by the greater part of judicious antiquaries been long rejected for a modern fable.

Nevertheless, there being others besides the first supposed author, men not unread nor unlearned in antiquity, who admit that for approved story which the former explode for fiction, and seeing that oft-times relations heretofore accounted fabulous have been after found to contain in them many footsteps and relics of something true (as we read in poets of the flood and giants little believed, till undoubted witnesses taught us that all was not feigned), I have therefore determined to bestow the telling-over even of these reputed tales, be it for nothing else but in favour of our English poets and rhetoricians, who by their art will know how to use them judiciously.

I might also produce example, as Diodorus among the Greeks, Livy and others of the Latins, Polydore and Virunius accounted among our own writers. But I intend not with controversies and quotations to delay and interrupt the smooth course of history, much less to argue and debate long who were the first inhabitants, with what probabilities, what authorities each opinion hath been upheld, but shall endeavour that which hitherto hath been needed most, with plain and lightsome brevity to relate well and orderly things worth the noting, so as may best instruct and benefit them that read. Which, imploring divine assistance that it may redound to his glory and the good of the British nation, I now begin.

That the whole earth was inhabited before the Flood, and to the utmost point of habitable ground, from those effectual words of God in the creation may be more than conjectured. Hence that this island also had her dwellers, her affairs and perhaps her stories, even in that old world those many hundred years, with much reason we may infer. After the Flood and the dispersing of nations, as they journeyed leisurely from the east, Gomer the eldest son of Japhet and his offspring, as by authorities, arguments and affinity of divers names is generally believed, were the first that peopled all these west and northern climes. But they of our own writers who thought they had done nothing unless with all circumstance they tell us when and who first set foot upon this island presume to name out of fabulous and counterfeit authors a certain Samothes or Dis, a fourth or sixth son of Japhet, whom they make, about 200 years after the Flood, to have planted with colonies first the continent of Celtica, or Gaul, and next this island; thence to have named it Samothea, to have reigned here, and after him lineally four kings, Magus, Saron, Druis and Bardus. But the forged Berosus, whom only they have to cite, nowhere mentions that either he or any of those whom they bring did ever pass into Britain, or send their people hither; so that this outlandish figment may easily excuse our not allowing it the room here so much as of a British fable. That which follows, perhaps as wide from truth, though seeming less impertinent, is that these Samotheans under the reign of Bardus were subdued by Albion, a giant, son of Neptune, who called the island after his own name and ruled it forty-four years, till at length, passing over into Gaul in aid of his brother Lestrygon, against whom Hercules was hasting out of Spain into Italy, he was there slain in fight, and Bergion also his brother.

Sure enough we are that Britain hath been anciently termed Albion, both by the Greeks and Romans; and Mela the geographer makes mention of a stony shore in Languedoc where by report such a battle was fought. The rest, as his giving his name to the isle, or ever landing here, depends altogether upon late surmises. But too absurd and too unconscionably gross is that fond invention that wafted hither the fifty daughters of a strange Dioclesian, king of Syria, brought in doubtless by some illiterate pretender to something mistaken in the common poetical story of Danaus king of Argos, while his vanity, not pleased with the obscure beginning which truest antiquity affords the nation, laboured to contrive us a pedigree, as he thought, more noble. These daughters, by appointment of

Danaus on the marriage-night having murdered all their husbands except Lynceus, whom his wife's loyalty saved, were by him, at the suit of his wife their sister, not put to death but turned out to sea in a ship unmanned, of which whole sex they had incurred the hate, and, as the tale goes, were driven on this island, where the inhabitants – none but devils, as some write, or as others, a lawless crew left here by Albion without head or governor – both entertained them and had issue by them, a second breed of giants, who tyrannized the isle till Brutus came.

The eldest of these dames in their legend they call Albina, and from thence, for which cause the whole scene was framed, will have the name Albion derived. Incredible it may seem so sluggish a conceit should prove so ancient as to be authorised by the elder Nennius, reputed to have lived above a thousand years ago. This I find not in him, but that Histion, sprung of Japhet, had four sons, Francus, Romanus, Alemannus and Britto, of whom the Britons; as true, I believe, as that those other nations whose names are resembled came of the other three, if these dreams give not just occasion to call in doubt the book itself which bears that title.

Hitherto the things themselves have given us a warrantable dispatch to run them soon over. But now of Brutus and his line, with the whole progeny of kings to the entrance of Julius Caesar, we cannot so easily be discharged: descents of ancestry long continued, laws and exploits not plainly seeming to be borrowed or devised, which on the common belief have wrought no small impression, defended by many, denied utterly by few. For what though Brutus and the whole Trojan pretence were yielded up, seeing they who first devised to bring us from some noble ancestor were content at first with Brutus the consul, till better invention, although not willing to forgo the name, taught them to remove it higher into a more fabulous age, and by the same remove, lighting on the Trojan tales, in affectation to make the Briton of one original with the Roman, pitched there; yet those old and inborn names of successive kings never any to have been real persons or done in their lives at least some part of what so long hath been remembered cannot be thought without too strict an incredulity.

For these and those causes above mentioned, that which hath received approbation from so many I have chosen not to omit. Certain or uncertain, be that upon the credit of those whom I must follow; so far as keeps aloof from impossible and absurd, attested by ancient writers from books more ancient, I refuse not as the due and proper subject of story. The principal author is well known to be Geoffrey of Monmouth. What he was, and whence his authority, who in his age or before him have delivered the same matter and suchlike general discourses will better stand in a treatise by themselves. All of them agree in this, that Brutus was the son of Silvius; he of Ascanius, whose father was Aeneas a Trojan prince who at the burning of that city, with his son Ascanius and a collected number that escaped, after long wandering on the sea arrived in Italy, where at length by the assistance of Latinus king of Latium, who had given him his daughter Lavinia, he obtained to succeed in that kingdom, and left it to Ascanius, whose son Silvius (though Roman histories deny Silvius to be son of Ascanius) had married secretly a niece of Lavinia. She being with child, the matter became known to Ascanius, who, commanding his magicians to inquire by art what sex the maid had conceived, had answer that it was one who should be the death of both his parents, and banished for the fact, should after all in a far country attain to highest honour. The prediction failed not; for in travail the mother died, and Brutus (the child was so called) at fifteen years of age, attending his father to the chase, with an arrow unfortunately killed him.

Banished therefore by his kindred he retires into Greece, where meeting with the race of Helenus, King Priam's son, held there in servile condition by Pandrasus then king, with them he abides. For Pyrrhus, in revenge of his father slain at Troy, had brought thither with him Helenus and many others into servitude. There Brutus among his own stock so thrives in virtue and in arms as renders him beloved to kings and great captains above all the youth of that land; whereby the Trojans not only begin to hope but secretly to move him that he would lead them the way to liberty. They allege their numbers, and the promised help of Assaracus, a noble Greekish youth, by his mother's side a Trojan, whom for that cause his brother went about to dispossess of certain castles bequeathed him by his father. Brutus, considering both the forces offered him and the strength of those holds, not unwillingly consents. First therefore having fortified those castles, he with Assaracus and the whole multitude betake them to the woods and hills, as the safest place from whence to expostulate, and in the name of all sends to Pandrasus this message, that the Trojans, holding it unworthy their ancestors to serve in a foreign kingdom, had retreated to the woods, choosing rather a savage life than a slavish; if that displeased him, that then with his leave they might depart to some other soil.

As this may pass with good allowance, that the Trojans might be many in these parts, for Helenus was by Pyrrhus made king of the Chaonians, and the sons of Pyrrhus by Andromache, Hector's wife, could not but be powerful through all Epirus, so much the more it may be doubted how these Trojans could be thus in bondage, where they had friends and countrymen so potent. But to examine these things with diligence were but to confute the fables of Britain with the fables of Greece or Italy; for of this age what we have to say, as well concerning most other countries as this island, is equally under question.

Be how it will, Pandrasus, not expecting so bold a message from the sons of captives, gathers an army; and marching towards the woods, Brutus, who had notice of his approach nigh to a town called Sparatinum (I know not what town, but certain of no Greek name), overnight planting himself there with good part of his men, suddenly sets upon him and with slaughter of the Greeks pursues him to the passage of a river which mine author names Akalon, meaning perhaps Achelous or Acheron, where at the ford he overlays them afresh. This victory obtained, and a sufficient strength left in Sparatinum, Brutus with Antigonus the king's brother and his friend Anacletus, whom he had taken in the fight, returns to the residue of his friends in the thick woods, while Pandrasus, with all speed recollecting, besieges the town. Brutus, to relieve his men besieged who earnestly called him, distrusting the sufficiency of his force, bethinks himself of this policy: calls to him Anacletus, and threatening instant death else both to him and his friend Antigonus, enjoins him that he should go at the second hour of night to the Greekish leaguer and tell the guards he had brought Antigonus by stealth out of prison to a certain woody vale, unable through the weight of his fetters to move further, entreating them to come speedily and fetch him in. Anacletus, to save both himself and his friend Antigonus, swears this, and at fit hour sets on alone toward the camp, is met, examined, and at last unquestionably known; to whom great profession of fidelity first made, he frames his tale as had been taught him, and they now fully assured, with a credulous rashness leaving their stations, fared accordingly by the ambush that there awaited them. Forthwith Brutus, dividing his men into three parts, leads on in silence to the camp, commanding first each part at a several place to enter, and forbear execution till he with his squadron possessed of the king's tent gave signal to them by trumpet; the sound whereof no sooner heard but huge havoc begins upon the sleeping and unguarded enemy, whom the besieged also now sallying forth on the other side assail. Brutus the while had special care to seize and secure the king's person, whose life still within his custody he knew was the surest pledge to obtain what he should demand. Day appearing, he enters the town, there distributes the king's treasury, and leaving the place better fortified returns with the king his prisoner to the woods. Straight the ancient and grave men he summons to counsel what they should now demand of the king.

After long debate Mempricius, one of the gravest, utterly dissuading them from thought of longer stay in Greece unless they meant to be deluded with a subtle peace and the awaited revenge of those whose friends they had slain, advises them to demand, first, the king's eldest daughter Innogen in marriage to their leader Brutus, with a rich dowry; next, shipping, money and fit provision for them all to depart the land. This resolution pleasing best, the king now brought in and placed in a high seat is briefly told that on these conditions granted he might be free, not granted he must prepare to die. Pressed with fear of death, the king readily yields, especially to bestow his daughter on whom he confessed so noble and valiant; offers them also the third part of his kingdom if they like to stay; if not, to be their hostage himself till he had made good his word.

The marriage therefore solemnized and shipping from all parts got together, the Trojans in a fleet, no less written than three hundred four and twenty sail, betake them to the wide sea, where with a prosperous course two days and a night bring them on a certain island long before dispeopled and left waste by sea-rovers, the name whereof was then Leogecia, now unknown. They who were sent out to discover came at length to a ruined city, where was a temple and image of Diana that gave oracles; but not meeting first or last save wild beasts, they return with this notice to their ships, wishing their general would inquire of that oracle what voyage to pursue. Consultation had, Brutus, taking with him Gerion his diviner and twelve of the ancientest, with wonted ceremonies before the inward shrine of the goddess, in verse, as it seems the manner was, utters his request, *Diva potens nemorum*, etc:

Goddess of shades and Huntress, who at will
Walk'st on the rolling sphere and through the deep,
On thy third reign the Earth look now, and tell
What land, what seat of rest thou bidst me seek,
What certain seat where I may worship thee
For aye, with temples vow'd and virgin choirs.

To whom, sleeping before the altar, Diana in a vision that night thus answered, *Brute sub occasum solis*, etc:

Brutus, far to the west, in th'ocean wide,
Beyond the realm of Gaul, a land there lies,
Sea-girt it lies, where giants dwelt of old.
Now void, it fits thy people; thither bend
Thy course, there shalt thou find a lasting seat,
There to thy sons another Troy shall rise,
And kings be born of thee, whose dreaded might
Shall awe the world, and conquer nations bold.

These verses, originally Greek, were put in Latin, saith Virunius, by Gildas, a British poet, and him to have lived under

Claudius; which granted true adds much to the antiquity of this fable. And indeed the Latin verses are much better than for the age of Geoffrey ap-Arthur, unless perhaps Joseph of Exeter, the only smooth poet of those times, befriended him. In this Diana overshot her oracle, thus ending, *Ipsis totius terrae subditus orbis erit*, that to the race of Brute, kings of this island, the whole earth shall be subject.

But Brutus, guided now as he thought by divine conduct, speeds him towards the west, and after some encounters on the Afric side arrives at a place on the Tyrrhene sea, where he happens to find the race of those Trojans who with Antenor came into Italy, and Corineus, a man much famed, was their chief; though by surer authors it be reported that those Trojans with Antenor were seated on the other side of Italy, on the Adriatic not the Tyrrhene shore. But these joining company, and past the Herculean Pillars, at the mouth of Ligeris in Aquitania cast anchor, where after some discovery made of the place, Corineus, hunting nigh the shore with his men, is by messengers of the king Goffarius Pictus met and questioned about his errand there, who not answering to their mind, Imbertus, one of them, lets fly an arrow at Corineus, which he avoiding slays him; and the Pictavian himself hereupon levying his whole force is overthrown by Brutus and Corineus, who with the battle-axe which he was wont to manage against the Tyrrhene giants is said to have done marvels. But Goffarius, having drawn to his aid the whole country of Gaul, at that time governed by twelve kings, puts his fortune to a second trial, wherein the Trojans, overborne by multitude, are driven back and besieged in their own camp, which by good foresight was strongly situate; whence Brutus unexpectedly issuing out and Corineus in the meanwhile, whose device it was, assaulting them behind from a wood where he had conveyed his men the night before, the Trojans are again victors, but with the loss of Turon, a valiant nephew of Brutus, whose ashes left in that place gave name to the city of Tours, built there by the Trojans. Brutus, finding now his powers much lessened, and this yet not the place foretold him, leaves Aquitaine, and with an easy course arriving at Totnes in Devonshire quickly perceives here to be the promised end of his labours.

The island, not yet Britain but Albion, was in a manner desert and inhospitable, kept only by a remnant of giants whose excessive force and tyranny had consumed the rest. Them Brutus destroys, and to his people divides the land, which with some reference to his own name he thenceforth calls Britain. To Corineus Cornwall, as we now call it, fell by lot, the rather by him liked for that the hugest giants in rocks and caves were said to lurk still there, which kind of monsters to deal with was his old exercise. And here (with leave bespoken to recite a grand fable, though dignified by our best poets), while Brutus on a certain festival-day, solemnly kept on that shore where he first landed, was with the people in great jollity and mirth, a crew of these savages breaking in upon them began on the sudden another sort of game than at such a meeting was expected. But at length by many hands overcome, Goemagog the hugest, in girth twelve cubits, is reserved alive, that with him Corineus, who desired nothing more, might try his strength; whom in a wrestle the giant catching aloft with a terrible hug broke three of his ribs. Nevertheless Corineus enraged, heaving him up by main force, threw him headlong all shattered into the sea and left his name on the cliff, called ever since Langoemagog, which is to say the giant's leap.

After this, Brutus in a chosen place builds Troia Nova, changed in time to Trinovantum, now London, and began to enact laws, Eli being then high priest in Judaea; and having governed the whole isle 24 years, died and was buried in his new Troy. His three sons Locrine, Albanact and Camber divide the land by consent. Locrine had the middle part, Loegria, Camber possessed Cambria or Wales, Albanact Albania, now Scotland; but he in the end by Humber king of the Huns, who with a fleet invaded that land, was slain in fight and his people driven back into Loegria. Locrine and his brother go out against Humber, who now marching onward was by them defeated, and in a river drowned which to this day retains his name. Among the spoils of his camp and navy were found certain young maids, and Estrildis above the rest passing fair, the daughter of a king in Germany, from whence Humber, as he went wasting the sea-coast, had led her captive; whom

Locrine, though before contracted to the daughter of Corineus, resolves to marry. But being forced and threatened by Corineus, whose authority and power he feared, Gwendolen the daughter he yields to marry, but in secret loves the other, and oft-times retiring as to some private sacrifice through vaults and passages made underground, and seven years thus enjoying her, had by her a daughter equally fair, whose name was Sabra. But when once his fear was off by the death of Corineus, not content with secret enjoyment, divorcing Gwendolen he makes Estrildis now his queen. Gwendolen all in rage departs into Cornwall, where Madan, the son she had by Locrine, was hitherto brought up by Corineus his grandfather, and gathering an army of her father's friends and subjects gives battle to her husband by the river Stour, wherein Locrine shot with an arrow ends his life. But not so ends the fury of Gwendolen; for Estrildis and her daughter Sabra she throws into a river, and to leave a monument of revenge proclaims that the stream be thenceforth called after the damsel's name, which by length of time is changed now to Sabrina, or Severn.

LEIR

Hitherto from father to son the direct line hath run on; but Leir, who next reigned, had only three daughters and no male issue, governed laudably, and built Caerleir, now Leicester, on the bank of Sora. But at last, failing through age, he determines to bestow his daughters, and so among them to divide his kingdom. Yet first, to try which of them loved him best (a trial that might have made him, had he known as wisely how to try, as he seemed to know how much the trying behooved him), he resolves a simple resolution, to ask them solemnly in order, and which of them should profess largest, her to believe.

Gonerill the eldest, apprehending too well her father's weakness, makes answer invoking Heaven that she loved him above her soul.

'Therefore', quoth the old man overjoyed, 'since thou so honourst my declined age, to thee and thy husband whom thou shalt choose I give the third part of my realm'.

So fair a speeding for a few words uttered was to Regan,

the second, ample instruction what to say. She on the same demand spares no protesting, and the gods must witness that otherwise to express her thoughts she knew not but that she loved him above all creatures; and so receives an equal reward with her sister.

But Cordelia, the youngest, though hitherto best beloved, and now before her eyes the rich and present hire of a little easy soothing, the danger also and the loss likely to betide plain dealing, yet moves not from the solid purpose of a sincere and virtuous answer.

'Father', saith she, 'my love towards you is as my duty bids. What should a father seek, what can a child promise more? They who pretend beyond this, flatter'. When the old man, sorry to hear this and wishing her to recall those words, persisted asking, with a loyal sadness at her father's infirmity, but something on the sudden harsh, and glancing rather at her sisters than speaking her own mind, 'two ways only', saith she, 'I have to answer what you require me. The former, your command is, I should recant. Accept then this other which is left me: look how much you have, so much is your value, and so much I love you'.

'Then hear thou', quoth Leir, now all in passion, 'what thy ingratitude hath gained thee. Because thou hast not reverenced thy aged father equal to thy sisters, part in my kingdom or what else is mine reckon to have none,' and without delay gives in marriage his other daughters, Gonerill to Maglaunus Duke of Albania, Regan to Henninus Duke of Cornwall, with them in present half his kingdom, the rest to follow at his death. In the meanwhile fame was not sparing to divulge the wisdom and other graces of Cordelia, insomuch that Aganippus, a great king in Gaul (however he came by his Greek name), seeks her to wife, and nothing altered at the loss of her dowry receives her gladly in such manner as she was sent him.

After this King Leir, more and more drooping with years, became an easy prey to his daughters and their husbands, who now by daily encroachment had seized the whole kingdom into their hands, and the old king is put to sojourn with his eldest daughter, attended only by threescore knights. But they in a short while, grudged at as too numerous and disorderly for continual guests, are reduced to thirty. Not brooking that affront, the old king betakes him to his second daughter; but there also, discord soon arising between the servants of differing masters in one family, five only are suffered to attend him. Then back again he returns to the other, hoping that she the eldest could not but have more pity on his grey hairs; but she now refuses to admit him unless he be content with only one of his followers. At last the remembrance of his youngest Cordelia comes to his thoughts; and now acknowledging how true her words had been, though with little hope from whom he had so injured, be it but to pay her the last recompense she can have from him, his confession of her wise forewarning, that so perhaps his misery, the proof and experiment of her wisdom, might something soften her, he takes his journey into France.

Now might be seen a difference between the silent or downright-spoken affection of some children to their parents, and the talkative obsequiousness of others, while the hope of inheritance overacts them and on the tongue's end enlarges their duty. Cordelia out of mere love, without the suspicion of expected reward, at the message only of her father in distress, pours forth true filial tears, and not enduring either that her own or any other eye should see him in such forlorn condition as his messenger declared, discreetly appoints one of her trusted servants first to convey him privately towards some good sea-town, there to array him, bathe him, cherish him, furnish him with such attendance and state as beseemed his dignity; that then, as from his first landing, he might send word of his arrival to her husband Aganippus, which done with all mature and requisite contrivance, Cordelia with the king her husband and all the barony of her realm, who then first had news of his passing the sea, go out to meet him. And after all honourable and joyful entertainment, Aganippus, as to his wife's father and his royal guest, surrenders him during his abode there the power and disposal of his whole dominion, permitting his wife Cordelia to go with an army and set her father upon his throne; wherein her piety so prospered as that she vanquished her impious sisters with those dukes, and Leir again (as saith the story) three years obtained the crown.

To whom dying, Cordelia with all regal solemnities gave burial in the town of Leicester, and then as right heir succeeding, and her husband dead, ruled the land five years in peace, until Marganus and Cunedagius, her two sisters' sons, not bearing that a kingdom should be governed by a woman, in the unseasonablest time to raise that quarrel against a woman so worthy, make war against her, depose her and imprison her; of which impatient, and now long unexercised to suffer, she there (as is related) killed herself. The victors between them part the land; but Marganus the eldest sister's son, who held by agreement from the north side of Humber to Caithness, incited by those about him to invade all as his own right, wars on Cunedagius, who soon met him, overcame and overtook him in a town in Wales, where he left his life, and ever since his name to the place. Cunedagius was now sole king, and governed with much praise many years, about the time when Rome was built. Him succeeded Rivallo, his son, wise also and fortunate, save what they tell us of three days raining blood, and swarms of stinging flies, whereof men died. In order then Gurgustius; Jago or Lago, his nephew; Sisillius; Kinmarcus; then Gorbogudo, whom others name Gorbodego and Gorbodion, who had two sons, Ferrex and Porrex. They in the old age of their father falling to contend who should succeed, Porrex, attempting by treachery his brother's life, drives him into France, and in his return, though aided with the force of that country, defeats and slays him, but by his mother Videna, who less loved him, is himself with the assistance of her women soon after slain in his bed; with whom ended, as is thought, the line of Brutus.

From Book 3

ARTHUR

Kerdic, the same in power though not so fond of the title, forbore the name twenty-four years after his arrival, but then founded so firmly the kingdom of West Saxons that it subjected all the rest at length and became the sole monarchy of England. The same year he had a victory against the Britons at Kerdics Ford by the river Avon, and after eight years another great fight at Kerdics Leage, but which won the day is not by any set down. Hitherto hath been collected what there is of certainty with circumstance of time and place to be found registered, and no more than barely registered, in annals of best note, without describing, after Huntingdon, the manner of those battles and encounters, which they who compare and can judge of books may be confident he never found in any current author whom he had to follow. But this disease hath been incident to many more historians; and the age whereof we now write hath had the ill hap, more than any other since the first fabulous times, to be surcharged with all the idle fancies of posterity. Yet, that we may not rely altogether on Saxon relaters, Gildas, in antiquity far before these and every way more credible, speaks of these wars in such a manner, though nothing conceited of the British valour, as declares the Saxons in his time and before to have been foiled not seldomer than the Britons. For besides that first victory of Ambrose, and the interchangeable success long after, he tells that the last overthrow which they received at Badon Hill was not the least, which they in their oldest annals mention not at all. And because the time of this battle, by any who could do more than guess, is not set down or any foundation given from whence to draw a solid compute, it cannot be much wide to insert it in this place; for such authors as we have to follow give the conduct and praise of this exploit to Arthur, and that this was the last of twelve great battles which he fought victoriously against the Saxons (the several places written by Nennius in their Welsh names were many hundred years ago unknown, and so here omitted).

But who Arthur was, and whether ever any such reigned in Britain, hath been doubted heretofore, and may again with good reason; for the monk of Malmesbury, and others whose credit hath swayed most with the learneder sort, we may well perceive to have known no more of this Arthur five hundred years past nor of his doings than we now living, and what they had to say transcribed out of Nennius, a very trivial writer yet extant, which hath already been related, or out of a British book, the same which he of Monmouth set forth, utterly unknown to the world till more than six hundred years after the days of Arthur, of whom, as Sigebert in his Chronicle confesses, all other histories were silent both foreign and domestic except only that fabulous book. Others of later time have sought to assert him by old legends and cathedral regests; but he who can accept of legends for good story may quickly swell a volume with trash, and had need be furnished with two only necessaries, leisure and belief, whether it be the writer or he that shall read.

As to Arthur, no less is in doubt who was his father; for if it be true, as Nennius or his notist avers, that Arthur was called Mab-Uther, that is to say 'a cruel son', for the fierceness that men saw in him of a child (and the intent of his name Arturus imports as much), it might well be that some in after ages who sought to turn him into a fable wrested the word Uther into a proper name, and so feigned him the son of Uther, since we read not in any certain story that ever such person lived, till Geoffrey of Monmouth set him off with the surname of Pendragon. And as we doubted of his parentage, so may we also of his puissance; for whether that victory at Badon Hill were his or no is uncertain, Gildas not naming him as he did Ambrose in the former. Next, if it be true, as Caradoc relates, that Melvas, king of that country which is now Somerset, kept from him Guinever his wife a whole year in the town of Glaston, and restored her at the entreaty of Gildas rather than for any enforcement that Arthur with all his chivalry could make against a small town defended only by a moory situation, had either his knowledge in war or the force he had to make been answerable to the fame they bear, that petty king had neither dared such an affront nor he been so long, and at last without effect, in revenging it. Considering lastly how the Saxons gained upon him everywhere all the time of his supposed reign, which began, as some write, in the tenth year of Kerdic, who wrung from him by long war the countries of Somerset and Hampshire, there will remain neither place nor circumstance in story which may administer any likelihood of those great acts which are ascribed him. This only is alleged by Nennius in Arthur's behalf, that the Saxons, though vanquished never so oft, grew still more numerous upon him by continual supplies out of Germany; and the truth is that valour may be overtoiled, and overcome at last with endless overcoming. But as for this battle of Mount Badon where the Saxons were hemmed in or beseiged, whether by Arthur won or whensoever, it seems indeed to have given a most undoubted and important blow to the Saxons and to have stopped their proceedings for a good while after, Gildas himself witnessing that the Britons, having thus compelled them to sit down with peace, fell thereupon to civil discord among themselves; which words may seem to let in some light toward the searching out when this battle was fought. And we shall find no time since the first Saxon war from whence a longer peace ensued than from the fight at Kerdics Leage in the year 527, which all the chronicles mention without victory to Kerdic, and give us argument, from the custom they have of magnifying their own deeds upon all occasions, to presume here his ill speeding. And if we look still onward, even to the forty-fourth year after wherein Gildas wrote (if his obscure utterance be understood), we shall meet with very little war between the Britons and Saxons. This only remains difficult, that the victory first won by Ambrose was not so long before this at Badon siege but that the same men living might be eye-witnesses of both; and by this rate hardly can the latter be thought won by Arthur, unless we reckon him a grown youth at least in the days of Ambrose, and much more than a youth if Malmesbury be heard, who affirms all the exploits of Ambrose to have been done chiefly by Arthur as his general, which will add much unbelief to the common assertion of his reigning after Ambrose and Uther, especially the fight at Badon, being the last of his twelve battles. But to prove by that which follows that the fight at Kerdics Leage, though it differ in name from that of Badon, may be thought the same by all effects, Kerdic three years after, not proceeding onward as his manner was on the continent, turns back his forces on the Isle of Wight, which, with the slaying of a few only in Withgarburgh, he soon masters, and not long surviving, left it to his nephews by his mother's side, Stuff and Withgar. The rest of what he had subdued Kenric his son held, and reigned twenty six years, in whose tenth year Withgar was buried in the town of that island which bore his name.

Notwithstanding all these unlikelihoods of Arthur's reign and great achievements, in a narration crept in I know not how among the Laws of Edward the Confessor Arthur the famous king of Britons is said not only to have expelled hence the Saracens, who were not then known in Europe, but to have conquered Friesland and all the north-east isles as far as Russia, to have made Lapland the eastern bound of his empire, and Norway the chamber of Britain. When should this be done? From the Saxons, till after twelve battles, he had no rest at home. After those, the Britons, contented with the quiet they had from their Saxon enemies, were so far from seeking conquests abroad that, by report of Gildas above cited, they fell to civil wars at home. Surely Arthur had much better made war in old Saxony, to repress their flowing hither, than to have won kingdoms as far as Russia, scarce able here to defend his own. Buchanan our neighbour historian reprehends him of Monmouth and others for fabling in the deeds of Arthur, yet what he writes thereof himself, as of better credit, shows not whence he had but from those fables, which he seems content to believe in part on condition that the Scots and Picts may be thought to have assisted Arthur in all his wars and achievements; whereof appears as little ground by any credible story as of that which he most counts fabulous. But not further to contest about such uncertainies.

From Book 6

THE NORMAN CONQUEST

Harold, whether by King Edward a little before his death ordained successor to the crown, as Simeon of Durham and others affirm, or by the prevalence of his faction excluding Edgar the right heir, grandchild to Edmund Ironside, as Malmesbury and Huntingdon agree, no sooner was the funeral of King Edward ended but on the same day was elected and crowned king; and no sooner placed in the throne but began to frame himself by all manner of compliances to gain affection, endeavoured to make good laws, repealed bad, became a great patron to Church and churchmen, courteous and affable to all reputed good, a hater of evil doers, charged all his officers to punish thieves, robbers and all disturbers of the peace, while he himself by sea and land laboured in the defence of his country: so good an actor is ambition. In the meanwhile a blazing star seven mornings together about the end of April was seen to stream terribly not only over England but other parts of the world, foretelling here, as was thought, the great changes approaching; plainliest prognosticated by Elmer, a monk of Malmesbury, who could not foresee, when time was, the breaking of his own legs for soaring too high. He in his youth strangely aspiring had made and fitted wings to his hands and feet; with these on the top of a tower spread out to gather air he flew more than a furlong, but the wind being too high, came fluttering down, to the maiming of all his limbs, yet so conceited of his art that he attributed the cause of his fall to the want of a tail, as birds have, which he forgot to make to his hinder parts. This story, though seeming otherwise too light in the midst of a sad narration, yet for the strangeness thereof I thought worthy enough the placing as I found it placed in my author.

But to digress no further, Tostig the king's brother coming from Flanders, full of envy at his younger brother's advancement to the crown, resolved what he might to trouble his reign. Forcing therefore them of Wight Isle to contribution, he sailed thence to Sandwich, committing piracies on the coast between. Harold, then residing at London, with a great number of ships drawn together and of horse troops by land prepares in person for Sandwich, whereof Tostig having notice directs his course with sixty ships towards Lindsey, taking with him all the seamen he found, willing or unwilling, where he burnt many villages and slew many of the inhabitants; but Edwin the Mercian duke and Morcar his brother, the Northumbrian earl, with their forces on either side soon drove him out of the country, who thence betook him to Malcolm the Scottish king and with him abode the whole summer. About the same time, Duke William sending ambassadors to admonish Harold of his promise and oath to assist him in his plea to the kingdom, he made answer that by the death of his daughter, betrothed to him on that condition, he was absolved of his oath; or not dead, he could not take her now, an outlandish woman, without consent of the realm; that it was presumptuously done and not to be persisted in if without consent and knowledge of the States he had sworn away the right of the kingdom; that what he swore was to gain his liberty, being in a manner then his prisoner; that it was unreasonable in the Duke to require or expect of him the forgoing of a kingdom conferred upon him with universal favour and acclamation of the people. To this flat denial he added contempt, sending the messengers back (saith Matthew Paris) on maimed horses.

The Duke, thus contemptuously put off, addresses himself to the Pope, setting forth the justice of his cause, which Harold, whether through haughtiness of mind or distrust or that the ways to Rome were stopped, sought not to do. Duke William, besides the promise and oath of Harold, alleged that King Edward by the advice of Seward, Godwin himself and Stigand the Archbishop had given him the right of succession and had sent him the son and nephew of Godwin, pledges of the gift. The Pope sent to Duke William, after this demonstration of his right, a consecrated banner; whereupon he, having with great care and choice got an army of tall and stout soldiers under captains of great skill and mature age, came in August to the port of St-Valéry. Meanwhile Harold from London comes to Sandwich, there expecting his navy, which also coming, he sails to the Isle of Wight, and having heard of Duke William's preparations and readiness to invade him kept good watch on the coast, and foot forces everywhere in fit places to guard the shore. But ere the middle of September, provision failing when it was most needed, both fleet and army return home; when on a sudden Harold Harvager King of Norway with a navy of more than five hundred great ships (others lessen them by two hundred, others augment them to a thousand) appears at the mouth of the Tyne, to whom Earl Tostig with his ships came as was agreed between them; whence both uniting set sail with all speed and entered the river

Humber, thence turning into Ouse as far as Riccall landed, and won York by assault.

At these tidings Harold with all his power hastes thitherward. But ere his coming, Edwin and Morcar at Fulford by York, on the north side of the Ouse, about the feast of Matthew had given them battle, successfully at first; but overborne at length with numbers, and forced to turn their backs, more of them perished in the river than in the fight. The Norwegians, taking with them five hundred hostages out of York and leaving there a hundred and fifty of their own, retired to their ships. But the fifth day after, King Harold with a great and well-appointed army coming to York, and at Stamford Bridge or Battle Bridge on Derwent assailing the Norwegians, after much bloodshed on both sides cut off the greatest part of them with Harvager their king and Tostig his own brother. But Olav the king's son and Paul Earl of Orkney, left with many soldiers to guard the ships, surrendering themselves with hostages and oath given never to return as enemies, he suffered freely to depart with twenty ships and the small remnant of their army. One man with the Norwegians is not to be forgotten, who with incredible valour keeping the bridge a long hour against the whole English army with his single resistance delayed their victory, and scorning offered life, till in the end, no man daring to grapple with him, either dreaded as too strong or contemned as one desperate, he was at length shot dead with an arrow, and by his fall opened the passage of pursuit to a complete victory. Wherewith Harold, lifted up in mind and forgetting now his former shows of popularity, defrauded his soldiers their due and well-deserved share of the spoils.

While these things thus passed in Northumberland, Duke William lay still at St-Valéry. His ships were ready, but the wind served not for many days, which put his soldiery into much discouragement and murmur, taking this for an unlucky sign of their success. At last the wind came favourable, the Duke first under sail awaited the rest at anchor, till all coming forth the whole fleet of nine hundred ships with a prosperous gale arrived at Hastings. At his going out of the boat, by a slip falling on his hands, to correct the omen a soldier standing by said aloud that their Duke had taken possession of England. Landed, he restrained his army from waste and spoil, saying that they ought to spare what was their own. But these are things related of Alexander and Caesar, and I doubt thence borrowed by the monks to inlay their story. The Duke for fifteen days after landing kept his men quiet within the camp, having taken the castle of Hastings, or built a fortress there. Harold, secure the while and proud of his new victory, thought all his enemies now under foot; but sitting jollily at dinner, news is brought him that Duke William of Normandy with a great multitude of horse and foot, slingers and archers, besides other choice auxiliaries which he had hired in France, was arrived at Pevensey. Harold, who had expected him all the summer, but not so late in the year as now it was (for it was October), with his forces much diminished after two sore conflicts and the departing of many others from him discontented, in great haste marches to London; thence, not tarrying for supplies which were on their way towards him, hurries into Sussex (for he was always in haste since the day of his coronation) and, ere the third part of his army could be well put in order, finds the Duke about nine miles from Hastings, and now drawing nigh, sent spies before him to survey the strength and number of his enemies. Them, discovered such, the Duke causing to be led about and after well filled with meat and drink sent back. They, not over wise, brought word that the Duke's army were most of them priests; for they saw their faces all over shaven, the English then using to let grow on their upper lip large moustachios, as did anciently the Britons. The King laughing answered that they were not priests but valiant and hardy soldiers. Therefore, said Girtha his brother, a youth of noble courage and understanding above his age, forbear thou thyself to fight, who art obnoxious to Duke William by oath; let us unsworn undergo the hazard of battle who may justly fight in the defence of our country; thou reserved to fitter time mayst either reunite us flying or revenge us dead. The King, not hearkening to this lest it might seem to argue fear in him or a bad cause, with like resolution rejected the offers of Duke William sent to him by a monk before the battle, with only this answer hastily delivered: let God judge between us. The offers were these, that Harold would either lay down the sceptre, or hold it of him, or try his title with him by single combat in the sight of both armies, or refer it to the Pope.

These rejected, both sides prepared to fight the next morning, the English from singing and drinking all night, the Normans from confession of their sins and communion of the host. The English were in a straight disadvantageous place, so that many, discouraged with their ill ordering, scarce having room where to stand, slipped away before the onset. The rest in close order with their battle-axes and shields made an impenetrable squadron. The King himself with his brothers on foot stood by the royal standard, wherein the figure of a man fighting was inwoven with gold and precious stones. The Norman foot, most bowmen, made the foremost front, on either side wings of horse somewhat behind. The Duke arming, and his corslet given him on the wrong side, said pleasantly, the strength of my dukedom will be turned now into a kingdom. Then the whole army singing the Song of Roland, the remembrance of whose exploits might hearten them, imploring lastly divine help, the battle began, and was fought sorely on either side; but the main body of the English foot by no means would be broken till the Duke, causing his men to feign flight, drew them out with desire of pursuit into open disorder, then turned suddenly upon them so routed by themselves, which wrought their overthrow. Yet so they died not unmanfully, but turning oft upon their enemies, by the advantage of an upper ground, beat them down by heaps and filled up a great ditch with their carcasses. Thus hung the victory wavering on either side from the third hour of day to evening, when Harold, having maintained the fight with unspeakable courage and personal valour, shot into the head with an arrow, fell at length and left his soldiers without heart longer to withstand the unwearied enemy. With Harold fell also his two brothers Leofwin and Girtha, with them greatest part of the English nobility. His body lying dead a knight or soldier wounding on the thigh was by the Duke presently turned out of military service. Of Normans or French were slain no small number. The Duke himself also that day not a little hazarded his person, having had three choice horses killed under him.

Victory obtained, and his dead carefully buried (the English also, by permission), he sent the body of Harold to his mother without ransom, though she offered very much to redeem it, which having received she buried at Waltham in a church built there by Harold. In the meanwhile Edwin and Morcar, who had withdrawn themselves from Harold, hearing of his death came to London, sending Aldgith the Queen their sister with all speed to Westchester. Aldred Archbishop of York and many of the nobles with the Londoners would have set up Edgar the right heir, and prepared themselves to fight for him; but Morcar and Edwin, not liking the choice, who each of them expected to have been chosen before him, withdrew their forces and returned home. Duke William, contrary to his former resolution (if Florence of Worcester and they who follow him say true) wasting, burning and slaying all in his way, or rather (as saith Malmesbury) not in hostile but in regal manner came up to London, met at Barcham by Edgar with the nobles, bishops, citizens and at length Edwin and Morcar, who all submitted to him, gave hostages, and swore fidelity, he to them promised peace and defence, yet permitted his men the while to burn and make prey. Coming to London with all his army, he was on Christmas day solemnly crowned in the great church at Westminster by Aldred Archbishop of York, having first given his oath at the altar in presence of all the people to defend the Church, well govern the people, maintain right law, prohibit rapine and unjust judgement.

Thus the English, while they agreed not about the choice of their native king, were constrained to take the yoke of an outlandish conqueror. With what minds and by what course of life they had fitted themselves for this servitude William of Malmesbury spares not to lay open. Not a few years before the Normans came the clergy, though in Edward the Confessor's days, had lost all good literature and religion, scarce able to read and understand their Latin service; he was a miracle to others who knew his grammar. The monks went clad in fine stuffs, and made no difference what they ate, which though in itself no fault, yet to their consciences was irreligious. The great men, given to gluttony and dissolute life, made a prey of the common people, abusing their daughters whom they had in service, then turning them off to the stews; the meaner sort, tippling together night and day, spent all they had in drunkenness, attended with other vices which effeminate men's minds; whence it came to pass that carried on with fury and rashness more than any true fortitude or skill of war they gave to William their conqueror so easy a conquest. Not but that some few of all sorts were much better among them, but such was the generality; and as the long suffering of God permits bad men to enjoy prosperous days with the good, so his severity ofttimes exempts not good men from their share in evil times with the bad. If these were the causes of such misery and thraldom to those our ancestors, with what better close can be concluded than here in fit season to remember this age in the midst of her security to fear from like vices without amendment the revolution of like calamities.

Samson Agonistes

Of that sort of dramatic poem
which is called tragedy

Tragedy, as it was anciently composed, hath been ever held the gravest, moralest and most profitable of all other poems: therefore said by Aristotle to be of power by raising pity and fear, or terror, to purge the mind of those and such like passions; that is, to temper and reduce them to just measure with a kind of delight stirred up by reading or seeing those passions well imitated. Nor is Nature wanting in her own effects to make good his assertion; for so in physic things of melancholic hue and quality are used against melancholy, sour against sour, salt to remove salt humours. Hence philosophers and other gravest writers, as Cicero, Plutarch and others, frequently cite out of tragic poets both to adorn and illustrate their discourse. The apostle Paul himself thought it not unworthy to insert a verse of Euripides into the text of holy scripture (I. *Cor.* 15. 33), and Paraeus, commenting on the *Revelation*, divides the whole book as a tragedy into acts, distinguished each by a chorus of heavenly harpings and song between. Heretofore men in highest dignity have laboured not a little to be thought able to compose a tragedy. Of that honour Dionysius the elder was no less ambitious than before of his attaining to the tyranny. Augustus Caesar also had begun his *Ajax*, but unable to please his own judgement with what he had begun, left it unfinished. Seneca the philosopher is by some thought the author of those tragedies (at least the best of them) that go under that name. Gregory Nazianzen, a father of the Church, thought it not unbeseeming the sanctity of his person to write a tragedy, which he entitled *Christ Suffering*. This is mentioned to vindicate tragedy from the small esteem, or rather infamy, which in the account of many it undergoes at this day with other common interludes, happening through the poets' error of intermixing comic stuff with tragic sadness and gravity, or introducing trivial and vulgar persons, which by all judicious hath been counted absurd, and brought in without discretion corruptly to gratify the people. And though ancient tragedy use no prologue, yet using sometimes, in case of self defence or explanation, that which Martial calls an epistle, in behalf of this tragedy, coming forth after the ancient manner, much different from what among us passes for best, thus much beforehand may be epistled, that Chorus is here introduced after the Greek manner, not ancient only but modern, and still in use among the Italians. In the modelling therefore of this poem, with good reason, the ancients and Italians are rather followed, as of much more authority and fame. The measure of verse used in the Chorus is of all sorts, called by the Greeks *monostrophic*, or rather *apolelymenon*, without regard had to *strophe*, *antistrophe* or *epode*, which were a kind of stanzas framed only for the music then used with the Chorus that sung, not essential to the poem and therefore not material; or, being divided into stanzas or pauses, they may be called *alloeostropha*. Division into act and scene, referring chiefly to the stage (to which this work never was intended), is here omitted. It suffices if the whole drama be found not produced beyong the fifth act.

Of the style and uniformity, and that commonly called the plot, whether intricate or explicit, which is nothing indeed but such economy or disposition of the fable as may stand best with verisimilitude and decorum, they only will best judge who are not unacquainted with Aeschylus, Sophocles and Euripides, the three tragic poets unequalled yet by any, and the best rule to all who endeavour to write tragedy. The circumscription of time wherein the whole drama begins and ends is, according to ancient rule and best example, within the space of twenty-four hours.

THE ARGUMENT

Samson, *made captive, blind, and now in the prison at* Gaza, *there to labour as in a common workhouse, on a festival day, in the general cessation from labour, comes forth into the open air to a place nigh, somewhat retired, there to sit a while and bemoan his condition; where he happens at length to be visited by certain friends and equals of his tribe, which make the Chorus, who seek to comfort him what they can; then by his old father* Manoah, *who endeavours the like, and withal tells him his purpose to procure his liberty by ransom; lastly, that this feast was proclaimed by the* Philistines *as a day of thanksgiving for their deliverance from the hands of* Samson, *which yet more troubles him.* Manoah *then departs to prosecute his endeavour with the* Philistian *lords for* Samson's *redemption, who in the meanwhile is visited by other persons, and lastly by a public officer to require his coming to the feast before the lords and people, to play or show his strength in their presence. He at first refuses, dismissing the public officer with absolute denial to come. At length, persuaded inwardly that this was from God, he yields to go along with him, who came now the second time with great threatenings to fetch him. The Chorus yet remaining on the place,* Manoah *returns full of joyful hope to procure ere long his son's deliverance; in the midst of which discourse an Hebrew comes in haste, confusedly at first and afterwards more distinctly relating the catastrophe, what* Samson *had done to the* Philistines, *and by accident to himself; wherewith the tragedy ends.*

The Persons

Samson
Manoah, the father of Samson
Dalila, his wife
Harapha of Gath
Public Officer
Messenger
Chorus of Danites

The scene before the prison in Gaza.

Samson. A little onward lend thy guiding hand
To these dark steps a little further on,
For yonder bank hath choice of sun or shade;
There am I wont to sit when any chance
Relieves me from my task of servile toil
Daily in the common prison else enjoin'd me,
Where I a pris'ner chain'd scarce freely draw
The air imprison'd also close and damp,
Unwholesome draught. But here I feel amends,
The breath of heav'n fresh blowing, pure and sweet,
With day-spring born; here leave me to respire.
This day a solemn feast the people hold
To Dagon their sea-idol, and forbid
Laborious works. Unwillingly this rest
Their superstition yields me; hence with leave
Retiring from the popular noise I seek
This unfrequented place to find some ease,
Ease to the body some, none to the mind
From restless thoughts, that like a deadly swarm
Of hornets arm'd, no sooner found alone,
But rush upon me thronging and present
Times past, what once I was, and what am now.
O wherefore was my birth from heav'n foretold
Twice by an angel, who at last in sight
Of both my parents all in flames ascended
From off the altar where an off'ring burn'd,
As in a fiery column charioting
His godlike presence, and from some great act
Or benefit reveal'd to Abraham's race?
Why was my breeding order'd and prescrib'd
As of a person separate to God,
Design'd for great exploits, if I must die
Betray'd, captiv'd, and both my eyes put out,
Made of my enemies the scorn and gaze,
To grind in brazen fetters under task
With this heav'n-gifted strength? O glorious strength
Put to the labour of a beast, debas'd

Lower than bondslave! Promise was that I
Should Israel from Philistian yoke deliver;
Ask for this great deliverer now, and find him
Eyeless in Gaza at the mill with slaves,
Himself in bonds under Philistian yoke.
Yet stay, let me not rashly call in doubt
Divine prediction. What if all foretold
Had been fulfill'd but through mine own default,
Whom have I to complain of but myself?
Who, this high gift of strength committed to me,
In what part lodg'd, how easily bereft me
Under the seal of silence could not keep
But weakly to a woman must reveal it,
O'ercome with importunity and tears.
O impotence of mind in body strong!
But what is strength without a double share
Of wisdom? Vast, unwieldy, burdensome,
Proudly secure, yet liable to fall
By weakest subtleties, not made to rule
But to subserve where wisdom bears command.
God, when he gave me strength, to show withal
How slight the gift was, hung it in my hair.
But peace, I must not quarrel with the will
Of highest dispensation, which herein
Haply had ends above my reach to know.
Suffices that to me strength is my bane,
And proves the source of all my miseries;
So many, and so huge, that each apart
Would ask a life to wail, but chief of all,
O loss of sight, of thee I most complain!
Blind among enemies, O worse than chains,
Dungeon, or beggary, or decrepit age!
Light the prime work of God to me is extinct,
And all her various objects of delight
Annull'd which might in part my grief have eased,
Inferior to the vilest now become
Of man or worm. The vilest here excel me:
They creep, yet see; I, dark in light, expos'd
To daily fraud, contempt, abuse and wrong,

Within doors or without still, as a fool,
In power of others, never in my own,
Scarce half I seem to live, dead more than half.
O dark, dark, dark, amid the blaze of noon,
Irrecoverably dark, total eclipse
Without all hope of day!
O first created beam, and thou great Word,
Let there be light, and light was over all,
Why am I thus bereav'd thy prime decree?
The sun to me is dark
And silent as the moon
When she deserts the night
Hid in her vacant interlunar cave.
Since light so necessary is to life,
And almost life itself, if it be true
That light is in the soul,
She all in every part, why was the sight
To such a tender ball as th'eye confin'd,
So obvious and so easy to be quench'd,
And not as feeling through all parts diffus'd
That she might look at will through every pore?
Then had I not been thus exil'd from light,
As in the land of darkness yet in light,
To live a life half dead, a living death,
And buried; but O yet more miserable!
Myself my sepulchre, a moving grave,
Buried, yet not exempt
By privilege of death and burial
From worst of other evils, pains and wrongs,
But made hereby obnoxious more
To all the miseries of life,
Life in captivity
Among inhuman foes.
But who are these? For with joint pace I hear
The tread of many feet steering this way;
Perhaps my enemies who come to stare
At my affliction, and perhaps to insult,
Their daily practice, to afflict me more.
Chorus. This, this is he; softly a while,

Let us not break in upon him.
O change beyond report, thought or belief!
See how he lies at random, carelessly diffus'd,
With languish'd head unpropp'd,
As one past hope, abandon'd
And by himself giv'n over,
In slavish habit, ill-fitted weeds
O'er worn and soil'd.
Or do my eyes misrepresent? Can this be he,
That heroic, that renown'd,
Irresistible Samson? Whom unarm'd
No strength of man or fiercest wild beast could withstand;
Who tore the lion as the lion tears the kid,
Ran on embattl'd armies clad in iron,
And weaponless himself
Made arms ridiculous, useless the forgery
Of brazen shield and spear, the hammer'd cuirass,
Chalybean temper'd steel and frock of mail
Adamantean proof,
But safest he who stood aloof
When insupportably his foot advanc'd,
In scorn of their proud arms and warlike tools,
Spurn'd them to death by troops. The bold Ascalonite
Fled from his lion ramp; old warriors turn'd
Their plated backs under his heel,
Or grov'lling soil'd their crested helmets in the dust.
Then with what trivial weapon came to hand,
The jaw of a dead ass, his sword of bone,
A thousand foreskins fell, the flower of Palestine,
In Ramathlechi famous to this day;
Then by main force pull'd up and on his shoulders bore
The gates of Azza, post and massy bar,
Up to the hill by Hebron, seat of giants old,
No journey of a Sabbath day, and loaded so
Like whom the Gentiles feign to bear up heav'n.
Which shall I first bewail,
Thy bondage or lost sight,
Prison within prison

Inseparably dark?
Thou art become (O worst imprisonment!)
The dungeon of thy self; thy soul
(Which men enjoying sight oft without cause complain)
Imprison'd now indeed
In real darkness of the body dwells,
Shut up from outward light
To incorporate with gloomy night;
For inward light alas
Puts forth no visual beam.
O mirror of our fickle state,
Since man on earth unparallel'd!
The rarer thy example stands,
By how much from the top of wondrous glory,
Strongest of mortal men,
To lowest pitch of abject fortune thou art fall'n.
For him I reckon not in high estate
Whom long descent of birth
Or the sphere of fortune raises;
But thee whose strength, while virtue was her mate,
Might have subdu'd the earth,
Universally crown'd with highest praises.
Samson. I hear the sound of words; their sense the air
Dissolves unjointed ere it reach my ear.
Chorus. He speaks, let us draw nigh. Matchless in might,
The glory late of Israel, now the grief,
We come thy friends and neighbours not unknown
From Eshtaol and Zora's fruitful vale
To visit or bewail thee, or if better,
Counsel and consolation we may bring,
Salve to thy sores; apt words have power to suage
The tumours of a troubl'd mind,
And are as balm to fester'd wounds.
Samson. Your coming, friends, revives me, for I learn
Now of my own experience, not by talk,
How counterfeit a coin they are who friends
Bear in their superscription (of the most
I would be understood); in prosperous days
They swarm, but in adverse withdraw their head,

Not to be found though sought. Ye see, O friends,
How many evils have enclos'd me round;
Yet that which was the worst now least afflicts me,
Blindness, for had I sight, confus'd with shame,
How could I once look up or heave the head,
Who like a foolish pilot have shipwrack'd
My vessel trusted to me from above
Gloriously rigg'd, and for a word, a tear,
Fool, have divulg'd the secret gift of God
To a deceitful woman. Tell me, friends,
Am I not sung and proverb'd for a fool
In every street? Do they not say, how well
Are come upon him his deserts? Yet why?
Immeasurable strength they might behold
In me, of wisdom nothing more than mean.
This with the other should at least have pair'd;
These two proportion'd ill drove me transverse.
Chorus. Tax not divine disposal. Wisest men
Have err'd, and by bad women been deceiv'd,
And shall again, pretend they ne'er so wise.
Deject not then so overmuch thyself,
Who hast of sorrow thy full load besides.
Yet, truth to say, I oft have heard men wonder
Why thou shouldst wed Philistian women rather
Than of thine own tribe fairer, or as fair
At least of thy own nation, and as noble.
Samson. The first I saw at Timna, and she pleas'd
Me, not my parents that I sought to wed
The daughter of an infidel. They knew not
That what I motion'd was of God; I knew
From intimate impulse, and therefore urg'd
That marriage on, that by occasion thence
I might begin Israel's deliverance,
The work to which I was divinely call'd.
She proving false, the next I took to wife
(O that I never had! fond wish too late)
Was in the vale of Sorec, Dalila,
That specious monster, my accomplish'd snare.
I thought it lawful from my former act

And the same end, still watching to oppress
Israel's oppressors. Of what now I suffer
She was not the prime cause, but I myself,
Who vanquish'd with a peal of words (O weakness!)
Gave up my fort of silence to a woman.
Chorus. In seeking just occasion to provoke
The Philistine, thy country's enemy,
Thou never wast remiss, I bear thee witness.
Yet Israel still serves with all his sons.
Samson. That fault I take not on me, but transfer
On Israel's governors and heads of tribes,
Who seeing those great acts which God had done
Singly by me against their conquerors
Acknowledg'd not, or not at all consider'd
Deliverance offer'd. I on th'other side
Us'd no ambition to commend my deeds;
The deeds themselves, though mute, spoke loud the doer.
But they persisted deaf, and would not seem
To count them things worth notice, till at length
Their lords the Philistines with gather'd powers
Enter'd Judea seeking me, who then
Safe to the rock of Etham was retir'd,
Not flying, but forecasting in what place
To set upon them, what advantag'd best.
Meanwhile the men of Judah, to prevent
The harass of their land, beset me round;
I willingly on some conditions came
Into their hands, and they as gladly yield me
To the uncircumcis'd a welcome prey,
Bound with two cords. But cords to me were threads
Touch'd with the flame; on their whole host I flew
Unarm'd and with a trivial weapon fell'd
Their choicest youth; they only liv'd who fled.
Had Judah that day join'd, or one whole tribe,
They had by this possess'd the towers of Gath
And lorded over them whom now they serve.
But what more oft in nations grown corrupt
And by their vices brought to servitude
Than to love bondage more than liberty,

Bondage with ease than strenuous liberty,
And to despise or envy or suspect
Whom God hath of his special favour rais'd
As their deliverer? If he aught begin,
How frequent to desert him, and at last
To heap ingratitude on worthiest deeds!
Chorus. Thy words to my remembrance bring
How Succoth and the fort of Penuel
Their great deliverer contemn'd,
The matchless Gideon, in pursuit
Of Madian and her vanquish'd kings;
And how ungrateful Ephraim
Had dealt with Jephtha, who by argument
Not worse than by his shield and spear
Defended Israel from the Ammonite,
Had not his prowess quell'd their pride
In that sore battle when so many died,
Without reprieve adjudg'd to death
For want of well pronouncing 'shibboleth'.
Samson. Of such examples add me to the roll;
Me easily indeed mine may neglect,
But God's propos'd deliverance not so.
Chorus. Just are the ways of God,
And justifiable to men,
Unless there be who think not God at all:
If any be, they walk obscure,
For of such doctrine never was there school
But the heart of the fool,
And no man therein doctor but himself.
Yet more there be that doubt his ways not just
As to his own edicts, found contradicting;
Then give the reins to wand'ring thought,
Regardless of his glory's diminution,
Till by their own perplexities involv'd
They ravel more, still less resolv'd,
But never find self-satisfying solution.
As if they would confine th'interminable
And tie him to his own prescript,

Who made our laws to bind us, not himself,
And hath full right to exempt
Whom so it pleases him by choice
From national obstriction, without taint
Of sin, or legal debt;
For with his own laws he can best dispense.
He would not else, who never wanted means,
Nor in respect of th'enemy just cause
To set his people free,
Have prompted this heroic Nazarite
Against his vow of strictest purity
To seek in marriage that fallacious bride,
Unclean, unchaste.
Down reason then, at least vain reasonings down,
Though reason here aver
That moral verdict quits her of unclean:
Unchaste was subsequent, her stain not his.
But see, here comes thy reverend sire
With careful step, locks white as down,
Old Manoah. Advise
Forthwith how thou oughtst to receive him.
Samson. Ay me, another inward grief awak'd
With mention of that name renews th'assault.
Manoah. Brethren and men of Dan, for such ye seem
Though in this uncouth place; if old respect,
As I suppose, towards your once glori'd friend,
My son now captive, hither hath inform'd
Your younger feet, while mine cast back with age
Came lagging after, say if he be here.
Chorus. As signal now in low dejected state
As erst in highest, behold him where he lies.
Manoah. O miserable change! Is this the man,
That invincible Samson far renown'd,
The dread of Israel's foes, who with a strength
Equivalent to angel's walked their streets,
None offering fight; who single combatant
Duell'd their armies rank'd in proud array,
Himself an army, now unequal match
To save himself against a coward arm'd

At one spear's length? O ever failing trust
In mortal strength! And O what not in man
Deceivable and vain? Nay what thing good
Pray'd for but often proves our woe, our bane?
I pray'd for children, and thought barrenness
In wedlock a reproach: I gain'd a son,
And such a son as all men hail'd me happy.
Who now would be a father in my stead?
O wherefore did God grant me my request,
And as a blessing with such pomp adorn'd?
Why are his gifts desirable, to tempt
Our earnest prayers, then giv'n with solemn hand
As graces, draw a scorpion's tail behind?
For this did th'angel twice descend? For this
Ordain'd thy nurture holy, as of a plant
Select and sacred, glorious for a while,
The miracle of men; then in an hour
Ensnar'd, assaulted, overcome, led bound,
Thy foes' derision, captive, poor, and blind
Into a dungeon thrust to work with slaves?
Alas, methinks whom God hath chosen once
To worthiest deeds, if he through frailty err,
He should not so o'erwhelm and as a thrall
Subject him to so foul indignities,
Be it but for honour's sake of former deeds.
Samson. Appoint not heavenly disposition, father.
Nothing of all these evils hath befall'n me
But justly; I myself have brought them on,
Sole author I, sole cause. If aught seem vile,
As vile hath been my folly who have profan'd
The mystery of God giv'n me under pledge
Of vow, and have betray'd it to a woman,
A Canaanite, my faithless enemy.
This well I knew, nor was at all surpris'd,
But warn'd by oft experience: did not she
Of Timna first betray me, and reveal
The secret wrested from me in her height
Of nuptial love profess'd, carrying it straight

To them who had corrupted her, my spies
And rivals? In this other was there found
More faith, who also in her prime of love,
Spousal embraces, vitiated with gold
Though offer'd only, by the scent conceiv'd
Her spurious first-born, treason against me?
Thrice she assay'd with flattering prayers and sighs
And amorous reproaches to win from me
My capital secret, in what part my strength
Lay stor'd, in what part summ'd, that she might know.
Thrice I deluded her and turn'd to sport
Her importunity, each time perceiving
How openly and with what impudence
She purpos'd to betray me, and (which was worse
Than undissembl'd hate) with what contempt
She sought to make me traitor to myself.
Yet the fourth time, when must'ring all her wiles
With blandish'd parleys, feminine assaults,
Tongue-batteries, she surceas'd not day nor night
To storm me overwatch'd and weari'd out
At times when men seek most repose and rest,
I yielded, and unlock'd her all my heart,
Who with a grain of manhood well resolv'd
Might easily have shook off all her snares;
But foul effeminacy held me yok'd
Her bond-slave. O indignity, O blot
To honour and religion! Servile mind
Rewarded well with servile punishment!
The base degree to which I now am fall'n,
These rags, this grinding, is not yet so base
As was my former servitude, ignoble,
Unmanly, ignominious, infamous,
True slavery, and that blindness worse than this,
That saw not how degenerately I serv'd.
Manoah. I cannot praise thy marriage choices, son,
Rather approv'd them not; but thou didst plead
Divine impulsion prompting how thou mightst
Find some occasion to infest our foes.

I state not that; this I am sure, our foes
Found soon occasion thereby to make thee
Their captive and their triumph. Thou the sooner
Temptation found'st or over-potent charms
To violate the sacred trust of silence
Deposited within thee, which to have kept
Tacit was in thy power. True; and thou bear'st
Enough and more the burden of that fault.
Bitterly hast thou paid and still art paying
That rigid score. A worse thing yet remains:
This day the Philistines a popular feast
Here celebrate in Gaza, and proclaim
Great pomp and sacrifice and praises loud
To Dagon as their God who hath deliver'd
Thee Samson bound and blind into their hands,
Them out of thine, who slew'st them many a slain.
So Dagon shall be magnifi'd, and God,
Besides whom is no God, compar'd with idols,
Disglorifi'd, blasphem'd and had in scorn
By th'idolatrous rout amidst their wine;
Which to have come to pass by means of thee,
Samson, of all thy sufferings think the heaviest,
Of all reproach the most with shame that ever
Could have befall'n thee and thy father's house.
Samson. Father, I do acknowledge and confess
That I this honour, I this pomp have brought
To Dagon, and advanc'd his praises high
Among the heathen round; to God have brought
Dishonour, obloquy, and op'd the mouths
Of idolists and atheists; have brought scandal
To Israel, diffidence of God and doubt
In feeble hearts, propense enough before
To waver, or fall off and join with idols:
Which is my chief affliction, shame and sorrow,
The anguish of my soul, that suffers not
Mine eye to harbour sleep, or thoughts to rest.
This only hope relieves me, that the strife
With me hath end; all the contest is now
Twixt God and Dagon. Dagon hath presum'd,

Me overthrown, to enter lists with God,
His deity comparing and preferring
Before the God of Abraham. He, be sure,
Will not connive or linger, thus provok'd,
But will arise and his great name assert.
Dagon must stoop, and shall ere long receive
Such a discomfit as shall quite despoil him
Of all these boasted trophies won on me,
And with confusion blank his worshippers.
Manoah. With cause this hope relieves thee, and these words
I as a prophecy receive; for God,
Nothing more certain, will not long defer
To vindicate the glory of his name
Against all competition, nor will long
Endure it doubtful whether God be lord
Or Dagon. But for thee what shall be done?
Thou must not in the meanwhile here forgot
Lie in this miserable loathsome plight
Neglected. I already have made way
To some Philistian lords, with whom to treat
About thy ransom. Well they may by this
Have satisfi'd their utmost of revenge
By pains and slaveries, worse than death inflicted
On thee, who now no more canst do them harm.
Samson. Spare that proposal, father; spare the trouble
Of that solicitation. Let me here
As I deserve pay on my punishment,
And expiate if possible my crime,
Shameful garrulity. To have reveal'd
Secrets of men, the secrets of a friend,
How heinous had the fact been, how deserving
Contempt and scorn of all, to be excluded
All friendship, and avoided as a blab,
The mark of fool set on his front! But I
God's counsel have not kept, his holy secret
Presumptuously have publish'd, impiously,
Weakly at least, and shamefully: a sin
That Gentiles in their parables condemn

To their abyss and horrid pains confin'd.
Manoah. Be penitent and for thy fault contrite,
But act not in thy own affliction, son.
Repent the sin, but if the punishment
Thou canst avoid, self-preservation bids;
Or th'execution leave to high disposal,
And let another hand, not thine, exact
Thy penal forfeit from thyself. Perhaps
God will relent, and quit thee all his debt,
Who ever more approves and more accepts
(Best pleas'd with humble and filial submission)
Him who imploring mercy sues for life
Than who self-rigorous chooses death as due,
Which argues over-just, and self-displeas'd
For self-offence more than for God offended.
Reject not then what offer'd means who knows
But God hath set before us, to return thee
Home to thy country and his sacred house,
Where thou mayst bring thy offerings to avert
His further ire with prayers and vows renew'd.
Samson. His pardon I implore; but as for life,
To what end should I seek it? When in strength
All mortals I excell'd, and great in hopes
With youthful courage and magnanimous thoughts
Of birth from Heav'n foretold and high exploits,
Full of divine instinct, after some proof
Of acts indeed heroic, far beyond
The sons of Anak famous now and blaz'd,
Fearless of danger, like a petty god
I walk'd about admir'd of all and dreaded
On hostile ground, none daring my affront.
Then swoll'n with pride into the snare I fell
Of fair fallacious looks, venereal trains,
Soften'd with pleasure and voluptuous life,
At length to lay my head and hallow'd pledge
Of all my strength in the lascivious lap
Of a deceitful concubine, who shore me
Like a tame wether all my precious fleece,

Then turn'd me out ridiculous, despoil'd,
Shav'n and disarm'd among my enemies.
Chorus. Desire of wine and all delicious drinks,
Which many a famous warrior overturns,
Thou couldst repress, nor did the dancing ruby
Sparkling outpour'd, the flavour or the smell
Or taste that cheers the hearts of gods and men,
Allure thee from the cool crystalline stream.
Samson. Wherever fountain or fresh current flow'd
Against the eastern ray translucent, pure
With touch ethereal of heav'n's fiery rod,
I drank, from the clear milky juice allaying
Thirst and refresh'd, nor envi'd them the grape
Whose heads that turbulent liquor fills with fumes.
Chorus. O madness, to think use of strongest wines
And strongest drinks our chief support of health,
When God with these forbidd'n made choice to rear
His mighty champion, strong above compare,
Whose drink was only from the liquid brook.
Samson. But what avail'd this temperance, not complete
Against another object more enticing?
What boots it at one gate to make defence
And at another to let in the foe,
Effeminately vanquish'd? By which means
Now blind, dishearten'd, sham'd, dishonour'd, quell'd,
To what can I be useful, wherein serve
My nation and the work from Heav'n impos'd,
But to sit idle on the household hearth,
A burdenous drone, to visitants a gaze
Or pitied object, these redundant locks,
Robustious to no purpose, clust'ring down,
Vain monument of strength, till length of years
And sedentary numbness craze my limbs
To a contemptible old age obscure?
Here rather let me drudge and earn my bread,
Till vermin or the draff of servile food
Consume me, and oft-invocated death
Hasten the welcome end of all my pains.
Manoah. Wilt thou then serve the Philistines with that gift

Which was expressly giv'n thee to annoy them?
Better at home lie bed-rid, not only idle,
Inglorious, unemploy'd, with age outworn.
But God, who caus'd a fountain at thy prayer
From the dry ground to spring thy thirst to allay
After the brunt of battle, can as easy
Cause light again within thy eyes to spring,
Wherewith to serve him better than thou hast.
And I persuade me so: why else this strength
Miraculous yet remaining in those locks?
His might continues in thee not for naught,
Nor shall his wondrous gifts be frustrate thus.
  Samson. All otherwise to me my thoughts portend,
That these dark orbs no more shall treat with life,
Nor th'other light of life continue long,
But yield to double darkness near at hand.
So much I feel my genial spirits droop,
My hopes all flat; nature within me seems
In all her functions weary of herself,
My race of glory run, and race of shame,
And I shall shortly be with them that rest.
  Manoah. Believe not these suggestions, which proceed
From anguish of the mind and humours black
That mingle with thy fancy. I however
Must not omit a father's timely care
To prosecute the means of thy deliverance
By ransom or how else. Meanwhile be calm,
And healing words from these thy friends admit.
  Samson. O that torment should not be confin'd
To the body's wounds and sores
With maladies innumerable
In heart, head, breast and reins,
But must secret passage find
To th' inmost mind,
There exercise all his fierce accidents,
And on her purest spirits prey
As on entrails, joints and limbs,
With answerable pains, but more intense,
Though void of corporal sense.

My griefs not only pain me
As a ling'ring disease,
But, finding no redress, ferment and rage,
Nor less than wounds immedicable
Rankle, and fester, and gangrene
To black mortification.
Thoughts, my tormentors, arm'd with deadly stings
Mangle my apprehensive tenderest parts,
Exasperate, exulcerate, and raise
Dire inflammation which no cooling herb
Or med'cinal liquor can assuage,
Nor breath of vernal air from snowy alp.
Sleep hath forsook and giv'n me o'er
To death's benumbing opium as my only cure;
Thence faintings, swoonings of despair,
And sense of Heav'n's desertion.
I was his nursling once and choice delight,
His destin'd from the womb,
Promis'd by heav'nly message twice descending.
Under his special eye
Abstemious I grew up and thriv'd amain.
He led me on to mightiest deeds
Above the nerve of mortal arm
Against th'uncircumcis'd, our enemies,
But now hath cast me off as never known,
And to those cruel enemies,
Whom I by his appointment had provok'd,
Left me all helpless with th'irreparable loss
Of sight, reserv'd alive to be repeated
The subject of their cruelty or scorn.
Nor am I in the list of them that hope;
Hopeless are all my evils, all remediless.
This one prayer yet remains, might I be heard,
No long petition: speedy death,
The close of all my miseries, and the balm.
Chorus. Many are the sayings of the wise
In ancient and in modern books enroll'd
Extolling patience as the truest fortitude,
And to the bearing well of all calamities,

All chances incident to man's frail life,
Consolatories writ
With studi'd argument and much persuasion sought,
Lenient of grief and anxious thought;
But with th'afflicted in his pangs their sound
Little prevails, or rather seems a tune
Harsh and of dissonant mood from his complaint,
Unless he feel within
Some source of consolation from above,
Secret refreshings that repair his strength
And fainting spirits uphold.
  God of our fathers, what is man!
That thou towards him with hand so various,
Or might I say contrarious,
Temper'st thy providence through his short course
Not evenly, as thou rul'st
Th'angelic orders and inferior creatures mute,
Irrational and brute.
Nor do I name of men the common rout
That, wand'ring loose about,
Grow up and perish as the summer fly,
Heads without name no more remember'd;
But such as thou hast solemnly elected,
With gifts and graces eminently adorn'd,
To some great work, thy glory
And people's safety, which in part they effect.
Yet toward these thus dignifi'd thou oft
Amidst their height of noon
Changest thy countenance and thy hand, with no regard
Of highest favours past
From thee on them, or them to thee of service.
  Nor only dost degrade them, or remit
To life obscur'd, which were a fair dismission,
But throw'st them lower than thou didst exalt them high,
Unseemly falls in human eye,
Too grievous for the trespass or omission;
Oft leav'st them to the hostile sword
Of heathen and profane, their carcasses

To dogs and fowls a prey, or else captiv'd,
Or to th'unjust tribunals, under change of times,
And condemnation of th'ungrateful multitude.
If these they scape, perhaps in poverty
With sickness and disease thou bow'st them down,
Painful diseases and deform'd,
In crude old age,
Though not disordinate, yet causeless suff'ring
The punishment of dissolute days: in fine,
Just or unjust alike seem miserable,
For oft alike both come to evil end.
  So deal not with this once thy glorious champion,
The image of thy strength and mighty minister.
What do I beg? How hast thou dealt already?
Behold him in this state calamitous, and turn
His labours, for thou canst, to peaceful end.
  But who is this? What thing of sea or land?
Female of sex it seems,
That so bedeck'd, ornate and gay
Comes this way sailing
Like a stately ship
Of Tarsus, bound for th'isles
Of Javan or Gadier
With all her bravery on, and tackle trim,
Sails fill'd and streamers waving,
Courted by all the winds that hold them play.
An amber scent of odorous perfume
Her harbinger, a damsel train behind,
Some rich Philistian matron she may seem;
And now at nearer view, no other, certain,
Than Dalila thy wife.
  Samson. My wife, my traitress; let her not come near me.
  Chorus. Yet on she moves, now stands and eyes thee fix'd,
About t'have spoke, but now with head declin'd
Like a fair flower surcharg'd with dew she weeps,
And words address'd seem into tears dissolv'd,
Wetting the borders of her silken veil.
But now again she makes address to speak.

Dalila. With doubtful feet and wavering resolution
I came, still dreading thy displeasure, Samson,
Which to have merited without excuse
I cannot but acknowledge; yet if tears
May expiate (though the fact more evil drew
In the perverse event than I foresaw)
My penance hath not slacken'd, though my pardon
No way assur'd. But conjugal affection
Prevailing over fear and timorous doubt
Hath led me on, desirous to behold
Once more thy face and know of thy estate,
If aught in my ability may serve
To lighten what thou suffer'st, and appease
Thy mind with what amends is in my power,
Though late, yet in some part to recompense
My rash but more unfortunate misdeed.
Samson. Out, out, hyena! These are thy wonted arts,
And arts of every woman false like thee,
To break all faith, all vows, deceive, betray,
Then as repentant to submit, beseech,
And reconcilement move with feign'd remorse,
Confess, and promise wonders in her change,
Not truly penitent, but chief to try
Her husband how far urg'd his patience bears,
His virtue or weakness which way to assail;
Then with more cautious and instructed skill
Again transgresses, and again submits,
That wisest and best men full oft beguil'd
With goodness principl'd not to reject
The penitent, but ever to forgive,
Are drawn to wear out miserable days
Entangl'd with a pois'nous bosom snake,
If not with quick destruction soon cut off,
As I by thee, to ages an example.
Dalila. Yet hear me, Samson; not that I endeavour
To lessen or extenuate my offence,
But that on th'other side if it be weigh'd
By itself, with aggravations not surcharg'd,
Or else with just allowance counterpois'd,

I may, if possible, thy pardon find
The easier towards me, or thy hatred less.
First granting, as I do, it was a weakness
In me, but incident to all our sex,
Curiosity inquisitive, importune
Of secrets, then with like infirmity
To publish them, both common female faults;
Was it not weakness also to make known
For importunity, that is for naught,
Wherein consisted all thy strength and safety?
To what I did thou show'dst me first the way.
But I to enemies reveal'd, and should not;
Nor shouldst thou have trusted that to woman's frailty.
Ere I to thee, thou to thyself wast cruel.
Let weakness then with weakness come to parle
So near related, or of the same kind,
Thine forgive mine. That men may censure thine
The gentler, if severely, thou exact not
More strength from me than in thyself was found.
And what if love, which thou interpret'st hate,
The jealousy of love, powerful of sway
In human hearts, nor less in mine towards thee,
Caus'd what I did? I saw thee mutable
Of fancy, fear'd lest one day thou wouldst leave me
As her at Timna, sought all means therefore
How to endear and hold thee to me firmest:
No better way I saw than by importuning
To learn thy secrets, get into my power
Thy key of strength and safety. Thou wilt say,
Why then reveal'd? I was assur'd by those
Who tempted me that nothing was design'd
Against thee but safe custody and hold,
That made for me. I knew that liberty
Would draw thee forth to perilous enterprises,
While I at home sat full of cares and fears,
Wailing thy absence in my widow'd bed;
Here I should still enjoy thee day and night,
Mine and love's prisoner, not the Philistines',

Whole to myself, unhazarded abroad,
Fearless at home of partners in my love.
These reasons in love's law have pass'd for good,
Though fond and reasonless to some, perhaps,
And love hath oft, well-meaning, wrought much woe,
Yet always pity or pardon hath obtain'd.
Be not unlike all others, not austere
As thou art strong, inflexible as steel.
If thou in strength all mortals dost exceed,
In uncompassionate anger do not so.
Samson. How cunningly the sorceress displays
Her own transgressions, to upbraid me mine!
That malice, not repentance, brought thee hither
By this appears: I gave, thou say'st, th'example,
I led the way; bitter reproach, but true,
I to myself was false ere thou to me.
Such pardon therefore as I give my folly
Take to thy wicked self, which when thou seest
Impartial, self-severe, inexorable,
Thou wilt renounce thy seeking, and much rather
Confess it feign'd. Weakness is thy excuse,
And I believe it: weakness to resist
Philistian gold. If weakness may excuse,
What murderer, what traitor, parricide,
Incestuous, sacrilegious, but may plead it?
All wickedness is weakness; that plea therefore
With God or man will gain thee no remission.
But love constrain'd thee: call it furious rage
To satisfy thy lust. Love seeks to have love;
My love how couldst thou hope, who tookst the way
To raise in me inexpiable hate,
Knowing, as needs I must, by thee betray'd?
In vain thou striv'st to cover shame with shame,
Or by evasions thy crime uncover'st more.
Dalila. Since thou determin'st weakness for no plea
In man or woman, though to thy own condemning,
Hear what assaults I had, what snares besides,
What sieges girt me round ere I consented,
Which might have awed the best resolv'd of men,

The constantest to have yielded without blame.
It was not gold, as to my charge thou lay'st,
That wrought with me: thou knowst the magistrates
And princes of my country came in person,
Solicited, commanded, threaten'd, urg'd,
Adjur'd by all the bonds of civil duty
And of religion, press'd how just it was,
How honourable, how glorious to entrap
A common enemy who had destroy'd
Such numbers of our nation; and the priest
Was not behind, but ever at my ear
Preaching how meritorious with the gods
It would be to ensnare an irreligious
Dishonourer of Dagon. What had I
To oppose against such powerful arguments?
Only my love of thee held long debate
And combated in silence all these reasons
With hard contest; at length that grounded maxim
So rife and celebrated in the mouths
Of wisest men, that to the public good
Private respects must yield, with grave authority
Took full possession of me and prevail'd,
Virtue, as I thought, truth, duty so enjoining.
Samson. I thought where all thy circling wiles would end,
In feign'd religion, smooth hypocrisy.
But had thy love, still odiously pretended,
Been as it ought sincere, it would have taught thee
Far other reasonings, brought forth other deeds.
I before all the daughters of my tribe
And of my nation chose thee from among
My enemies, lov'd thee, as too well thou knew'st,
Too well, unbosom'd all my secrets to thee,
Not out of levity, but over-power'd
By thy request, who could deny thee nothing,
Yet now am judg'd an enemy. Why then
Didst thou at first receive me for thy husband,
Then, as since then, thy country's foe profess'd?
Being once a wife, for me thou wast to leave
Parents and country; nor was I their subject,

Nor under their protection but my own,
Thou mine, not theirs. If aught against my life
Thy country sought of thee, it sought unjustly,
Against the law of nature, law of nations,
No more thy country but an impious crew
Of men conspiring to uphold their state
By worse than hostile deeds, violating the ends
For which our country is a name so dear,
Not therefore to be obey'd. But zeal mov'd thee;
To please the gods thou didst it: gods unable
To acquit themselves and prosecute their foes
But by ungodly deeds, the contradiction
Of their own deity, gods cannot be,
Less therefore to be pleas'd, obey'd or fear'd.
These false pretexts and varnish'd colours failing,
Bare in thy guilt how foul thou must appear!
Dalila. In argument with men a woman ever
Goes by the worst, whatever be her cause.
Samson. For want of words, no doubt, or lack of breath!
Witness when I was worried with thy peals.
Dalila. I was a fool, too rash and quite mistak'n
In what I thought would have succeeded best.
Let me obtain forgiveness of thee, Samson.
Afford me place to show what recompense
Towards thee I intend for what I have misdone
Misguided. Only what remains past cure
Bear not too sensibly, nor still insist
To afflict thyself in vain. Though sight be lost,
Life yet hath many solaces, enjoy'd
Where other senses want not their delights
At home in leisure and domestic ease,
Exempt from many a care and chance to which
Eyesight exposes daily men abroad.
I to the lords will intercede, not doubting
Their favourable ear, that I may fetch thee
From forth this loathsome prison-house to abide
With me, where my redoubl'd love and care
With nursing diligence, to me glad office,

May ever tend about thee to old age
With all things grateful cheer'd and so suppli'd
That what by me thou hast lost thou least shall miss.
Samson. No, no, of my condition take no care;
It fits not, thou and I are long since twain.
Nor think me so unwary or accurs'd
To bring my feet again into the snare
Where once I have been caught. I know thy trains,
Though dearly to my cost, thy gins and toils.
Thy fair enchanted cup and warbling charms
No more on me have power, their force is null'd,
So much of adder's wisdom I have learnt
To fence my ear against thy sorceries.
If in my flower of youth and strength, when all men
Lov'd, honour'd, fear'd me, thou alone could hate me
Thy husband, slight me, sell me and forgo me,
How wouldst thou use me now, blind and thereby
Deceivable, in most things as a child
Helpless, thence easily contemn'd and scorn'd,
And last neglected? How wouldst thou insult
When I must live uxorious to thy will
In perfect thraldom, how again betray me,
Bearing my words and doings to the lords
To gloss upon and, censuring, frown or smile?
This gaol I count the house of liberty
To thine, whose doors my feet shall never enter.
Dalila. Let me approach at least, and touch thy hand.
Samson. Not for thy life, lest fierce remembrance wake
My sudden rage to tear thee joint by joint.
At distance I forgive thee; go with that.
Bewail thy falsehood, and the pious works
It hath brought forth to make thee memorable
Among illustrious women, faithful wives;
Cherish thy hasten'd widowhood with the gold
Of matrimonial treason: so farewell.
Dalila. I see thou art implacable, more deaf
To prayers than winds and seas. Yet winds to seas
Are reconcil'd at length, and sea to shore;
Thy anger unappeasable still rages,

Eternal tempest never to be calm'd.
Why do I humble thus myself, and suing
For peace, reap nothing but repulse and hate,
Bid go with evil omen and the brand
Of infamy upon my name denounc'd?
To mix with thy concernments I desist
Henceforth, nor too much disapprove my own.
Fame, if not double-fac'd, is double-mouth'd
And with contrary blast proclaims most deeds,
On both his wings, one black, the other white,
Bears greatest names in his wild airy flight.
My name perhaps among the circumcis'd
In Dan, in Judah and the bordering tribes
To all posterity may stand defam'd,
With malediction mention'd, and the blot
Of falsehood most unconjugal traduc'd.
But in my country, where I most desire,
In Ecron, Gaza, Asdod and in Gath
I shall be nam'd among the famousest
Of women, sung at solemn festivals,
Living and dead recorded, who to save
Her country from a fierce destroyer chose
Above the faith of wedlock bands, my tomb
With odours visited and annual flowers;
Not less renown'd than in Mount Ephraim
Jael, who with inhospitable guile
Smote Sisera sleeping through the temples nail'd.
Nor shall I count it heinous to enjoy
The public marks of honour and reward
Conferr'd upon me for the piety
Which to my country I was judg'd to have shown.
At this whoever envies or repines,
I leave him to his lot, and like my own.
Chorus. She's gone, a manifest serpent by her sting
Discover'd in the end, till now conceal'd.
Samson. So let her go. God sent her to debase me
And aggravate my folly, who committed
To such a viper his most sacred trust
Of secrecy, my safety and my life.

Chorus. Yet beauty, though injurious, hath strange power,
After offence returning, to regain
Love once possess'd, nor can be easily
Repuls'd without much inward passion felt
And secret sting of amorous remorse.
Samson. Love-quarrels oft in pleasing concord end,
Not wedlock-treachery endangering life.
Chorus. It is not virtue, wisdom, valour, wit,
Strength, comeliness of shape or amplest merit
That woman's love can win or long inherit;
But what it is, hard is to say,
Harder to hit,
Whichever way soever men refer it,
Much like thy riddle, Samson, in one day
Or seven, though one should musing sit.
If any of these, or all, the Timnian bride
Had not so soon preferr'd
Thy paranymph, worthless to thee compar'd,
Successor in thy bed,
Nor both so loosely disallied
Their nuptials, nor this last so treacherously
Had shorn the fatal harvest of thy head.
Is it for that such outward ornament
Was lavish'd on their sex, that inward gifts
Were left for haste unfinish'd, judgement scant,
Capacity not rais'd to apprehend
Or value what is best
In choice, but oftest to affect the wrong?
Or was too much of self-love mix'd,
Of constancy no root infix'd,
That either they love nothing, or not long?
What e'er it be, to wisest men and best
Seeming at first all heav'nly under virgin veil,
Soft, modest, meek, demure,
Once join'd the contrary she proves, a thorn
Intestine, far within defensive arms
A cleaving mischief, in his way to virtue
Adverse and turbulent, or by her charms
Draws him awry enslav'd

With dotage and his sense deprav'd
To folly and shameful deeds which ruin ends.
What pilot so expert but needs must wreck
Embark'd with such a steers-mate at the helm?
  Favour'd of Heav'n who finds
One virtuous, rarely found,
That in domestic good combines:
Happy that house! His way to peace is smooth;
But virtue, which breaks through all opposition
And all temptation can remove,
Most shines and most is acceptable above.
  Therefore God's universal law
Gave to the man despotic power
Over his female in due awe,
Nor from that right to part an hour,
Smile she or lour:
So shall he least confusion draw
On his whole life, not sway'd
By female usurpation, nor dismay'd.
  But had we best retire? I see a storm.
  Samson. Fair days have oft contracted wind and rain.
  Chorus. But this another kind of tempest brings.
  Samson. Be less abstruse, my riddling days are past.
  Chorus. Look now for no enchanting voice, nor fear
The bait of honey'd words; a rougher tongue
Draws hitherward, I know him by his stride:
The giant Harapha of Gath, his look
Haughty as is his pile high-built and proud.
Comes he in peace? What wind hath blown him hither
I less conjecture than when first I saw
The sumptuous Dalila floating this way.
His habit carries peace, his brow defiance.
  Samson. Or peace or not, alike to me he comes.
  Chorus. His fraught we soon shall know, he now arrives.
  Harapha. I come not, Samson, to condole thy chance,
As these perhaps, yet wish it had not been,
Though for no friendly intent. I am of Gath,
Men call me Harapha, of stock renown'd
As Og or Anak and the Emims old

That Kiriathaim held. Thou know'st me now
If thou at all art known. Much I have heard
Of thy prodigious might and feats perform'd
Incredible to me, in this displeas'd
That I was never present on the place
Of those encounters, where we might have tri'd
Each other's force in camp or listed field;
And now am come to see of whom such noise
Hath walk'd about, and each limb to survey,
If thy appearance answer loud report.
Samson. The way to know were not to see but taste.
Harapha. Dost thou already single me? I thought
Gyves and the mill had tam'd thee. O that fortune
Had brought me to the field where thou art fam'd
To have wrought such wonders with an ass's jaw;
I should have forc'd thee soon wish other arms,
Or left thy carcass where the ass lay thrown.
So had the glory of prowess been recover'd
To Palestine, won by a Philistine
From the unforeskinn'd race, of whom thou bear'st
The highest name for valiant acts. That honour,
Certain to have won by mortal duel from thee,
I lose, prevented by thy eyes put out.
Samson. Boast not of what thou wouldst have done, but do
What then thou wouldst, thou seest it in thy hand.
Harapha. To combat with a blind man I disdain,
And thou hast need much washing to be touch'd.
Samson. Such usage as your honourable lords
Afford me assassinated and betray'd,
Who durst not with their whole united powers
In fight withstand me single and unarm'd,
Nor in the house with chamber ambushes
Close-banded durst attack me, no, not sleeping,
Till they had hir'd a woman with their gold
Breaking her marriage faith to circumvent me.
Therefore without feign'd shifts let be assign'd
Some narrow place enclos'd, where sight may give thee,
Or rather flight, no great advantage on me.

Then put on all thy gorgeous arms, thy helmet
And brigandine of brass, thy broad habergeon,
Vantbrace and greaves and gauntlet; add thy spear,
A weaver's beam, and seven-times-folded shield.
I only with an oaken staff will meet thee,
And raise such outcries on thy clatter'd iron,
Which long shall not withold me from thy head,
That in a little time, while breath remains thee,
Thou oft shalt wish thyself at Gath to boast
Again in safety what thou wouldst have done
To Samson, but shalt never see Gath more.
Harapha. Thou durst not thus disparage glorious arms
Which greatest heroes have in battle worn,
Their ornament and safety, had not spells
And black enchantments, some magician's art,
Arm'd thee or charm'd thee strong, which thou from Heaven
Feign'dst at thy birth was giv'n thee in thy hair,
Where strength can least abide, though all thy hairs
Were bristles rang'd like those that ridge the back
Of chaf'd wild boars or ruffl'd porcupines.
Samson. I know no spells, use no forbidden arts.
My trust is in the living God who gave me
At my nativity this strength, diffus'd
No less through all my sinews, joints and bones
Than thine, while I preserv'd these locks unshorn,
The pledge of my unviolated vow.
For proof hereof, if Dagon be thy god,
Go to his temple, invocate his aid
With solemnest devotion, spread before him
How highly it concerns his glory now
To frustrate and dissolve these magic spells,
Which I to be the power of Israel's God
Avow, and challenge Dagon to the test,
Offering to combat thee his champion bold
With th'utmost of his godhead seconded.
Then thou shalt see, or rather to thy sorrow
Soon feel, whose God is strongest, thine or mine.
Harapha. Presume not on thy God, whate'er he be.

Thee he regards not, owns not, hath cut off
Quite from his people and deliver'd up
Into thy enemies' hand, permitted them
To put out both thine eyes and fetter'd send thee
Into the common prison, there to grind
Among the slaves and asses thy comrades,
As good for nothing else, no better service
With those thy boist'rous locks, no worthy match
For valour to assail, nor by the sword
Of noble warrior, so to stain his honour,
But by the barber's razor best subdu'd.
Samson. All these indignities, for such they are
From thine, these evils I deserve and more,
Acknowledge them from God inflicted on me
Justly, yet despair not of his final pardon
Whose ear is ever open, and his eye
Gracious to readmit the suppliant;
In confidence whereof I once again
Defy thee to the trial of mortal fight,
By combat to decide whose god is God,
Thine or whom I with Israel's sons adore.
Harapha. Fair honour that thou dost thy god, in trusting
He will accept thee to defend his cause,
A murderer, a revolter and a robber.
Samson. Tongue-doughty giant, how dost thou prove me these?
Harapha. Is not thy nation subject to our lords?
Their magistrates confess'd it when they took thee
As a league-breaker and deliver'd bound
Into our hands; for hadst thou not committed
Notorious murder on those thirty men
At Ascalon, who never did thee harm,
Then like a robber stripp'd them of their robes?
The Philistines, when thou hadst broke the league,
Went up with armed powers thee only seeking,
To others did no violence or spoil.
Samson. Among the daughters of the Philistines
I chose a wife, which argu'd me no foe,

And in your city held my nuptial feast;
But your ill-meaning politician lords
Under pretence of bridal friends and guests
Appointed to await me thirty spies,
Who threat'ning cruel death constrain'd the bride
To wring from me and tell to them my secret
That solv'd the riddle which I had propos'd.
When I perceiv'd all set on enmity,
As on my enemies, wherever chanc'd,
I us'd hostility, and took their spoil
To pay my underminers in their coin.
My nation was subjected to your lords.
It was the force of conquest: force with force
Is well ejected when the conquer'd can.
But I, a private person, whom my country
As a league-breaker gave up bound, presum'd
Single rebellion and did hostile acts.
I was no private but a person rais'd
With strength sufficient and command from Heav'n
To free my country. If their servile minds
Me their deliverer sent would not receive,
But to their masters gave me up for naught,
Th'unworthier they; whence to this day they serve.
I was to do my part from Heav'n assign'd,
And had perform'd it if mine own offence
Had not disabl'd me, not all your force.
These shifts refuted, answer thy appellant,
Though by his blindness maim'd for high attempts,
Who now defies thee thrice to single fight
As a petty enterprise of small enforce.
Harapha. With thee, a man condemn'd, a slave enroll'd,
Due by the law to capital punishment?
To fight with thee no man of arms will deign.
Samson. Cam'st thou for this, vain boaster, to survey me,
To descant on my strength and give thy verdict?
Come nearer, part not hence so slight inform'd;
But take good heed my hand survey not thee.
Harapha. O Baalzebub! Can my ears unus'd

Hear these dishonours and not render death?
Samson. No man witholds thee, nothing from thy hand
Fear I incurable. Bring up thy van:
My heels are fetter'd, but my fist is free.
Harapha. This insolence other kind of answer fits.
Samson. Go baffl'd coward, lest I run upon thee
Though in these chains, bulk without spirit vast,
And with one buffet lay thy structure low,
Or swing thee in the air, then dash thee down
To the hazard of thy brains and shatter'd sides.
Harapha. By Astaroth, ere long thou shalt lament
These braveries in irons loaden on thee.
Chorus. His giantship is gone, somewhat crestfall'n,
Stalking with less unconscionable strides
And lower looks, but in a sultry chafe.
Samson. I dread him not, nor all his giant brood,
Though fame divulge him father of five sons
All of gigantic size, Goliath chief.
Chorus. He will directly to the lords, I fear,
And with malicious counsel stir them up
Some way or other yet further to afflict thee.
Samson. He must allege some cause, and offer'd fight
Will not dare mention lest a question rise
Whether he durst accept the offer or not,
And that he durst not plain enough appear'd.
Much more affliction than already felt
They cannot well impose, nor I sustain,
If they intend advantage of my labours,
The work of many hands, which earns my keeping
With no small profit daily to my owners.
But come what will, my deadliest foe will prove
My speediest friend, by death to rid me hence,
The worst that he can give, to me the best.
Yet so it may fall out, because their end
Is hate not help to me, it may with mine
Draw their own ruin who attempt the deed.
Chorus. O how comely it is and how reviving
To the spirits of just men long oppress'd
When God into the hands of their deliverer

Puts invincible might
To quell the mighty of the earth, th'oppressor,
The brute and boist'rous force of violent men
Hardy and industrious to support
Tyrannic power, but raging to pursue
The righteous and all such as honour truth.
He all their ammunition
And feats of war defeats
With plain heroic magnitude of mind
And celestial vigour arm'd,
Their armouries and magazines contemns,
Renders them useless, while
With winged expedition
Swift as the lightning glance he executes
His errand on the wicked, who surpris'd
Lose their defence distracted and amaz'd.
  But patience is more oft the exercise
Of saints, the trial of their fortitude,
Making them each his own deliverer
And victor over all
That tyranny or fortune can inflict.
Either of these is in thy lot,
Samson, with might endu'd
Above the sons of men; but sight bereav'd
May chance to number thee with those
Whom patience finally must crown.
  This idol's day hath been to thee no day of rest,
Labouring thy mind
More than the working day thy hands.
And yet perhaps more trouble is behind,
For I descry this way
Some other tending; in his hand
A sceptre or quaint staff he bears,
Comes on amain, speed in his look.
By his habit I discern him now
A public officer, and now at hand.
His message will be short and voluble.
  Officer. Hebrews, the prisoner Samson here I seek.

Chorus. His manacles remark him. There he sits.
Officer. Samson, to thee our lords thus bid me say:
This day to Dagon is a solemn feast,
With sacrifices, triumph, pomp and games.
Thy strength they know surpassing human rate,
And now some public proof thereof require
To honour this great feast and great assembly.
Rise therefore with all speed and come along
Where I will see thee hearten'd and fresh clad
To appear as fits before th'illustrious lords.
Samson. Thou knowst I am an Hebrew, therefore tell them
Our law forbids at their religious rites
My presence; for that cause I cannot come.
Officer. This answer, be assur'd, will not content them.
Samson. Have they not sword-players, and every sort
Of gymnic artists, wrestlers, riders, runners,
Jugglers and dancers, antics, mummers, mimics,
But they must pick me out with shackles tir'd
And over-labour'd at their public mill
To make them sport with blind activity?
Do they not seek occasion of new quarrels
On my refusal, to distress me more,
Or make a game of my calamities?
Return the way thou cam'st; I will not come.
Officer. Regard thyself; this will offend them highly.
Samson. Myself? My conscience and internal peace.
Can they think me so broken, so debas'd
With corporal servitude that my mind ever
Will condescend to such absurd commands,
Although their drudge, to be their fool and jester,
And in my midst of sorrow and heart-grief
To show them feats, and play before their god,
The worst of all indignities, yet on me
Join'd with extreme contempt? I will not come.
Officer. My message was impos'd on me with speed,
Brooks no delay. Is this thy resolution?
Samson. So take it with what speed thy message needs.
Officer. I am sorry what this stoutness will produce.

Samson. Perhaps thou shalt have cause to sorrow indeed.
Chorus. Consider, Samson. Matters now are strain'd
Up to the height, whether to hold or break.
He's gone, and who knows how he may report
Thy words by adding fuel to the flame?
Expect another message more imperious,
More lordly thundering than thou well wilt bear.
Samson. Shall I abuse this consecrated gift
Of strength, again returning with my hair
After my great transgression? So requite
Favour renew'd, and add a greater sin
By prostituting holy things to idols,
A Nazarite in place abominable
Vaunting my strength in honour to their Dagon?
Besides, how vile, contemptible, ridiculous,
What act more execrably unclean, profane?
Chorus. Yet with this strength thou serv'st the Philistines
Idolatrous, uncircumcis'd, unclean.
Samson. Not in their idol-worship, but by labour
Honest and lawful to deserve my food
Of those who have me in their civil power.
Chorus. Where the heart joins not, outward acts defile not.
Samson. Where outward force constrains the sentence holds;
But who constrains me to the temple of Dagon,
Not dragging? The Philistian lords command.
Commands are no constraints. If I obey them,
I do it freely, venturing to displease
God for the fear of man, and man prefer,
Set God behind; which in his jealousy
Shall never unrepented find forgiveness.
Yet that he may dispense with me or thee
Present in temples at idolatrous rites
For some important cause thou needst not doubt.
Chorus. How thou wilt here come off surmounts my reach.
Samson. Be of good courage, I begin to feel
Some rousing motions in me which dispose
To something extraordinary my thoughts.

I with this messenger will go along,
Nothing to do, be sure, that may dishonour
Our Law or stain my vow of Nazarite.
If aught there be of presage in the mind,
This day will be remarkable in my life
By some great act, or of my days the last.
Chorus. In time thou hast resolv'd; the man returns.
Officer. Samson, this second message from our lords
To thee I am bid say: art thou our slave,
Our captive, at the public mill the drudge,
And dar'st thou at our sending and command
Dispute thy coming? Come without delay,
Or we shall find such engines to assail
And hamper thee as thou shalt come of force,
Though thou wert firmlier fasten'd than a rock.
Samson. I could be well content to try their art,
Which to no few of them would prove pernicious;
Yet knowing their advantages too many,
Because they shall not trail me through their streets
Like a wild beast, I am content to go.
Masters' commands come with a power resistless
To such as owe them absolute subjection;
And for a life who will not change his purpose?
So mutable are all the ways of men.
Yet this be sure, in nothing to comply
Scandalous or forbidden in our Law.
Officer. I praise thy resolution; doff these links.
By this compliance thou wilt win the lords
To favour and perhaps to set thee free.
Samson. Brethren, farewell. Your company along
I will not wish, lest it perhaps offend them
To see me girt with friends; and how the sight
Of me, as of a common enemy
So dreaded once, may now exasperate them
I know not. Lords are lordliest in their wine,
And the well-feasted priest then soonest fir'd
With zeal, if aught religion seem concern'd;
No less the people on their holy-days
Impetuous, insolent, unquenchable.

Happen what may, of me expect to hear
Nothing dishonourable, impure, unworthy
Our God, our Law, my nation or myself;
The last of me or no I cannot warrant.
Chorus. Go, and the Holy One
Of Israel be thy guide
To what may serve his glory best, and spread his name
Great among the heathen round;
Send thee the angel of thy birth to stand
Fast by thy side, who from thy father's field
Rode up in flames after his message told
Of thy conception, and be now a shield
Of fire. That spirit that first rush'd on thee
In the camp of Dan
Be efficacious in thee now at need.
For never was from Heav'n imparted
Measure of strength so great to mortal seed
As in thy wondrous actions hath been seen.
But wherefore comes old Manoah in such haste
With youthful steps? Much livelier than erewhile
He seems – supposing here to find his son,
Or of him bringing to us some glad news?
Manoah. Peace with you, brethren. My inducement hither
Was not at present here to find my son,
By order of the lords new-parted hence
To come and play before them at their feast.
I heard all as I came: the city rings,
And numbers thither flock. I had no will,
Lest I should see him forc'd to things unseemly.
But that which mov'd my coming now was chiefly
To give ye part with me what hope I have
With good success to work his liberty.
Chorus. That hope would much rejoice us to partake
With thee. Say, reverend sire; we thirst to hear.
Manoah. I have attempted one by one the lords,
Either at home or through the high street passing,
With supplication prone and father's tears
To accept of ransom for my son their pris'ner.

Some much averse I found and wondrous harsh,
Contemptuous, proud, set on revenge and spite:
That part most reverenc'd Dagon and his priests;
Others more moderate seeming, but their aim
Private reward, for which both god and state
They easily would set to sale; a third
More generous far and civil, who confess'd
They had enough reveng'd, having reduc'd
Their foe to misery beneath their fears;
The rest was magnanimity to remit
If some convenient ransom were propos'd.
What was that noise or shout? It tore the sky.
Chorus. Doubtless the people shouting to behold
Their once great dread captive and blind before them,
Or at some proof of strength before them shown.
Manoah. His ransom, if my whole inheritance
May compass it, shall willingly be paid
And number'd down. Much rather I shall choose
To live the poorest in my tribe, than richest
And he in that calamitous prison left.
No, I am fix'd not to part hence without him.
For his redemption all my patrimony,
If need be, I am ready to forgo
And quit. Not wanting him, I shall want nothing.
Chorus. Fathers are wont to lay up for their sons,
Thou for thy son art bent to lay out all;
Sons wont to nurse their parents in old age,
Thou in old age car'st how to nurse thy son
Made older than thy age through eyesight lost.
Manoah. It shall be my delight to tend his eyes,
And view him sitting in the house, ennobl'd
With all those high exploits by him achiev'd,
And on his shoulders waving down those locks
That of a nation arm'd the strength contain'd;
And I persuade me God had not permitted
His strength again to grow up with his hair
Garrison'd round about him like a camp
Of faithful soldiery, were not his purpose

To use him further yet in some great service,
Not to sit idle with so great a gift
Useless and thence ridiculous about him.
And since his strength with eyesight was not lost,
God will restore him eyesight to his strength.
Chorus. Thy hopes are not ill-founded nor seem vain
Of his delivery, and thy joy thereon
Conceiv'd agreeable to a father's love;
In both which we as next participate.
Manoah. I know your friendly minds and . . . .O what noise!
Mercy of Heav'n, what hideous noise was that,
Horribly loud, unlike the former shout?
Chorus. Noise call you it, or universal groan,
As if the whole inhabitation perish'd?
Blood, death and deathful deeds are in that noise,
Ruin, destruction at the utmost point.
Manoah. Of ruin indeed methought I heard the noise.
O it continues – they have slain my son.
Chorus. Thy son is rather slaying them; that outcry
From slaughter of one foe could not ascend.
Manoah. Some dismal accident it needs must be.
What shall we do? Stay here, or run and see?
Chorus. Best keep together here, lest running thither
We unawares run into danger's mouth.
This evil on the Philistines is fallen;
From whom could else a general cry be heard?
The sufferers then will scarce molest us here;
From other hands we need not much to fear.
What if his eyesight (for to Israel's God
Nothing is hard) by miracle restor'd
He now be dealing dole among his foes,
And over heaps of slaughter'd walk his way?
Manoah. That were a joy presumptuous to be thought.
Chorus. Yet God hath wrought things as incredible
For his people of old; what hinders now?
Manoah. He can, I know, but doubt to think he will;
Yet hope would fain subscribe, and tempts belief.

A little stay will bring some notice hither.
Chorus. Of good or bad so great, of bad the sooner,
For evil news rides post while good news baits.
And to our wish I see one hither speeding,
An Hebrew, as I guess, and of our tribe.
Messenger. O whither shall I run, or which way fly
The sight of this so horrid spectacle
Which erst my eyes beheld and yet behold,
For dire imagination still pursues me.
But providence or instinct of nature seems
Or reason, though disturb'd and scarce consulted,
To have guided me aright, I know not how,
To thee first, reverend Manoah, and to these
My countrymen, whom here I knew remaining
As at some distance from the place of horror,
So in the sad event too much concern'd.
Manoah. The accident was loud and here before thee
With rueful cry, yet what it was we hear not.
No preface needs, thou seest we long to know.
Messenger. It would burst forth, but I recover breath
And sense distract, to know well what I utter.
Manoah. Tell us the sum, the circumstance defer.
Messenger. Gaza still stands, but all her sons are fall'n,
All in a moment overwhelm'd and fall'n.
Manoah. Sad, but thou know'st to Israelites not saddest
The desolation of a hostile city.
Messenger. Feed on that first; there may be grief in surfeit.
Manoah. Relate by whom.
Messenger. By Samson.
Manoah. That still lessens
The sorrow and converts it nigh to joy.
Messenger. Ah Manoah, I refrain too suddenly
To utter what will come at last too soon,
Lest evil tidings with too rude irruption
Hitting thy aged ear should pierce too deep.
Manoah. Suspense in news is torture; speak them out.
Messenger. Then take the worst in brief: Samson is dead.
Manoah. The worst indeed; O all my hopes defeated
To free him hence! But death who sets all free

Hath paid his ransom now and full discharge.
What windy joy had I this day conceiv'd,
Hopeful of his delivery, which now proves
Abortive as the first-born bloom of spring
Nipp'd with the lagging rear of winter's frost.
Yet ere I give the reins to grief, say first
How died he? Death to life is crown or shame.
All by him fell, thou say'st. By whom fell he?
What glorious hand gave Samson his death's wound?
Messenger. Unwounded of his enemies he fell.
Manoah. Wearied with slaughter, then, or how? Explain.
Messenger. By his own hands.
Manoah. Self-violence? What cause
Brought him so soon at variance with himself
Among his foes?
Messenger. Inevitable cause
At once both to destroy and be destroy'd.
The edifice where all were met to see him
Upon their heads and on his own he pull'd.
Manoah. O lastly over-strong against thyself!
A dreadful way thou took'st to thy revenge.
More than enough we know; but while things yet
Are in confusion, give us if thou canst,
Eye-witness of what first and last was done,
Relation more particular and distinct.
Messenger. Occasions drew me early to this city,
And as the gates I enter'd with sunrise
The morning trumpets festival proclaim'd
Through each high street. Little I had dispatch'd
When all abroad was rumour'd that this day
Samson should be brought forth to show the people
Proof of his mighty strength in feats and games.
I sorrow'd at his captive state, but minded
Not to be absent at that spectacle.
The building was a spacious theatre,
Half round on two main pillars vaulted high,
With seats where all the lords and each degree
Of sort might sit in order to behold.

The other side was open, where the throng
On banks and scaffolds under sky might stand.
I among these aloof obscurely stood.
The feast and noon grew high, and sacrifice
Had fill'd their hearts with mirth, high cheer and wine
When to their sports they turn'd. Immediately
Was Samson as a public servant brought,
In their state livery clad; before him pipes
And timbrels, on each side went armed guards,
Both horse and foot, before him and behind,
Archers and slingers, cataphracts and spears.
At sight of him the people with a shout
Rifted the air, clamouring their god with praise
Who had made their dreadful enemy their thrall.
He, patient but undaunted where they led him,
Came to the place, and what was set before him
Which without help of eye might be assay'd,
To heave, pull, draw or break, he still perform'd
All with incredible, stupendous force,
None daring to appear antagonist.
At length for intermission sake they led him
Between the pillars. He his guide requested
(For so from such as nearer stood we heard)
As over-tir'd to let him lean awhile
With both his arms on those two massy pillars
That to the arched roof gave main support.
He unsuspicious led him; which when Samson
Felt in his arms, with head a while inclin'd
And eyes fast fix'd he stood, as one who pray'd,
Or some great matter in his mind revolv'd;
At last with head erect thus cried aloud,
'Hitherto, lords, what your commands impos'd
I have perform'd, as reason was, obeying,
Not without wonder or delight beheld.
Now of my own accord such other trial
I mean to show you of my strength, yet greater,
As with amaze shall strike all who behold'.
This utter'd, straining all his nerves he bow'd;
As with the force of winds and waters pent

When mountains tremble, those two massy pillars
With horrible convulsion to and fro
He tugg'd, he shook, till down they came and drew
The whole roof after them with burst of thunder
Upon the heads of all who sat beneath,
Lords, ladies, captains, counsellors or priests,
Their choice nobility and flower, not only
Of this but each Philistian city round,
Met from all parts to solemnise this feast.
Samson, with these immix'd, inevitably
Pull'd down the same destruction on himself.
The vulgar only scap'd who stood without.
Chorus. O dearly-bought revenge, yet glorious!
Living or dying thou hast fulfill'd
The work for which thou wast foretold
To Israel, and now li'st victorious
Among thy slain, self-kill'd
Not willingly but tangl'd in the fold
Of dire necessity, whose law in death conjoin'd
Thee with thy slaughter'd foes in number more
Than all thy life had slain before.
Semichorus 1. While their hearts were jocund and sublime,
Drunk with idolatry, drunk with wine
And fat regorg'd of bulls and goats,
Chanting their idol and preferring
Before our living dread who dwells
In Shiloh his bright sanctuary,
Among them he a spirit of frenzy sent,
Who hurt their minds
And urg'd them on with mad desire
To call in haste for their destroyer.
They, only set on sport or play,
Unweetingly importun'd
Their own destruction to come speedy upon them.
So fond are mortal men,
Fall'n into wrath divine,
As their own ruin on themselves to invite,
Insensate left or to sense reprobate,
And with blindness internal struck.

Semichorus 2. But he, though blind of sight,
Despis'd and thought extinguish'd quite,
With inward eyes illuminated
His fiery virtue rous'd
From under ashes into sudden flame,
And as an evening dragon came
Assailant on the perched roosts
And nests in order rang'd
Of tame villatic fowl, but as an eagle
His cloudless thunder bolted on their heads.
So virtue giv'n for lost,
Depress'd and overthrown, as seem'd,
Like that self-begotten bird
In the Arabian woods emboss'd
That no second knows nor third,
And lay erewhile a holocaust,
From out her ashy womb now teem'd
Revives, reflourishes, then vigorous most
When most unactive deem'd,
And though her body die, her fame survives,
A secular bird, ages of lives.
Manoah. Come, come, no time for lamentation now,
Nor much more cause. Samson hath quit himself
Like Samson, and heroically hath finish'd
A life heroic, on his enemies
Fully reveng'd, hath left them years of mourning
And lamentation to the sons of Caphtor
Through all Philistian bounds; to Israel
Honour hath left and freedom, let but them
Find courage to lay hold on this occasion,
To himself and father's house eternal fame;
And which is best and happiest yet, all this
With God not parted from him, as was fear'd,
But favouring and assisting to the end.
Nothing is here for tears, nothing to wail
Or knock the breast, no weakness, no contempt,
Dispraise or blame, nothing but well and fair
And what may quiet us in a death so noble.
Let us go find the body where it lies

Soak'd in his enemies' blood, and from the stream
With lavers pure and cleansing herbs wash off
The clotted gore. I with what speed the while
(Gaza is not in plight to say us nay)
Will send for all my kindred, all my friends
To fetch him hence and solemnly attend
With silent obsequy and funeral train
Home to his father's house. There will I build him
A monument and plant it round with shade
Of laurel ever green and branching palm,
With all his trophies hung and acts enroll'd
In copious legend or sweet lyric song.
Thither shall all the valiant youth resort,
And from his memory inflame their breasts
To matchless valour and adventures high.
The virgins also shall on feastful days
Visit his tomb with flowers, only bewailing
His lot unfortunate in nuptial choice,
From whence captivity and loss of eyes.
  Chorus. All is best, though we oft doubt,
What th'unsearchable dispose
Of highest wisdom brings about,
And ever best found in the close.
Oft he seems to hide his face,
But unexpectedly returns,
And to his faithful champion hath in place
Bore witness gloriously, whence Gaza mourns
And all that band them to resist
His uncontrollable intent;
His servants he with new acquist
Of true experience from this great event
With peace and consolation hath dismiss'd,
And calm of mind all passion spent.

Critical commentary

> His face is turned towards the past. Where we perceive a chain of events, he sees one single catastrophe which keeps piling wreckage upon wreckage and hurls it in front of his feet. The angel would like to stay, awaken the dead, and make whole what has been smashed. But a storm is blowing from Paradise; it has got caught in his wings with such violence that the angel can no longer close them. The storm irresistibly propels him into the future to which his back is turned, while the pile of debris before him grows skyward. This storm is what we call progress.
>
> (Walter Benjamin, *On the Philosophy of History*[1])

The purpose of epic, Milton had written in 1642, is 'to imbreed and cherish in a great people the seeds of virtue and public civility' (*CPW* I, 816); and had *Paradise Lost* been written then, or any time in the next decade, it might have shown something of the expansive nationalism and messianic triumphalism of the earlier prose works. What gives it its very different timbre, and perhaps even its choice of subject, is the bitter disillusion of the fifties, as the revolution lost its way, and the defeat and humiliation of the Restoration. The ominous turn at the beginning of Book IX ('I now must change/These notes to tragic'), a turn which radically redefines the nature of epic itself, looks back to the early treatment of the story as a tragedy; but it locates the poem firmly, too, in that later moment when the 'great people' have fallen into 'foul distrust and breach/Disloyal' (*PL* IX, 6–7), when the epic nurturing of virtue will be directed no longer to the 'public civility' of a thriving commonwealth but to the 'patience and heroic martyrdom/Unsung' of its survivors, a persecuted remnant in a hostile world. From this springs the striking interiority of the poem. For all its cosmic scale, its freewheeling fantasy and a rhetorical energy that borders at times on brutality, the real action is all turned inwards. Satan inhabits a 'Hell within him' (IV, 20), contained by what he contains. Adam is promised a 'paradise within thee, happier far' than the outer Paradise he has lost (XII, 587). Characters are shown in moments of dramatic introspection and (Greenblatt's phrase) 'self-fashioning', somewhere between stage soliloquy and the free indirect speech of that most interiorised of genres, the psychological novel (IV, 32ff, IV, 358ff, IX, 745ff, IX, 896ff, X, 720ff). In counterpoint with this, the text has an introspective turn of its own, insistently scrutinising its own genre, narrative and circumstances of composition in passages, unprecedented in earlier epic, that present the authorial voice in intimate colloquy with its readers and itself (VII, 24ff; IX, 13–47). But above all, the interiority of *Paradise Lost* can be felt in the kind of reading it provokes, a reading at once distanced and engaged, entranced and watchful, a model of the critical and active consciousness itself. As Stanley Fish argues, the poem does not merely narrate the Fall; it encourages the reader, by subtle shifts and reversals of perspective and identification, directly to experience it, at once 'a participant in the action and a critic of his own performance' (Fish 1967: xiii).

To experience it, I'd add, not as a token representative of 'the English people', still less of some generalised 'human condition', but as a private individual whose understanding of herself and the world is expressed primarily not through the big public discourses of politics or history or even religion but through intimate personal *relationships*. In the *Second Defence* (1654) Milton had distinguished 'three main kinds of liberty . . . religious, domestic or private, and civil', and although *Paradise Lost* is far from neglecting the first and third of these spheres of life, its central meanings and commitments are rooted in the second. Locating the climactic action of epic not on a battlefield but in a garden, and so affirming the priority of the 'domestic or private' over the public and forensic, the poem attests its modernity, reconstructing the biblical narratives in terms of relationships – wife and husband, child and parent, pupil and teacher – that belong not to the tribal world of the Old Testament but to Milton's own, and ours. When Adam resolves to eat the fruit, opting for 'sin and death' rather than separation from Eve because 'loss of thee/Would never from my heart . . . / . . . from thy state/Mine never shall be parted, bliss or woe' (IX, 912-16), he is appealing to ideas of married love that are modern, not biblical. Commentators may chide him for this (Alastair Fowler quotes St Paul and St Augustine with relish, adding pontifically that 'Adam becomes corrupt because he refuses to divorce Eve'); but the passage forms a crucial focus of identification for readers (well, for this male reader anyway, but I'd guess for others, and perhaps for women too), making 'man's first disobedience' intelligible not through doctrinal exposition but by an appeal to the recognition of shared intimate experience and feeling, a common 'link of nature'.

The link of nature (the word itself is a vortex of ideological turbulence in the period) is very much a matter of culture, in this case of ideas and feelings inseparable from a particular and historically-specific set of relationships, about which there's nothing remotely 'natural': the nuclear family, founded on what historians of the period call 'companionate marriage'[2] and what Milton, in a passage of impassioned propaganda, calls 'wedded love' (IV, 750). That, for a seventeenth-century middle-class protestant intellectual, is the fundamental thing, the basic unit and generative matrix not only of society but of individuality and the capacity for relationship: 'by thee . . ./ Relations dear and all the charities/Of father, son and brother first were known'. Of masculine individuality and patriarchal society, some readers will want to add, noting the absence from this – from the poem as a whole – of the relations and charities of mother, daughter, sister; and of course that is true. Patriarchy – 'he for God only, she for God in him' (IV, 299) – structures the most fundamental of Miltonic relationships not only around love but around power and inequality; and Milton would have agreed with Engels that in the relations between the sexes we find the source of private property ('sole propriety/ In Paradise, of all things common else') and the first division of labour ('For contemplation he and valour form'd/For softness she and sweet attractive grace').[3] Milton's patriarchalism can hardly be avoided; it permeates his writing as it permeated the intellectual traditions, humanist and protestant, that formed him as a writer.

But as in those traditions, so in *Paradise Lost* patriarchal attitudes are not allowed to have it all their own way. It is not just that the 'contemplation' and 'valour' for which the masculine character is formed are found in the highest degree in Satan (who is very clearly male, despite the supposed androgyny of the angels), or that the poem's critique and rejection of the traditionally 'heroic' (the wrath of Achilles or the 'tedious havoc' of 'fabl'd knights/In battles feign'd') in favour of 'the better fortitude/Of patience and heroic martyrdom' (IX, 30–2) is, by strong implication at least, a rejection of Homeric and Satanic machismo. For there's nothing particularly 'masculine' about patience; rather the reverse, as the long-suffering Grizelda of Chaucer's *Clerk's Tale* or Shakespeare's Viola 'like patience on a monument/Smiling at grief'[4] attest. For Joan Webber, indeed, the major difference between *Paradise Lost* and other renaissance epics, such as *The Faerie Queene*, 'still dominated by the actions of male heroes', lies precisely in the fact that 'what women have always stood for, the apparent passivity of their patience and heroic fortitude, has become for Milton an essential attribute of the hero' (Webber 1979: 161). For her, this makes it the first epic 'to accept absolutely the joint necessity and active heroism of male and female'. But Eve is at once a more powerful and a more ambivalent figure than this suggests; for at an even more fundamental level, the justification, imaginatively and intellectually, of 'the ways of God to men' must also involve in some way both a condemnation and a justification of Eve's action in eating the fruit. Everyone who has puzzled about the logic of the story has realised how nonsensical the whole thing would have been if she hadn't eaten it: what, after all, was the Messiah supposed to be for? So that people who answer the old chestnut about who is the real hero of *Paradise Lost* by saying 'Eve' (see

McColley 1983, Wittreich 1987) may be closer to the paradoxical heart of the text than those who see her only as an emblem of womanly frailty (as Lewis and Fowler do, for example) or of Miltonic sexism.

Milton would have written a better epic, John Dryden suggested, 'if the Devil had not been his hero, instead of Adam; if the giant had not foiled the knight, and driven him out of his stronghold, to wander through the world with his lady errant'.[5] As a thumbnail sketch of *Paradise Lost* this leaves some room for improvement, and nothing could more clearly demonstrate the stark gulf that separates the poem from the style and expectations of cultivated restoration taste, which Dryden did so much to establish. But just as a hostile critic can sometimes get closer to the crux of the matter than a sympathetic one, so in its flippant way this comment makes clear the extent to which Milton's poem stands the usual features of heroic poetry on their head. In renaissance epic, as in the folktales which its narratives closely resemble, the knight drives the giant from his castle and rescues the lady ('lady errant' puns wittily on Eve's 'error' in eating the fruit, and parodies 'knight errant' to suggest an inversion of the sexual hierarchy, with Eve taking the initiative that belongs by tradition to her husband). In *Paradise Lost* all this is reversed: the villainous giant (Satan) seduces the lady (Eve) and drives the knight (Adam) out of Paradise. Worse still, Dryden suggests, Milton has allowed the giant to usurp the role and the characteristics – courage, eloquence, singlemindedness – of the epic hero.

Any number of readers since Dryden have agreed with the last point. Blake's own devil, we have seen, thought the poet 'of the Devil's party without knowing it'. Shelley found Milton's Satan 'a moral being far superior to his God', though flawed by malice and too personal a sense of grievance, lacking the magnanimous objectivity of the ideal revolutionary (Wittreich 1970: 534–5). Empson attacks Milton's God as a tyrant and bully ('the reason why the poem is so good is that it makes God so bad', 1961: 275), and mounts a brilliant defence of his fallen adversary. And I know from years of teaching the poem, and from my own reading of it, that for many people the tragic grandeur of Satan in the first two books remains their most enduring impression of the poem. In part, no doubt, this is because it is their first impression, following inevitably from Milton's decision to start the narrative in Hell. In part it reflects an inclination, of which he was well aware, to identify sympathetically with the defeated, especially when they justify their cause so eloquently. There has been a tendency, too, to associate Satan with Milton himself, another fallen rebel, and to read his heroic obduracy and defiance as the poet's own. Pope slyly hinted at a Satanic pride and malice in all Milton's writings:

> Milton's strong pinion now not Heaven can bound,
> Now serpent-like, in prose he sweeps the ground.[6]

And the nineteenth-century cult of the doomed rebellious anti-hero, from Byron's Manfred to Bronte's Heathcliff and Wilde's Dorian Gray, has its modern representatives, existential wild-siders like Brando's sexily menacing biker in *The Wild Ones*, and his real-life counterparts, the Miltonically-named Hell's Angels. When Joyce's Stephen Dedalus rejects the Catholic Church with the defiant words 'I will not serve', he consciously echoes the primordial apostate who thought it 'better to reign in Hell than serve in Heaven'.[7]

For all the bravado of his great refusal, though, Dedalus remains, in a friend's words, 'supersaturated with the religion in which you say you disbelieve'; and Satan too cannot escape the order he struggles to subvert. Locked into antithesis (reign/serve, 'Evil, be thou my Good' IV, 110), his most strenuous efforts serve only to reinforce the ideological dominant, of which he remains a kind of inverted reflection. Many readers have observed the element of parody that shadows all his exploits, turning him into a photographic negative of God (so forming, with Sin and Death, a grisly trinity) or the Messiah (both journey across Chaos, and Satan has his own incarnation, 'constrain'd/Into a beast, and mix'd with bestial slime,/ This essence to incarnate and imbrute/That to the height of deity aspir'd', IX, 164–7). C.S. Lewis found all this comic; but the Satan of his once-influential essay, a strutting narcissist and prurient keyhole-peeper, his 'sense of injur'd merit' (I, 98) little more than a fit of adolescent sulks, seems to me a creature of Lewis's own invention, grounded in a reading too complacently at home with its own cheerfully uncomplicated orthodoxies ever to engage deeply with this most protean and disconcerting of texts. Satan is a tragic hero – Helen Gardner compares him to Marlowe's Faustus and Shakespeare's Macbeth (Barker 1965: 205-17) – and the doublings and mirrorings with which his predicament is worked out evoke not a chuckle of donnish amusement but 'pity and fear, or terror' (see p. 213) and a vertiginous awareness of the dangers of choosing, the radical complexity of a world in which 'the knowledge of good is so involved and interwoven with the knowledge of evil, and in so many cunning resemblances hardly to be discerned, that those confused seeds which were imposed on Psyche as an incessant labour to cull out and sort asunder were not more intermixed' (*SSPP* 87).

But Satanic heroism is undercut, nonetheless; not by ironic or mock-heroic parallels with God or Messiah, nor even by those 'authorial' comments (e.g. 'high words that bore/ Semblance of worth, not substance', I, 528-9) that, some critics have argued, seek to restrain the reader's (and writer's) perilously easy identification with the character (Waldock 1961: 77ff), but by a thoroughgoing critique and redefinition of heroism itself. The heroic (Milton prefers the term to 'epic') is at once a literary, a moral and a political concept. The opening of the ninth book rejects the 'long and tedious havoc' of renaissance epic for the 'better fortitude/Of patience and heroic martyrdom/Unsung'. Michael, recounting the final confrontation between Satan and the Son, warns Adam to 'dream not of their fight/As of a duel, or the local wounds/Of head or heel' (XII, 386-8), stressing instead the moral and spiritual character of Christ's victory. And *Paradise Regained*, in which that victory is adumbrated, brings out the political implications, rejecting those 'conquerors who leave behind/Nothing but ruin wheresoe'er they rove' in favour of a pacifist conception of personal and political 'glory':

> But if there be in glory aught of good,
> It may by means far different be attain'd

Without ambition, war, or violence;
By deeds of peace, by wisdom eminent,
By patience, temperance.

(*Paradise Regained* III, 88-92)

Lycidas, it is true, had warned the hated bishops of the 'two-handed engine' of justice that, in 1638, 'stands ready to smite once, and smites no more', and *Areopagitica* (1644) speaks enthusiastically of 'the true warfaring Christian' (*SSPP* 59, 87); but as early as 1648, Milton had reminded the victorious general Fairfax that 'a nobler task awaits thy hand,/For what can war but endless war still breed/Till truth and right from violence be freed', and the 1652 sonnet to Cromwell insists that 'peace hath her victories/No less renown'd than war' (*SSPP* 126, 136). In the post-restoration writings the rejection of violence, even in a good cause, is elaborated into a revisionist critique of all forms of heroic militancy. 'Unhappy the land that has no heroes', cries the disillusioned apprentice Andrea in Brecht's *Life of Galileo*. 'No', the old scientist replies; 'unhappy the land that is in need of heroes'.[8] This need not be seen as a retreat, a recantation of earlier radicalism. Milton remained a revolutionary; but we might say, adopting a later vocabulary, that from the second civil war onward the ex-schoolteacher who had written that education could 'repair the ruins of our first parents' (*CPW* II, 366-7) increasingly rejected the heroic rhetoric of armed struggle, in metaphor and in life, in favour of the less spectacular but perhaps more enduring revolution that Gramsci called 'intellectual and moral reform'.[9]

Such a reading shifts the centre of gravity of the poem from the first two books, magnificent as they are, and from the rebellion in Heaven described in books five and six, to the second half, where the climactic account of 'man's first disobedience' is framed by a past and a future of human scale and interest, four books recounting the education of Adam, first by Raphael, who explains the creation of 'a new world and new kind of creature' (books seven and eight), and then by Michael, who shows him the long unfolding of history that follows from the loss of Eden; shifts its focus, that is, from the supernatural to the human, from the heroic to the domestic, from the aggressive, paranoid and overwhelmingly masculine world of God and Satan to the domestic exchanges of Adam, Eve and the androgynous Raphael, whose last words to Adam are about love, happiness and sexuality, 'attractive, human, rational' (VIII, 587).

That break between the two halves of the poem can itself be seen in historical terms. Christopher Hill reads the war in Heaven as an allegory of the Civil Wars (Hill 1979: 371-5). Fredric Jameson disagrees, finding in the first six books 'a reminiscence of the distant feudal past that would seem to have little enough relevance to the war aims of the New Model Army or the visions of the radical reformation' (Barker 1986: 49). We must not expect Milton, historian though he was, to see the events of his lifetime in terms drawn from later historiography of the transition from feudal to capitalist society; but the two interpretations may not be as irreconcile-able as they seem. For Milton as for many like-minded contem-poraries, the real rebel, 'though of rebellion others he accuse' (XII, 37), was not Cromwell but the would-be absolutist Charles Stuart, who abolished Parliament, conferred secular power on favoured prelates and courtiers and claimed an unpre-cedented and unaccountable degree of kingly power for himself – at once a dangerous innovation and a return, it seemed to many, to the most arbitrary and repugnant manifestations of the feudal 'Norman yoke'. But by the mid-fifties, Cromwell himself seemed, like some later revolutionary leaders, to have become no more than the mirror-image of his adversary, a tyrant by merit rather than birth, perhaps, but a tyrant none-theless. Satan, 'the first prelate angel' (*CPW* I, 762), with his 'imperial ensign' (I, 536) and 'throne of royal state' (II, 1), compared by Jameson to 'a great feudal baron' and character-ised in the poem as a 'sultan', 'monarch' and 'dread emperor' (I, 348, II, 467, 510), prompts comparisons with Charles (or rather, with what he would have liked to be). The brilliant general and orator, 'by merit rais'd' (II, 5) to preeminence among his peers and presiding over a 'great consult' (I, 798) that recalls the strategic and constitutional debates in the Army Council and the Council of State, seems more like Cromwell. A composite figure, he allows an exploration, and ultimately a rejection, of the whole historical mode of the heroic, in its modern (revolutionary–absolutist) as well as its traditional (feudal–romantic) forms. Heaven, hierarchical and courtly, represents the *ancien régime*, no doubt. Satan rebels against it, but in its own terms. The true children of the new order are not Satan and his fellow-insurrectionists. They are Adam and, above all, Eve.

One of the most intriguing moments in the trial in 1960 of D. H. Lawrence's novel *Lady Chatterley's Lover* occurred when the critic Richard Hoggart, defending the book against the charge that its frank descriptions of lovemaking had 'a tendency to deprave and corrupt', called Lawrence a 'puritan'. Incredulous, the judge asked him to repeat what he had said. Hoggart replied that in his seriousness and moral integrity Lawrence was indeed in a tradition of English puritan writing that included Bunyan and Milton. In fact, neither Milton nor Lawrence was a puritan in any useful sense; but the exchange illustrates a common confusion over the word, which we tend to associate with an excessively priggish and censorious attitude towards sex; and many readers, approaching the poem with ideas about Milton's supposed puritanism, have been surprised by the prominence it gives to questions of sexuality, even pursuing them into contexts where neither the source-materials nor the narrative seem to require them. Not only does the text insist on the 'conjugal attraction unreprov'd' (IV, 493) of the two lovers, and dwell at length on their idyllic lovemaking, castigating those 'hypocrites' who 'austerely talk/ Of purity and place and innocence' and deny the sexuality of unfallen humankind (IV, 744–5); the sight of them 'imparadis'd in one another's arms' wrings from Satan the recognition that 'not the least' of the torments of the fallen angels is the frustration of 'fierce desire . . . still unfulfill'd' (IV, 509–11). Adam, indeed, suspects that Satan's principal motive may be to 'disturb/ Conjugal love', since 'perhaps no bliss/Enjoy'd by us excites his envy more' (IX, 262–4); and his close questioning of the decorous Raphael extracts the blushing acknowledgement that 'whatever pure thou in the body enjoy'st . . . we enjoy', though without the physical inconvenience of 'membrane, joint or limb' (VIII, 622–9). Meanwhile, the surrounding universe itself is charged with sexual energies and polarities, prompting Stevie Davies to describe the poem as 'a great fertility-myth' (Davies 1986: 241). An androgynous spirit, mother-father of the world, sits ''brooding' on the abyss of chaos and makes it 'pregnant' (I, 21-2). The heavens, Adam learns, are full of suns 'with their attendant moons . . . /Communicating male and female light,/Which two great sexes animate the world' (VIII, 149-51). On the final day of creation, the earth 'op'ning her fertile womb teem'd at a birth/Innumerous living creatures', then, her labour over, 'in her rich attire/Consummate lovely smil'd' (VII, 454-5, 501-2), a moment recalled with tragic hindsight when Adam eats the fruit, and 'Earth trembl'd from her entrails, as again/In pangs' (IX, 1000-1). Against this, in stark contrast and counterpoint, the relationship between Satan, his daughter Sin and their son Death (II, 747-802) is a gruesome phantasmagoria of 'embraces forcible and foul', a nightmare by Goya or Hieronymus Bosch, its incestuous and violent entanglements a horrible parody not only of the trinity but of the oedipal patternings of family life itself.

But if sexual joy, the touchstone of all relationships, good and bad, lies at the creative core of life itself, sexual difference is the root of politics, a microcosm of all future societies. Here the text repays a careful reading. 'Was she thy God, that her thou didst obey?' asks the Messiah reproachfully, preparing to judge the guilty couple. 'Her gifts/Were such as under government well seem'd,/Unseemly to bear rule, which was thy part' (X, 145-55). The language of 'rule' and 'government' looks back to the divorce pamphlets of the mid-forties, which couple the little domestic hierarchy of marriage securely to the overtly political responsibilities of the society outside. But although the lines enshrine a Miltonic commonplace, that women are unfitted for authority, in the home or outside, 'well *seem'd'* (underlined immediately by a kind of pun in 'un*seem*ly') recalls another passage that has been taken as more straightforwardly doctrinaire than perhaps it really is:

> Two of far nobler shape, erect and tall,
> Godlike erect, with naked honour clad
> In naked majesty seem'd lords of all,

And worthy seem'd, for in their looks divine
The image of their glorious maker shone,
Truth, wisdom, sanctitude severe and pure,
Severe but in true filial freedom plac'd,
Whence true authority in men; though both
Not equal, as their sex not equal seem'd:
For contemplation he and valour form'd,
For softness she and sweet attractive grace,
He for God only, she for God in him.
His fair large front and eye sublime declar'd
Absolute rule . . .

(IV, 288-301)

Here the repeated 'seem'd' reminds us that the whole passage is presented not as the definitive authorial statement it is often taken for but as speculative interpretation. This is the first time we, as readers, have seen these remarkable creatures, and we are invited to attribute various moral and psychological qualities to them on the basis of physical clues (most of all, it seems, their hair) which are not themselves necessarily decisive one way or the other. With 'not equal seem'd', in particular (where 'seem'd' must be taken with both parts of the phrase: 'they seemed physically different, and therefore presumably different in other ways'), we are caught up in a powerful, virtually universal process of ideological ascription, in which biological differences are read as an index of supposedly natural and immutable cultural inequalities between men and women. Whether or not Milton himself endorsed that inference is not really the point here. The text, operating as narrative rather than statement, presents it as provisional, as (quite literally) a point of view. And it is easy to forget, as we watch them passing through the garden, that the point of view from which we first see Adam and Eve, the speculative gaze to which the mute language of their bodies yields up its portentous cultural meanings, is Satan's. He, at this stage in the story, is the only one to know that their erect bearing is 'godlike'. He alone is in a position positively to recognise 'the image of their glorious maker'. It is his patriarchal arrogance that attributes a Satanic (or Stuart) 'absolute rule' to Adam on the basis of his supposed physical superiority. Above all, his recent reminder of the 'attractive graces' of his daughter Sin (II, 762) enables him to interpret Eve's appearance as a sign of 'sweet attractive grace' and to formulate the difference in abstract and characteristically hierarchical terms: 'He for God only, she for God in him'.

This is a striking example not only of the 'novelistic' interiority of *Paradise Lost* (very different from the olympian objectivity of classical epic) but also of its profound *duplicity*, its way of presenting ideas (in this instance ideas that Milton himself strongly believed, as we know from his other writings) as authoritative and at the same time of allowing us to look beyond them, to see them not as unchanging truths but as subjective viewpoints or 'readings' of experience, and so to glimpse the possibility of an alternative – in this case, perhaps, a true sexual equality that the text nowhere explicitly endorses, in a world where *difference* need not always be decoded as *inequality*. Recent theory tempts me to call this reading a kind of 'deconstruction';[10] but I prefer here to put it in moral and political terms closer to Milton's own. The subjection of women to the authority of men, like other forms of hierarchy, inequality and exploitation, is a 'fact' about the world, seemingly unchangeable, maybe even (some will say) right and proper and natural. But it is also a Satanic view of the world, and if we endorse it we do so through his eyes. The effort to imagine an alternative, even (especially) to one's own deepest convictions and prejudices, is itself a kind of political struggle, as well as a moral necessity. But the imagined alternative will be a weak thing, a mere 'fugitive and cloistered virtue', unless it is grounded in the recognition that the Satanic regime, which the poem associates not only with the heroic pomp of kingly power and the glamour of rebellion but with the revolutionary energies of expansive colonial capitalism (II, 632–42; IV, 159–65), is tremendously powerful, resourceful and tempting. 'Perhaps', as *Areopagitica* puts it, 'this is that doom which Adam fell into of knowing good and evil, that is to say of knowing good by evil. As therefore the state of man now is, what wisdom can there be to choose, what continence to forbear, without the knowledge of evil?' (*SSPP* 87).

This semantic and narrative duplicity, where the story is

purveyed from a series of shifting and overlapping points of view and the overall responsibility rests sometimes with an authorial 'I', sometimes with a higher authority identified variously and provisionally as 'heavenly Muse', 'Spirit', 'goddess', ought to make us wary of any straightforward reading of the poem, whether as theological treatise, confessional autobiography, political allegory or whatever. Satan tempts Eve with the humanistic arguments of *Areopagitica*: a 'fugitive and cloistered virtue' is useless; virtue is active, courageous, adventurous; the world of knowledge and experience is there to be encountered, engaged with, not feared and shunned. Whether he himself believes any of this is beside the point. He is using the Miltonic arguments, quite coldly, to enslave and destroy a creature he admires, envies, for a moment almost loves. That doesn't mean that the arguments are wrong, that the poem repudiates its author's earlier idealism, though we can see, what neither of them can, that they will mean little to Eve, to whom 'evil' and 'death' are as yet no more than words, and that they are true (for Milton did believe that the daughters and sons of Eve would at the last 'be as gods' IX, 710) in ways beyond the understanding of Satan, who thinks he is simply a brilliant liar. What the great central encounter of the poem does is to put the arguments about experience, self-knowledge and freedom in a new and critical perspective and to force us to think them through again, uncomfortably. The reader's innocence, if it has survived this far, is lost here, with Eve's. For I must agree with what Satan says, as Milton himself did, even while I can see quite clearly what he is really up to. Otherwise Eve is simply – as Fowler, who is fond of reminding us of her intellectual inferiority (see Fowler 1971: notes on IX, 824, 832, 905), thinks she is – silly, vain and inconsequential, and the poem falls to pieces with her.

Such doublings and complexities permeate the language and structure of the poem, down to the smallest verbal texture and detail. The famous 'latinisms', such as *invests* (I, 208), *horrid* (I, 224), *orient* (I, 546), *infantry* (I, 575), *partial* (II, 552), *charm* (IV, 647), *ponders* (IV, 1001), *prolific* (VII, 280), *opportune* (IX, 481) and *capital* (XII, 383), sometimes dismissed (or worse, relished) as mere pedantry, are actually a kind of pun. In each case, a familiar word opens out to disclose a range of meanings, sometimes (partial, prolific) closely related, sometimes (orient, opportune) richly and evocatively complex, sometimes, like 'charm' or the Miltonic favourite 'horror/horrid', disconcertingly different and unexpected. Whatever the effect, the reader, as Richardson nicely puts it, 'is surrounded with sense, it rises in every line' (Darbishire 1932: 315). And always, a historical dimension is revealed. We see language, as we see the action of the poem, unfolding through time from a point of origin too distant and perhaps, like innocence, too strange to be conceived, though it can be glimpsed in such odd, powerful concatenations as the recurrent cluster of puns on 'savour', 'sapience' and 'taste' (see IX, 1017n) and in the general tendency to pursue metaphor and abstraction back to some primitive grounding in material reality. The actual sun rising gives us the location of the 'orient', with all its connotations, as well as the changing glories of the morning sky. Horror, plumed on Satan's crest (IV, 988-9), really does make your hair stand up like bristle.

At the same time, the multiple perspectives on meaning opened up at this level are duplicated in the larger organisation of language and narrative: in the structural placing of books and episodes, of course, but also in the virtuoso handling of verse-sentences and verse-paragraphs, with their long-delayed main verbs ('Of man's first disobedience . . . Sing, heavenly Muse', I, 1-6; 'High on a throne . . . Satan exalted sat', II, 1-5; 'Into this wild abyss . . . the wary fiend/Stood', II, 910-18), their syntactical deferrals and ambiguities, and their wonderfully inventive use of the three distinctive strengths of blank verse, internal rhyme ('Brought her in naked beauty more *adorn*ed,/More lovely than P*andor*a, whom the gods/*Endow*ed with all their gifts, *and* O too like/In sad event', IV, 713-16), rhythmic syncopation ('Drópp'd frŏm thĕ zénĭth lĭke ă fállĭng stár . . . ') and line-breaks ('. . . On Lemnos, th'Aegean isle; thus they relate/Erring' II, 745-7). Milton uses the unrhymed iambic pentameter he inherited from Marlowe, Jonson and Shakespeare as Beethoven used classical sonata-form and Charlie Parker the twelve-bar blues; that is to say, he reinvents it, finding in it unprecedented resources of sound, rhythm and structure. (It may be that there is nothing left for others to do after such feats but to repeat, or to start again somewhere else. Keats thought so, and Hopkins, who, acknowledging the poem's inexhaustible variety and brilliance of 'sprung rhythm', was content to 'admire, and do otherwise'). The dislocated structure and word-order of these larger units, another so-called latinism sometimes thought perverse and artificial, can be compared with the organisation of the poem as a whole. Plunging *in medias res*, into the midst of the grammatical action, its double-headed conjunctions looking back and forward, its pursuit of coherence and finality constantly waylaid by the sensual temptations of simile and the unforeseen enticements of the subordinate clause, the whole serpentine elaboration converges at last on the verb that will explain, organise and justify it, only to find yet further vistas of possibility unfolding on the other side: a microcosm of the epic narrative itself. Like Eve and Adam at the end that is also a beginning, setting out to meet a world that lies 'all before them, where to choose', a reader of *Paradise Lost* confronts at every turn, syntactic, semantic, interpretative, the question of *choice*; a question, the poem suggests ('reason also is choice', III, 108), inseparable from the radical groundings of human freedom, indeed of conscious life itself.

'The author is ever distinguished from the person he introduces', Milton had written in 1642 (*CPW* I, 880), a crucial distinction no less to be observed when the 'person', the character in story or play, is, or seems to be, the writer himself, as in the personal allusions and authorial intrusions in *Paradise Lost*. In spite of this warning, Milton's critics have often found it hard to resist the biographical urge, obsessively searching out points of identification between the writer and his characters; and no work has suffered more in this way than the tragedy *Samson Agonistes*. The blind Nazarite, humiliated in defeat, tormented by the memory of his lost strength and his two disastrous marriages: who can this be but a scarcely-disguised self-portrait of the poet himself, 'fall'n on evil days . . . In darkness, and with dangers compass'd round' (*PL* VII, 25-7)? This was the view of Milton's eighteenth-century editor Thomas Newton, who suggested that the poet was attracted to the story 'by the similitude of his own circumstances to those of Samson blind among the Philistines'; and his Victorian biographer David Masson argued not only that Samson was the writer himself but that Dalila represented his first wife, Mary Powell, and Harapha the French scholar Claude de Saumaise (Salmasius) whose royalist propaganda had prompted the first *Defence of the English People*. This reading, in which the eventual destruction of the Philistines projects the writer's own vengeful fantasies about post-restoration England, helped to confirm the picture of the ageing Milton as an embittered, misogynistic puritan, underlining the Hebraic narrowness and contentiousness deplored by Matthew Arnold and recalling Johnson's sour description of 'a tragedy which ignorance has admired and bigotry applauded'; and it has played its part, too, in the continuing debate about the date of composition (prompted by the remark of Milton's nephew Edward Phillips that 'it cannot certainly be concluded when he wrote his excellent tragedy entitled *Samson Agonistes*', Darbishire 1932: 75), in which competing claims rest not only on analyses of prosody or imagery but on assumptions about Milton's supposed state of mind in the sixteen-fifties or sixties.[11]

This is an extreme instance of the post-romantic desire to see all poetry as autobiography, a Wordsworthian 'overflow' of directly personal experiences and emotions. I call it extreme because in the case of *Samson* it has to fight the text, or to ignore it, every inch of the way. It would be silly to deny that there are striking similarities between Milton and the hero of the play (blindness is the most obvious), and that these undoubtedly give the writing a special intensity and authority. But in most respects it would be an interesting challenge to try to find a biblical figure less promising as a Milton-surrogate than the violent braggart and witless bully of *Judges* who sleeps with harlots, kills foreigners for fun, blabs out his secrets to a woman not once but twice, and kills himself in a final orgy of genocidal slaughter; 'an overgrown juvenile delinquent', as one critic has called him, who 'never does anything good-natured or unselfish' (Frye 1966: 113). Editors remind us that medieval and renaissance commentators interpreted Samson allegorically as a 'type of Christ', a tribute to their hermeneutic ingenuity, and proof that you can make anything into a 'type' of anything else if you try hard enough (Carey 1971: 331-3). But there's nothing remotely Christian about the *Judges* story, and nothing noticeably so in Milton's version either. Some details of the story are discreetly overlooked (he drops the harlot, and omits the incident in which Samson destroys the Philistian harvest by setting fire to the tails of foxes and releasing them into the corn); but others cannot be avoided, and the text betrays some unease in its handling of the hero's death. In the biblical account he prays, suicidally, to 'die with the Philistines'. In the play he only stands 'as one who pray'd/Or some great matter in his mind revolv'd' (1637-8), and the Chorus attempts to clear him of the suspicion of suicide, claiming on no evidence that he was 'self-kill'd/Not willingly, but tangl'd in the fold/Of dire necessity' – the same 'necessity', no doubt, as that invoked by Satan in justification of his destruction of Adam and Eve (*PL* IV, 393), and described there as 'the tyrant's plea'. As for indiscriminate slaughter, the text reveals its discomfort with the wholesale butchery of *Judges* by limiting the destruction to the Philistine ruling-class ('Lords, ladies, captains, counsellors or priests,/Their choice nobility and flower', 1653-4) and exempting 'the vulgar . . . who stood without', a small but highly significant emendation to the biblical narrative.

All this suggests not uncritical identification between author and hero but deliberate distancing, a suggestion supported by the classical form of the play, to which the preface draws such emphatic attention. Like Sophocles' *Oedipus at Colonus, Samson Agonistes* is a drama in which, as one reviewer said of Beckett's *Waiting for Godot*, 'nothing happens, twice'. That is to say, the external action is all offstage, occurring either before the play begins (the protagonist's heroic exploits) or after Samson has left the scene (his death, and the destruction of the theatre). We encounter both, not as action, directly and unequivocally presented, but through a screen of third-person narration, with all its unavoidable problems of arrangement, selection and interpretation. Between, there is only the passing of time; and nothing in the exchanges with the Chorus, his father, his wife, Harapha or the Philistine official prepares us for the 'rousing motions' (1382) that impel Samson finally towards his bloody destiny. Johnson was right: the play 'must be allowed to want a middle, since nothing passes between the first act and the last, that either hastens or delays the death of Samson'; nothing, that is, that can be observed in a theatre or (since 'this work never was intended' (see p. 199) for the stage) read off from the text. Like the ways of 'highest wisdom', the passing of time, the meaning of that interim in which we all live, perpetually stranded between past and future, promise and fulfilment, remains 'unsearchable' (1746). Carey points out that the imagery of the poem, its recurring ships and serpents, water and fire, not only 'reinforce the drama's triumphant upward arc'; by hinting at correspondences between Samson and his enemies, they suggest 'meanings which threaten to invert this arc and bring the weak-minded, vengeful hero to the level of Dalila and the Philistines' (Carey 1971: 341). For him, this is an index of the work's 'moral maturity'. I prefer to see it as a sign of critical disengagement: the story is neither endorsed nor rejected, but pondered. All the characters are allowed their say, not least the much-abused Dalila. And the fatalistic 'calm of mind' with which the Chorus ends the play does nothing to resolve the many questions it has raised. It is the calm of resignation, not of understanding.

Above all, there is the question of consequences, of the future. From the 'fresh woods, and pastures new' that beckon the swain of *Lycidas* (*SSPP* 61), to the world that lies 'all before them' as Eve and Adam make their solitary way through Eden and the mission that awaits Christ as he returns 'home to his mother's house' at the end of *Paradise Regained* (Carey 1971: 521), Milton's poems open out at their endings towards a fresh start, illuminated by a new understanding of everything that has gone before; and he cannot have expected his readers to forget that the consequence of Samson's 'dearly-bought revenge' was not the 'honour . . . and freedom' promised by the Chorus (1715) but a period of bloody tribal warfare and idolatry, followed by the loss of the ark of the covenant to the Philistines and the humiliating submission of the Israelites to kingship. Robert Wilcher points out how closely Samson's replies to Dalila and Harapha follow the arguments of the

Tenure of Kings and Magistrates (Wilcher 1982: 115-17); but why assume, with the painful knowledge of all that had happened since, that Milton still uncritically endorsed those arguments, and the 'rousing motions' through which they seem to be vindicated? It is Manoah and the Chorus who discern the hand of God 'favouring and assisting' Samson's final act (1720), not the poet. In 1644 he had seen in his mind's eye 'a noble and puissant nation rousing herself like a strong man after sleep, and shaking her invincible locks' (*SSPP* 103); but Samson's locks proved far from 'invincible', and if in the years from the execution of Laud and Strafford to the death of Charles I the English Samson had exacted her own vengeance on the 'choice nobility and flower' (1654), she had delivered herself back into idolatry and bondage soon enough. There is no need to look for detailed allegory here, but the *Areopagitica* passage lends support to J.M.Steadman's preference for 'readings [of *Samson Agonistes*] which regard Samson rather as a representative of the English nation than as a surrogate for the poet himself and which associate his fate with that of the Good Old Cause' (Steadman 1987: 259). The hero of the play, Steadman suggests, is 'a type of a regenerated England'; but Samson's regeneration is also his death, and the treacherous ambiguities of a figure both 'puissant' and, like the English people in the *Ready and Easy Way*, all too easily 'misguided and abused' (*SSPP* 147) point to a more guarded reading of the story and its hero. England's regeneration may be already in the past, with which it is futile to argue. The Chorus, ever hopeful, and still believing in the efficacy of heroes, cannot see what is to come. The poem's readers, who have learned that heroes solve nothing, can. But for them too, the future remains 'unsearchable', the meaning of history opaque. If Satan is Milton's critique of kingly power, *Samson* may voice, no less searchingly and with a more personal involvement, his doubts about the cause he had made his own, its historical certainty, its anger and frustration, its dreams of a final, victorious reckoning.

'If these were the causes of such misery and thraldom to those our ancestors, with what better close can be concluded than here in fit season to remember this age in the midst of her security to fear from like vices the revolution of like calamities'. The ominous final words of the *History of Britain*, published three years after *Paradise Lost* and a few months before *Samson Agonistes* and *Paradise Regained*, restate the humanist conception of historiography as a record of the past and a source of instructive knowledge and example for the present. The writing of history enjoyed a renewed intellectual prestige in renaissance Europe, and its wide popularity in England is attested by the remarkable number of history plays performed in the public theatres in the later sixteenth and early seventeenth centuries. Three traditions converge on the English historian in this period. First is the medieval conception of history as the concrete realisation of a providential plan, the unfolding revelation through time of 'the ways of God to men'. Second is the high standing of history in classical antiquity, succinctly expressed in Cicero's often-quoted definition as 'the witness of the times, the light of truth, the life of memory, the governess of life, the messenger of the past'.[12] Third is the intense protestant nationalism of post-reformation England, which fired a new enthusiasm for British history and its (mythical or actual) Greco-Roman antecedents. And to these we can add, with Milton's own literary ambitions in mind, the words of his favourite historian, the Roman Sallust:

> It is a glorious thing to serve one's country in action, but to serve her by words is not contemptible either. Fame can be won in peace as well as in war, and not only the doers but also those who record their deeds can win praise.[13]

Milton began reading British history seriously soon after his return from Italy in 1639, and he probably worked on his own *History* intermittently from 1645 onwards, revising and correcting it up to and during the printing in 1671. A narrative of the British Isles from their first settlement by a mythical grandson of Noah to the Norman conquest, it is far more than a mechanical compilation of existing accounts. His attitude to his sources, particularly the clerical ones on which he relies for much of the early Anglo-Saxon material, is characteristically critical. 'This we must expect', he writes of the historians of post-Roman Britain, 'in civil matters to find them dubious relaters, and still to the best advantage of what they term holy Church, meaning indeed themselves; in most other matters of religion, blind, astonished, and struck with superstition as with a planet: in one word, monks' (*CPW* V, 127-8). The legendary and prehistoric 'matter of Britain', including the exploits of the Trojan Brute from whom the islands were supposed to have derived their name, is recounted at length, if only 'in favour of our English poets and rhetoricians, who by their art will know how to use them judiciously' (as Spenser, Shakespeare and Drayton had already done), but it is firmly distinguished from the 'daylight and truth' of authentic history (see p. 174). And the opportunity of a good story is not allowed to cloud the historian's primary obligation to 'follow truth most of all' (*CPW* V, xlv), as the sceptical treatment of Arthur, once the subject of Milton's epic enthusiasm, demonstrates (see pp. 12–13). On the whole, he declines to draw out explicit parallels with contemporary events. A long digression comparing England after the departure of the Romans with the activities of Parliament in 1647-8 was removed before publication (it was printed separately in 1681 as the *Character of the Long Parliament*); and the closing sentence already quoted offers only a generalised judgement, of which history could presumably supply countless instances, though Milton's readers were free to draw their own more detailed parallels, if they cared to, between the first imposition of Norman tyranny in 1066 and its restoration six centuries later.

For most readers nowadays, the *History* is likely to be of interest not as an example of seventeenth-century historiography but because it is by Milton. Working from sources that are often obscure, longwinded and incoherent, the narrative strives for clarity and concision (one of the major virtues of a historian, he had written, was 'conjunction of brevity with abundance . . . the despatch of much in few words', *CPW* V, xlv-xlvi), and the writing denies itself the coloratura effects and visionary cadences of an earlier historical essay like *Of Reformation* (1641; see *SSPP* 61-85). It is interesting to compare, for tone as much as detail, the *History*'s version of the Sabrina story (183) with the treatment in *Comus* (*SSPP* 50-1), of Arthur (186ff.) with the verse-letter to Manso (Carey 1971: 260-7), of

Lear (183ff.) with Shakespeare's play. The coolness, the measured sceptical rationality, the careful objectivity of the narrative voice (in which only a flickering anticlericalism recalls from time to time an earlier Milton), above all the concern, not with the apocalyptic Truth of *Areopagitica* but with the verifiable truths of empirical research: all these locate the text in the epistemological universe of Locke, Newton and the Royal Society, whose members, in the words of Thomas Sprat, resolved 'to reject all the amplifications, digressions and swellings of style; to return back to the primitive purity, and shortness, when men delivered so many things, almost in an equal number of words'.[14] In similar terms does Christ in *Paradise Regained* sweep aside the writings of the classical poets and philosophers,

> to our prophets far beneath,
> As men divinely taught, and better teaching
> The solid rules of civil government
> In their majestic unaffected style
> Than all the oratory of Greece and Rome.
> In them is plainliest taught and easiest learnt
> What makes a nation happy, and keeps it so.
> (IV, 356–62)

The plain style, clearly, signals no slackening of seriousness. The *History of Britain* is not hack-work but central to Milton's project. Clio, the Muse of history, was the oldest of the daughters of Memory, and history-writing should be as 'doctrinal and exemplary to a nation' as he had earlier claimed her sisters Calliope (epic) and Melpomene (tragedy) to be (*CPW* I, 815). To 'justify the ways of God to men', it is first necessary to untangle the ravelled threads of history, to tease out their hidden logic and pattern. And the reason for doing so, the compulsion that animates all Milton's writing early and late, poem and prose, epic, tragedy or history, is ultimately the question of politics, the great unsolved conundrum of modernity, that haunted the defeated revolutionaries of 1660 as it has haunted their successors ever since: 'What makes a nation happy, and keeps it so'.

Here once more I want to stress the modernity of Milton;

but it is important to remember that the word means something more than a merely superficial 'relevance' or fashionable topicality. On the contrary: Milton fought his battles, those with language and genre as much as those with bigotry and superstition, with weapons forged in the past. 'Just when they seem engaged in revolutionising themselves and things', wrote Marx, people 'conjure up the spirits of the past to their service and borrow from them names, battle-cries and costumes in order to present the new scene of world history in a time-honoured disguise and a borrowed language'.[18] Like Benjamin's angel of history, the new Israelites of the English revolution forged the future with their faces turned immovably towards the past. And like Satan's Niphates top, the 'specular mount' from which, in *Paradise Regained* (III, 236), he surveys all the beauty and richness of the mediterranean world, the texts collected here offer an unparalleled prospect of biblical and classical antiquity, as well as of the nearer landscapes of medieval and reformation Europe. But those ancient narratives and meanings are reworked by an imagination already unmistakably modern, formed by beliefs and institutions – intellectual and religious liberty, the nuclear family, the independent nation-state – that belong not to the past, classical or feudal, but to the future. So for us, denizens of that future, his writings afford another prospect too, towards the still indistinct and distant places where we live ourselves; and perhaps even, on a clear day, beyond.

NOTES

1 In *Illuminations*, New York, Schocken Books (1969) 257–8.

2 See Lawrence Stone, *The Family, Sex and Marriage in England, 1560–1800*, London, Weidenfeld & Nicolson (1977).

3 Frederick Engels, *The Origin of the Family, Private Property and the State* (1884). Milton would not of course have endorsed Engels's argument that the nuclear family exploits women and children, an exploitation that will disappear with the advent of socialist society.

4 *Twelfth Night*, II, iv, 113-14. Viola, disguised as the page

Cesario, is telling Orsino about an imaginary sister, but actually talking about herself.

5 John Dryden, 'Dedication to the Aeneis', in *Essays*, edited by W.P.Ker, 2 vols, Oxford University Press (1926), II, 165.

6 Alexander Pope, *Imitations of Horace* (1737), II, i, 99–100.

7 James Joyce, *A Portrait of the Artist as a Young Man*, Harmondsworth, Penguin (1960), 239–40.

8 Bertolt Brecht, *The Life of Galileo*, trans. Desmond I. Vesey, London, Methuen (1963), 107–8.

9 Antonio Gramsci, *Selections from the Prison Notebooks* ed. Quentin Hoare and Geoffrey Nowell Smith, London, Lawrence & Wishart (1971), 132–3. Gramsci stresses the importance of 'intellectual and moral reform' – of winning the 'hearts and minds' of ordinary people and establishing a new 'common sense' – in the consolidation of any revolutionary seizure of power.

10 Deconstruction, a critical enterprise associated with the French philosopher Jacques Derrida and the American critic Paul de Man, is defined by M.H. Abrams (*A Glossary of Literary Terms*, New York, Holt, Reinhart, Winston (1981)) as 'a mode of reading which subverts the implicit claim of a text to possess adequate grounds, in the system of language that it deploys, to establish its own structure, unity and determinate meanings' (38).

11 For the debate about the dating of *Samson Agonistes*, see Parker (1968), II, 903–17; Wittreich (1971), 163–74; Hill (1977), 481ff. The important point, of course, is that whenever Milton may have written the poem, he *published* it in 1671, without any indication (of the kind he prefixed to some of the 1645 poems) that it had been written earlier.

12 Cicero, *De Oratore*, London, Loeb (1942), I, 223 (my translation).

13 Sallust, *Bellum Catilinae*, London, Loeb (1920), 7 (my translation).

14 Thomas Sprat, *The History of the Royal Society of London*, London (1667), 113.

15 Karl Marx, *The Eighteenth Brumaire of Louis Bonaparte*

(1851), in *Selected Works*, London, Lawrence & Wishart (1968), 96–7.

Bibliography

The range and sheer quantity of writing about Milton is vast, and this list is neither exhaustive nor representative. Most books referred to in the introduction, commentary and notes will be found here, as well as others which are here for no better reason than that I have found them informative and stimulating. Collections like Barker (1965), Kermode and Rudrum provide a useful introduction to the last fifty years of Milton criticism. Of more recent work, some of the most interesting (Belsey, Ferguson and Nyquist, Jameson, McColley, Wilding, Wittreich) shows the invigorating influence of literary and social theory (feminist, Marxist, poststructuralist) and, often, a polemical engagement that Milton himself would certainly have relished.

Aers, David, Hodge, Bob and Kress, Gunther (1981) *Literature, Language and Society in England 1580-1680*, Dublin, Gill & Macmillan.

Arnold, Matthew (1888) *Essays in Criticism, Second Series*, London, Macmillan.

Barker, Arthur E. (ed.) (1965) *Milton: Modern Essays in Criticism*, Oxford, Oxford University Press.

Barker, Francis (ed.) (1986) *Literature, Politics and Theory*, London, Methuen.

Belsey, Catherine (1988) *Milton: Language, Gender, Power*, Oxford, Blackwell.

Blake, William (1959) *Poems and Prophecies*, ed. Max Plowman and Geoffrey Keynes, London, Dent.

Bloom, Harold (1973) *The Anxiety of Influence*, London, Galaxy.
—— (1982) *The Breaking of the Vessels*, Chicago, University of Chicago Press.
—— (1987) *Ruin the Sacred Truths*, Cambridge, Harvard University Press.
Broadbent, John B. (1960) *Some Graver Subject: an Essay on 'Paradise Lost'*, London, Chatto & Windus.
Bush, Douglas (1945) *'Paradise Lost' in Our Time*, New York, Cornell University Press.
Carey, John (ed.) (1971) *Milton: Complete Shorter Poems*, London, Longman.
CPW Milton: Complete Prose Works, New Haven, Yale University Press (vol. V, 1971, contains the *History of Britain*, edited by French Fogle).
Darbishire, Helen (ed.) (1932) *The Early Lives of Milton*, London, Constable.
Davies, Stevie (1986) *The Idea of Woman in Renaissance Literature*, Brighton, Harvester.
Eliot, T.S. (1957) *On Poetry and Poets*, London, Faber & Faber.
Empson, William (1961, revised 1965) *Milton's God*, London, Chatto & Windus.
Evelyn, John (1890) *Diary*, ed. William Bray, London, Gibbings.
Ferguson, Margaret and Mary Nyquist (1987) *Re-membering Milton: Essays on Texts and Traditions*, London, Methuen.
Fish, Stanley (1967) *Surprised By Sin: the Reader in 'Paradise Lost'*, London, Macmillan.
Fowler, Alastair (ed.) (1971) *Milton: Paradise Lost*, London, Longman.
Frye, Northrop (1966) *Five Essays on Milton's Epics*, London, Routledge & Kegan Paul.
Greenblatt, Stephen (1980) *Renaissance Self-Fashioning*, Chicago, University of Chicago Press.
Hill, Christopher (1977) *Milton and the English Revolution*, London, Faber & Faber.
Jameson, Fredric (1986) 'Religion and ideology: a political reading of *Paradise Lost*', in Barker (1986), 35-56.

Johnson, Samuel (1906) 'Life of Milton', in *Lives of the Poets*, London, Oxford University Press (first published 1779).
Kermode, Frank (ed.) (1960) *The Living Milton*, London, Routledge & Kegan Paul.
Leavis, F.R. (1952) *The Common Pursuit*, London, Chatto & Windus.
Lewalski, Barbara (1974) 'Milton on women', *Milton Studies* 6.
Lewis, C.S. (1942) *A Preface to 'Paradise Lost'*, London, Oxford University Press.
McColley, Diane K. (1983) *Milton's Eve*, Urbana, University of Illinois Press.
Milton Encyclopedia (1978–83), ed. J. T. Shawcross and J. M. Steadman, 9 vols, Lewisburg, Bucknell University Press.
Parker, William R. (1968) *Milton: a Biography*, 2 vols, Oxford, Clarendon Press
Pattison, Mark (1879) *Milton*, London, Macmillan
Ricks, Christopher (1963) *Milton's Grand Style*, Oxford, Clarendon Press.
_____ (ed.) (1970) *English Poetry and Prose 1540-1674*, London, Sphere.
Rudrum, Alan (1968) *Milton: Modern Judgements*, London, Macmillan.
Saurat, Denis (1925) *Milton, Man and Thinker*, London.
Shawcross, J.T. (ed.) (1970) *Milton: the Critical Heritage 1628-1731*, London, Routledge & Kegan Paul.
_____ (ed.) (1972) *Milton: the Critical Heritage 1732-1801*, London, Routledge & Kegan Paul.
Shelley, Percy B. (1971) *Poetical Works*, ed. Thomas Hutchinson, London, Oxford University Press.
Sinfield, Alan (1983) *Literature in Protestant England*, London, Croom Helm.
SSPP Milton: Selected Shorter Poems and Prose (1988), ed. Tony Davies, London, Routledge.
Steadman, John M. (1987) *Milton and the Paradoxes of Renaissance Heroism*, Chapel Hill, University of North Carolina.
Thompson, Edward P. (1968) *The Making of the English Working Class*, Harmondsworth, Penguin.
Waldock, A.J.A. (1961) *'Paradise Lost' and its Critics*, Cambridge, Cambridge University Press.

Webber, Joan (1979) *Milton and His Epic Tradition*, Seattle, University of Washington Press.
Wilcher, Robert (1982) '*Samson Agonistes* and the problem of history', *Renaissance and Modern Studies*, vol. XXVI, 108-33.
Wilding, Michael (1987) *Dragons Teeth: Literature in the English Revolution*, Oxford, Clarendon Press.
Wilson, A.N. (1983) *The Life of John Milton*, London, Oxford University Press.
Wittreich, J.A. (1970) *The Romantics on Milton*, Cleveland, Case Western Reserve University Press.
—— (1971) *Calm of Mind*, Cleveland, Case Western Reserve University Press.
—— (1979) *Visionary Poetics*, San Marino, University of California Press.
—— (1987) *Feminist Milton*, New York, Cornell University Press.
Wolfe, Don M. (1941) *Milton in the Puritan Revolution*, New York.

Notes

PARADISE LOST

Book I

This first book proposes, first in brief, the whole subject, man's disobedience, and the loss thereupon of Paradise wherein he was placed; then touches the prime cause of his fall, the serpent, or rather Satan in the serpent, who revolting from God, and drawing to his side many legions of angels, was by the command of God driven out of Heaven with all his crew into the great deep. Which action passed over, the poem hastes into the midst of things, presenting Satan with his angels now fallen into Hell, described here not in the centre (for heaven and earth may be supposed as not yet made, certainly not yet accursed) but in a place of utter darkness, fitliest called Chaos. Here Satan with his angels lying on the burning lake, thunderstruck and astonished, after a certain space recovers, as from confusion, calls up him who next in order and dignity lay by him. They confer of their miserable fall. Satan awakens all his legions, who lay till then in the same manner confounded; they rise, their numbers, array of battle, their chief leaders named according to the idols known afterwards in Canaan and the countries adjoining. To these Satan directs his speech, comforts them with hope yet of regaining Heaven, but tells them lastly of a new world and a new kind of creature to be created, according to an ancient prophecy or report in Heaven; for that angels were long before this visible creation was the opinion of many ancient Fathers. To find out the truth of this prophecy, and what to determine thereupon, he refers to a full council. What his associates thence attempt. Pandaemonium the palace of Satan rises, suddenly built out of the deep. The infernal peers there sit in council.

4 *one greater man* Christ, often referred to as the 'second Adam'.

6 *heavenly Muse* see the opening of Book VII, where she is tentatively identified as Urania, a christianised form of the classical muse of astronomy.

7 *Of Oreb or of Sinai* the mountain (Oreb or Horeb, modern Gebel Musa, one of the summits of the Sinai massif) where Jehovah first spoke to Moses ('that shepherd') while he was looking after his father-in-law Jethro's sheep. The top is 'secret' because shrouded 'with darkness, clouds, and thick darkness. And the Lord spake unto [Moses] out of the midst of the fire' (*Deuteronomy* 4, 11-12).

8 *chosen seed* the Israelites, the chosen people of God. As the (supposed) author of the Pentateuch (the first five books of the Old Testament), Moses 'first taught' them about the creation and early history of the world.

10 *Sion hill* the site of the Temple in Jerusalem. The spring of Siloa rises nearby. Together they form a biblical parallel to the classical Muses, whose sacred spring, Pieria, rises 'from beneath the seat of Jove' (*Lycidas*, 16) on Mount Olympus.

14 *no middle flight* Milton's biblical epic will outsoar its classical and renaissance predecessors, rising higher than the Greek Helicon (th' Aeonian mount), sacred mountain of the Muses. cf. VII, 3: 'above th' Olympian hill I soar'.

17 *O Spirit* the Holy Spirit, Christian counterpart of the inspirational Muse of classical epic.

18 *Before all temples* cf. 1 *Corinthians* 3, 16: 'Know ye not that ye are the temple of God, and that the Spirit of God dwelleth in you?'

21 *Dove-like sat'st brooding* 'And the earth was without form, and void: and darkness was upon the face of the deep. And the spirit of God moved upon the face of the waters' (*Genesis* 1, 2). By invoking the help of the Holy Spirit, Milton suggests a direct analogy between the creation of the world (the subject-matter of Book VII) and the creative impulse behind the poem.

57 *witness'd* revealed, bore witness to.

59 *as far as angels ken* as far as angels can see.

74 *As from the centre thrice* three times the distance from earth (the centre of the universe in Ptolemaic cosmology) to the outer limits of the cosmos.

78 *weltering* rocking to and fro on water, or here, on a 'fiery deluge'. cf. the 'weltering waves' of the Nativity Ode, 124, and *Lycidas*, 13.

80–1 *known in Palestine and nam'd/ Beelzebub* The Philistine 'god of Ekron' of *2 Kings* 1, 2. In the gospels, the Pharisees accuse Christ of using the help of this 'prince of the devils' to perform miracles (*Matthew* 12, 24). His name means 'Lord of the flies'.

82 *thence in heaven call'd Satan* the name means 'the adversary' in Hebrew.

117 *empyreal substance* the empyrean (from Greek *pyr*, fire) was the sphere of fire, highest of the heavenly spheres and home of the gods.

127 *compeer* comrade.

163 *Out of our evil . . . bring forth good* a formulation echoed near the end of the poem: 'That all this good of evil shall produce/And evil turn to good', XII, 470-1.

182 *livid flames* 'livid' is a leaden or bluish colour, with the metaphorical sense of 'angry'.

196 *rood* a quarter of an acre.

198 *Titanian or Earth-born* the Titans and the Giants, both sons of Gaia or Earth, waged war on the Olympian gods (Jove = Zeus). Briareus was a Titan, Typhon a Giant. Greek writers located Typhon's home in a

cave in Cilicia (southern Turkey), of which Tarsus was the principal city.

201 *Leviathan* The sea-monster of *Job* 41, who 'maketh the deep to boil like a pot' and is 'a king over all the children of pride', was generally identified as a whale, and, metaphorically, with Satan.

208 *Invests* combines the senses of 'clothes' and 'besieges'.

224 *horrid vale* alongside the modern meaning of 'horrid', Milton invariably retains the older Latin sense of 'bristling'. Here the 'vale' or parting opened up in the burning lake by Satan's sudden rearing upwards is 'horrid' with the 'pointing spires' of the liquid fire, driven back into 'billows'.

226 *incumbent* reclining

232 *Pelorus . . . Etna* Pelorus, modern Faro, is a rocky (but not volcanic) headland in north-east Sicily. The volcanic Mount Etna lies about fifty miles to the south. Ancient theory attributed volcanic activity to the pressure of 'subterranean wind', here aided by the 'sublim'd (= vaporised) entrails' of the mountain.

237 *such resting found the sole/Of unbless'd feet* there may be an implied contrast in this phrase with the promise given to Moses in *Deuteronomy* 11, 24–8: 'Every place whereon the soles of your feet shall tread shall be yours . . . Behold, I set before you this day a blessing and a curse; A blessing, if ye obey the commandments of the Lord your God, which I command you this day; And a curse, if ye will not obey the commandments of the Lord your God'.

239 *Stygian flood* because of its similarity to the Greek Styx, the river of the underworld; but 'stygian' has a more general sense of 'gloomy', 'hateful'. cf. II, 577.

266 *astonish'd* stronger than the modern sense: stunned, paralysed (literally 'thunderstruck'). The 'oblivious pool' (cf. the 'forgetful lake' of II, 74) induces (temporary) amnesia.

282 *pernicious* fatal, destructive.

285 *ethereal temper* of heavenly quality; tempered in heavenly fire.

288 *Tuscan artist* the scientist Galileo (1564–1642), one of the first astronomers to make detailed observations of the moon and other heavenly bodies with a telescope ('optic glass'). In *Areopagitica* Milton recalls a visit to him in 1638, when he was confined to his house by blindness and forbidden by the Church to publish the results of his research: 'there it was that I found and visited the famous Galileo grown old, a prisoner to the Inquisition, for thinking in astronomy otherwise than the Franciscan and Dominican licensers thought' (*CPW* II, 538). He lived at Arcetri, near Florence, in the Arno valley ('Valdarno'). Fiesole is in the Tuscan hills a few miles north-east of Florence.

293 *Norwegian hills* Norwegian fir was used for shipbuilding; but this is the second instance of the association of Satan with Norway (cf. 203); and later (351ff.) the rebel angels will be described as 'a multitude like which the populous north/Pour'd never from her frozen loins', an allusion to the barbarian invasions of central and southern Europe. The association of the devil with the north is traditional.

294 *ammiral* admiral: the flagship of a fleet, or the officer commanding it. The 17th-century spelling recalls its derivation from Arabic *amir*, commander.

296 *marl* clay.

299 *natheless* nevertheless.

303 *Vallombrosa* linking this part of the simile to the earlier references to Tuscany (ancient Etruria), Vallombrosa is a few miles east of Florence. The name means 'shady valley', perhaps here suggesting also the 'valley of the shadow of death' of Psalm 23.

304 *scatter'd sedge* in Hebrew, the Red Sea is called the 'sea of sedge' (i.e. seaweed). The evening setting in early November of the constellation Orion (named from a legendary hunter, and 'arm'd' because traditionally depicted as a hunter or warrior with sword and spear) often coincides in the mediterranean region

with a period of winter storms (cf. Horace, *Odes*, 28, 21-2); and *Job* 9 takes Orion, with other winter constellations, as a symbol of the anger and power of Jehovah, 'which doeth great things past finding out; yea, and wonders without number'.

307 *Busiris* Milton's name for the Pharaoh who, having agreed to let the Israelites leave Goshen (north-eastern Egypt), changed his mind and followed them with an army into the wilderness. Moses parted the waters of the Red Sea, but after the Israelites had crossed safely, Jehovah struck off the chariot-wheels of the pursuing Egyptian cavalry ('Memphian chivalry'), who were engulfed and destroyed by the returning water. The story is told in *Exodus* 13-14, and summarised by Milton in Book XII, 190-214.

332 *watch* stay awake and on guard.

339 *Amram's son* Moses, who used his rod to call up an east wind and with it a plague of locusts which 'covered the face of the whole earth, so that the land was darkened' (*Exodus* 10, 12-15). cf. XII, 185-8.

341 *warping* twisting and turning.

345 *cope* vault.

353 *Rhene or the Danaw* Rhine or Danube, crossed by the Barbarians on their successive invasions of western and southern Europe.

360 *powers . . . thrones* alluding to the orders of angels, derived from *Colossians* 1, 16 and elaborated in the renaissance into a quasi-feudal hierarchy: Seraphim, Cherubim, Thrones, Dominations, Virtues, Powers, Principalities, Archangels and Angels. Milton generally uses the names for rhetorical effect rather than theological precision.

371 *image of a brute* as the procession that follows shows in detail, near-eastern deities were often worshipped in the form of totemic animals, the 'brutish gods' of the Nativity Ode, vv. 22-94 (a passage worth comparing with the present one).

380 *promiscuous* mixed, not individually distinguishable.

386 *Jehovah thundering* like many other ancient deities (cf.

the Greek Zeus and Roman Jupiter), the biblical Jehovah is associated with thunder (see for example *Exodus* 19, 16). The tabernacle or sanctuary which he commanded Moses to make for him contained a throne (Authorised Version) or cover (New English Bible) framed by two gold cherubim. The tabernacle, and the ark of the covenant which it contained, were eventually placed in the temple in Jerusalem.

392 *Moloch, horrid king* the name Moloch means 'king'.

393 *human sacrifice and parents' tears* at Rabbah in Ammon (modern Jordan), Moloch was worshipped in the form of a hollow metal bull, in which children were roasted alive. 'Sullen Moloch', with his 'burning idol', is one of the pagan gods driven from their shrines at the birth of Christ in the Nativity Ode, v. 23.

401 *Solomon* the story of Solomon's idolatry is in *1 Kings* 11. His many wives from the surrounding kingdoms 'turned away his heart after other gods', including 'Molech, the abomination of the children of Ammon' and 'Chemosh, the abomination of Moab', for whom he built a temple on the Mount of Olives (the 'opprobrious hill').

411 *th'asphaltic pool* the Dead Sea.

412 *Peor* when the Israelites settled in Shittim on their journey from Egypt, the priest Balaam built altars to Baal (a generic name for local deities, here identified with Chemosh) on Mount Peor, a name which Milton here (as in the Nativity Ode 197) uses for the god; with the result that 'Israel joined himself unto Baal-peor: and the anger of the Lord was kindled against Israel', with predictably gory consequences (*Numbers* 23-5). King Josiah destroyed the shrines of Chemosh and Moloch in the hills around Jerusalem, including the 'hill of scandal', the Mount of Olives (*2 Kings* 23).

420 *Euphrates* the 'bordering flood' of the river Euphrates bounded biblical Syria to the north, the 'brook' Besor to the south. The Syrian deities include Astoreth, the

moon-goddess who also had a shrine on the 'offensive' Mount of Olives, built by the 'uxorious king' Solomon; her lover Thammuz, a vegetation-god with a shrine on the river Adonis (from which his Greek counterpart, also associated with the moon-goddess Aphrodite/Astarte, took his name), whose imported worship by Jewish women ('Sion's daughters') was denounced by the prophet Ezekiel in a later scourge of Israelite 'abomination' (*Ezekiel* 8, 13–14); Dagon, the Philistine god, who suffered the indignity described in II. 458–61 when the ark of the covenant was placed in his temple by its Philistine captors (*1 Samuel* 5); and Rimmon, whose worship was abjured by the Syrian general Naaman after Elisha had cured his leprosy (*2 Kings* 5), but later introduced into the temple by the apostate King Ahaz (*2 Kings* 16).

460 *groundsel edge* sill, threshhold.

464 *Azotus* the five principal cities of the Philistines were Ashdod (Latin Azotus), Gath (modern Qiryat), Askelon (Ascalon, modern Ashqelon), Ekron (Accaron) and Gaza. See *1 Samuel* 6,17 and *Samson* 138n.

478 *Osiris, Isis, Orus* Egyptian deities, often represented in animal form. The golden calf worshipped on Mount Horeb (cf. line 6) by the Israelites (*Exodus* 32), and the two ('doubl'd') made by King Jeroboam (*1 Kings* 12, 28) were thought to have been based on Egyptian idols.

488 *equall'd* levelled, destroyed. The feast of the Passover commemorated the divine vengeance visited on the Egyptians by Jehovah: 'For I will pass through the land of Egypt this night, and will smite all the first-born in the land of Egypt, both man and beast; and against all the gods of Egypt I will execute judgment' (*Exodus* 12, 12).

490 *Belial* the traditional personification of lust and sloth; his name is a Hebrew word meaning 'viciousness', only occurring in the Old Testament in generic phrases like 'children of Belial'. Milton alludes to three instances: the impiety of Eli's sons (*1 Samuel* 2,

12); Lot's offer of his daughters to the Sodomites in place of the male guests (actually angels) they were shouting for (*Genesis* 19, 4-9); and the rape and murder of a woman in the Benjamite city of Gibeah, offered to the 'sons of Belial' in place of her Levite master (*Judges* 19, 22ff.). Here and at II, 109-17 Milton gives him many of the characteristics of a Restoration rake, handsome, plausible, drunken, violent, bisexually predatory, and a coward. 'Reigns' (497) may even hint at similarities to Charles II himself.

502 *flown* overflowing.

508 *Th' Ionian gods* some biblical commentators derived the name Ionia (Greek Asia Minor) from Noah's grandson Javan, so 'Javan's issue' means Greeks. In this Miltonic mixture of ancient and post-classical folklore, the Greek gods, with their Roman counterparts, were descended from Ouranos and Gaia (Heaven and Earth) via Kronos (Saturn), who usurped his older brother Titan only to be himself overthrown by his son Zeus (Jupiter, Jove), born and nurtured on Mount Ida in Crete. They lived on Mount Olympus, with major cult centres at Delphi and Dodona, and others all over the Greek-speaking world ('Doric land'); and their worship spread across the Adriatic to Italy ('Hesperian fields'), France ('Celtic') and Britain ('the utmost isles').

537 *meteor* comet, perhaps with its traditional connotations of disaster.

543 *Chaos and old Night* the region ('reign') visited by Satan on his journey to Eden, II, 890ff.

546 *orient colours* literally 'rising'; hence the colour and brilliance of the sky at sunrise, perhaps with a suggestion of oriental magnificence. Satan is compared to 'the sun new risen' (594), and to an oriental potentate (II, 1-5).

550 *phalanx* a Greek term for a column of infantry in close order. Like the ancient Spartans in the advance on Mantinea (Thucydides, *History*, V, 70), the fallen

angels march to flutes. The 'Doric mood', doubly appropriate here because the Spartans were of Doric origin and dialect, is the Dorian mode of Greek music, permitted in Plato's utopian republic, where other modes were prohibited as unmanly. cf. Milton's sardonic comment in *Areopagitica* that under state censorship 'no music must be heard, no song be set or sung, but what is grave and Doric'.

575 *small infantry* the fallen angels in battle order are compared with other armies in folklore and literature, each associated with a specific epic tradition; so the comparison is also between *Paradise Lost* and its generic predecessors. The battle between the 'small infantry' of the Pygmies (with a pun on 'infantry': soldiers the size of children) and the cranes is from the *Iliad*, iii, 3-6. The Giants fought the gods at Phlegra in Hesiod's *Theogony*. Thebes and Ilium (Troy) are the sites of two of the major epic cycles of antiquity, Statius' *Thebaid* and the *Iliad*. 'Uther's son' Arthur and his British and Armoric (Breton) knights are the subject of the medieval 'matter of Britain', which Milton himself had once considered using for an epic poem. Lines 582-6 refer to the settings and protagonists of chivalric and romantic epics by Ariosto, Boiardo and others.

597 *dim eclipse* the solar eclipse is 'disastrous' (literally, 'ill-starred') because, like comets, eclipses were believed to forebode war and revolution. The sun is a traditional icon of monarchy, and according to Milton's early biographer John Toland the image of the sun 'shorn of his beams' and eclipsed, with associations of royal perplexity and 'fear of change', almost led to the suppression of the whole poem: 'I must not forget that we had like to be eternally depriv'd of this Treasure by the Ignorance or Malice of the Licenser [probably Roger L'Estrange or the ecclesiastical licenser Thomas Tomkins]; who, among other frivolous Exceptions, would needs suppress the

whole Poem for imaginary Treason in the following lines' (Darbishire 180).

603 *considerate* considered, self-conscious.

609 *amerc'd* punished by fine or confiscation.

675 *brigade* accented on the first syllable: *brigad.*

678 *Mammon* an Aramaic word, used in the New Testament, meaning 'wealth', left untranslated in the Authorised Version (as in the parable of the unjust steward, *Luke* 16), and later personified as the god of money.

686 *centre* of the earth.

692 *bane* poison.

694 *Babel* the tower of Babel (Greek *Babylon*), built by Nimrod (*Genesis* 10, 10 and 11, 3-9; cf. XII, 38ff.) and the pyramids built by the Egyptian ('Memphian') kings: examples of construction on a superhuman scale, both dwarfed by the size and speed of the building of Pandaemonium. cf. 'Babylon' and 'great Alcairo' below, 717-18.

704 *severing* separating out each kind of molten metal ('bullion'), and 'scumming' (skimming off) the dross.

713 *pilasters* rectangular columns, 'engaged' or attached to a wall. Like the Doric pillars supporting an entablature of architrave, cornice and frieze with sculpted bosses (projections), these identify the building as classical in style.

720 *Belus or Serapis* the Babylonian Baal and the bull-headed Egyptian deity.

729 *naphtha and asphaltus* naphtha is a petroleum oil, asphalt a bituminous pitch, burned in lamps and 'cressets' (baskets) to provide artificial lighting.

732 *the architect* the master-builder of Hell (and Heaven) is syncretically identified with the Greek Hephaistos, known in ancient Italy ('Ausonian land') as Vulcan or Mulciber. The 'fabled' account of his fall from Olympus onto the island of Lemnos is in the *Iliad*, i, 590-3.

756 *Pandaemonium* the name, Milton's invention, means 'place of all the demons'.

763 *like a cover'd field* the comparison is with the 'champ clos' or enclosed arena where Christian and Saracen ('paynim', heathen) champions fought single-handed in front of the Sultan ('soldan').

769 *Taurus* the sun moves from Aries into Taurus in April. The comparison with bees, in terms of size, number and social and political organisation, has close parallels in the *Iliad* and the *Aeneid*, and prepares figuratively for the actual shrinking of the devils, which is then registered in turn by the further similes of 'smallest forms', dwarfs, pygmies and elves. The effect has been called mock-heroic, and is certainly comic; but the fallen angels are not ridiculed as diminutive and helpless Lilliputians. They shrink themselves voluntarily, to prevent overcrowding ('straiten'd') in the outer hall, and the leading devils retain 'their own dimensions'.

797 *frequent and full* crowded.

Book II

The consultation begun, Satan debates whether another battle is to be hazarded for the recovery of Heaven. Some advise it, others dissuade. A third proposal is preferred, mentioned before by Satan, to search the truth of that prophecy or tradition in Heaven concerning another world and time to be created. Their doubt who shall be sent on this difficult search. Satan their chief undertakes alone the voyage, is honoured and applauded. The council thus ended, the rest betake them several ways and to several employments, as their inclinations lead them, to entertain the time till Satan return. He passes on his journey to Hell gates, finds them shut, and who sat there to guard them, by whom at length they are opened and discover to him the great gulf between Hell and Heaven; with what difficulty he passes through, directed by Chaos, the power of that place, to the sight of this new world which he sought.

2 *of Ormus or of Ind* Ormuz, or Hormuz, an island at the southern entrance to the Persian Gulf, a centre of

'very great trade of all sorts of spices, drugs, silk, cloth of silk, fine tapestry of Persia, great store of pearls' (Hakluyt); and the Indies, long exploited by European merchant adventurers as a source 'barbaric pearl and gold'.

5 *by merit rais'd* cf. the Messiah, who also 'by right of merit reigns' (VI, 43), and God's plan that unfallen humankind shall eventually enter heaven 'by degrees of merit rais'd' (VII, 157).

11 *Powers and dominions* two of the nine orders of angels. For a full list see I, 360n.

11 *sentence* judgement, opinion.

19 *Tartarean sulphur* Tartarus was the hell of Greek mythology.

71 *The way seems difficult* the whole passage is an inverted reworking of the warning given to Aeneas (*Aeneid* vi, 126ff.): 'the descent to hell is easy, but to retrace your steps and escape back to the upper air, that is the difficult task'. Fowler (1971: 93) suggests that the allusion 'gives the lie' to Moloch's argument, but that is to overlook the ironic distinction between the mortal (and wingless) Aeneas and the angels, for whom 'descent and fall . . . is adverse'. Satan invokes the Virgilian parallel more closely at lines 432–3.

82 *event* outcome, result.

258 *great things of small* Mammon's words are echoed by Adam at the end of the poem: 'by small Accomplishing great things, by things deem'd weak Subverting worldly strong' (XII, 566–8). Cf. I, 163 for a similar parallelism.

288 *o'erwatch'd* weary with being too long awake.

294 *sword of Michael* the archangel Michael commanded the heavenly army against the rebel angels. He fights with Satan, and wounds him (VI, 320ff.).

306 *Atlantean shoulders* Atlas, one of the rebellious Titans defeated by Zeus, was condemned to carry the heavens on his shoulders. The Atlas mountains of northwest Africa take their name from him; and the double mythological-geographical comparison (with

Titans and mountains) is sustained at IV, 987, where Satan is 'like Teneriffe or Atlas unremov'd'.

327 *iron sceptre . . . golden* the opposition of iron (punishment, exclusion) and gold (mercy, reconciliation) recalls St Peter's keys in *Lycidas* 111: 'The golden opes, the iron shuts amain'.

367 *puny* one of Milton's earliest editors, Patrick Hume (1695), pointed out the witty appropriateness of the word, which comes from French *puis-né*, born later, younger.

379 *first devis'd/By Satan* see I, 162–8, where Satan suggests the motive to Beelzebub, and I, 650–9, where he hints at the occasion.

406 *palpable obscure* the 'darkness which may be felt' of *Exodus*, 10, 21, rendered as 'palpable darkness' in Milton's version (XII, 188).

407 *uncouth* unknown.

412 *senteries* sentries.

436 *adamant* diamond.

439 *unessential* without essence or real existence. The 'abortive gulf' of uncreated chaos represents the negation of being.

467 *prevented* anticipated, forestalled.

513 *bright emblazonry* the political implications of Satan's 'monarchal pride' (428) are here reinforced by the ritual pomp of heraldic 'emblazonry' and 'arms'. 'Horrent' (cf. abhorrent) has the usual Miltonic sense of 'bristling'.

529 *swift race* the games with which the fallen angels pass the time till Satan's return are a generic feature of epic. Early examples are in *Iliad* xxiii, *Odyssey* viii and *Aeneid* v and vi. The unfallen angels have their own games at iv, 551–4. The Olympian and Pythian games (at Olympia and Delphi) were the principal athletic festivals of ancient Greece.

531 *shun the goal* avoid (perhaps with the sense 'narrowly miss') the turning-point of the circuit.

532 *fronted* confronting each other.

535 *van* the vanguard or leading ranks of an army. To

'prick', in chivalric literature, is to spur a horse forward, thus 'ride'. 'Couched' spears are lowered into the attacking position.

538 *welkin* sky.

539 *Typhoean rage* as at I, 199, Typhoeus, or Typhon, was one of the Giants who tore up mountains and piled them one on the other in their attempt to storm Olympus and overthrow the gods; but 'ride the air/ In whirlwind' suggests an association with 'typhoon'.

542 *Alcides* Hercules, here named after his grandfather Alceus, was killed by a poisoned robe unwittingly given to him by his companion Lichas. In his death agony, he hurled Lichas from Mount Oeta in Thessaly into the gulf of Euboea fifty miles away.

552 *partial* partisan, but also 'in parts', polyphonic.

564 *passion and apathy* apathy or dispassionate indifference to misfortune was the highest virtue in Stoic philosophy, described in *Paradise Regained* as 'contemning all/Wealth, pleasure, pain or torment, death and life', and there dismissed by Christ as merely 'philosophic pride' (IV, 304–5).

568 *obdured* obdurate, hardened.

575 *four infernal rivers* drawing on *Aeneid* vi, where six rivers are listed: 'Styx, Acheron, Lethe, Phlegethon, Cocytus, Avernus'. Of these, Milton omits the last, and separates Lethe from the others, perhaps to suggest a symmetry with the four rivers of Paradise (see IV, 233). Milton's epithets translate the Greek meaning of the names.

592 *Serbonian bog* Serbonis (modern Sabkhet Bardawil), a swampy coastal lake west of Damietta, a town at the mouth of the Nile (modern Dumyat). *Casius* is the Greco-Roman name for the coastal dunes of Ras el Kasrun.

595 *frore* frozen.

596 *Harpy-footed Furies* the winged and claw-footed Harpies who carried the souls of the dead to Hades are here conflated with the Furies, female deities who pursued wrongdoers and drove them to self-incrimination or

madness. There is a similar conflation, of Fate and Fury, in *Lycidas* 75.

603 *Periods of time* a 'period' (Greek = 'circuit', 'rotation') is the lapse of time between 'revolutions' (597) or recurrences of astronomical phenomena (the reappearance of comets etc).

611 *Medusa* one of the three Gorgons, of hideous appearance and with live snakes instead of hair. Her look was literally petrifying, turning her victims to stone.

614 *Tantalus* condemned for betraying the secrets of his father Zeus to stand up to his neck in a pool that receded whenever, tormented by thirst, he attempted to drink it; hence 'tantalize'. cf. *Samson* 500n.

628 *Gorgons, Hydras, Chimeras* see 611n. The hydra was a many-headed serpent-like monster. Chimeras combined goat, lion and dragon, and breathed fire. The grotesque inhabitants of hell are taken from Homeric and Virgilian descriptions of the underworld (*Odyssey* xi, *Aeneid* vi).

638 *Bengala* the later seventeenth century saw a rapid expansion of the trade in spices, coffee, silk and other luxury products with Bengal and the Indonesian archipelago (Ternate and Tidore are two of the Moluccas or Spice Islands). Here the ships are sailing south-west into the wind ('close sailing'), heading ('stemming') across the Indian Ocean ('wide Ethiopean') towards the (south) pole before rounding the Cape of Good Hope. The simile extends the association of Satan with the Orient (cf. II, 1-4) and with the sea (cf. I, 200-8, I, 292-4, II, 1043-4), and both are developed further at IV, 159-65.

655 *Cerberean mouths* Cerberus was the ferocious many-headed dog that guarded the entrance to the classical underworld.

660 *Scylla* one of a pair of sea-monsters (the other was Charybdis) guarding the straits of Messina between Calabria (south-west Italy) and Sicily (Trinacria, the Homeric Thrinakia). Her name is similar to the Greek for 'dog', and Homer (*Odyssey* xii) gives her a voice

'like a puppy'. This was elaborated by later writers into the story of a nymph whose lower body was transformed into a pack of snarling dogs. The 'night-hag' Hecate, moon-goddess and patroness of witchcraft, was traditionally accompanied by a pack of hell-hounds.

677 *admir'd* wondered.

701 *whip of scorpions* a Miltonic conflation based on *1 Kings* 12, 11: 'My father hath chastised you with whips, but I will chastise you with scorpions'. Fowler (123) takes it to mean that 'Satan would have done better to accept God's governance'; but the words are spoken by Solomon's tyrannical and apostate son Rehoboam, and Milton's earlier use of the phrase, in a description of the Laudian persecution of dissenters ('till all the land groan and cry out as against a whip of scorpions', *Of Reformation, SSPP* 62), suggests that he too took it as a symbol of tyranny rather than justice.

708 *like a comet* a large comet appeared in the northern constellation of Ophiuchus (the Serpent-bearer) in 1618, when Milton was nine. Some people thought it responsible for the Thirty Years War, which began in that year.

722 *so great a foe* Christ, eventual destroyer of both Satan and death (cf. 734).

757 *a goddess arm'd* the birth of Sin, fully-grown and armed, out of the head of Satan is based on the legendary birth of the goddess Athena from the head of Zeus.

768 *fields* battlefields, hence battles.

799 *gnaw* the 'hellhounds' that return to feed on the womb that bred them are an allegory of remorse (Latin *remorsus*, 'biting again').

815 *lore* knowledge, lesson.

825 *just pretences* rightful claims.

827 *uncouth* unfamiliar, strange, desolate.

829 *unfounded* bottomless.

833 *purlieus* outskirts, outlying parts.

842 *buxom* in its older sense of 'pliant', 'yielding'.

869 *at thy right hand* reinforcing the parallel between Sin/Satan and Messiah/God. Death completes the unholy trinity.

877 *wards* the projections and incisions on a key.

883 *Erebus* the Homeric word for 'darkness', mythologised as the offspring of Chaos and often used as a name for the underworld.

884 *Excell'd* exceeded.

889 *redounding* billowing.

894 *Chaos and Night* in Hesiod's *Theogony*, Chaos is the ancestor of the universe and father of Erebus (see 883n) and Night.

897 *endless wars* the passage elaborates the Greco-Roman idea (found in Lucretius and the first book of Ovid's *Metamorphoses*) of chaos as an unending struggle between the constituent elements of matter (earth/dry, air/cold, fire/hot, water/moist) into a full-scale allegory of tribal warfare.

904 *Barca or Cyrene* cities in ancient Cyrenaica (modern Libya).

919 *frith* firth, fiord.

922 *Bellona* the Roman goddess of war.

927 *vans* wings.

939 *a boggy Syrtis* quicksand, after a notorious shifting sandbank off the coast of Libya.

943 *gryphon* or griffin, a legendary Scythian dragon, half lion and half eagle. They guarded goldmines, and the attempts of the one-eyed Arimaspians to rob them of their hoard of gold are described by the Greek historian Herodotus.

964 *Orcus and Ades* interchangeable names, respectively Latin and Greek, for the god of the underworld. Demogorgon is an infernal deity in Statius' *Thebaid*, whose very name is feared by the ghosts of the dead.

982 *behoof* advantage, benefit.

1017 *Argo* the ship in which Jason and the Argonauts sailed in pursuit of the golden fleece. Passing through the

Bosphorus, they were almost wrecked on the Symplegades, the 'clashing rocks'.

1019 *Ulysses* the Latin form of Odysseus. After leaving Circe's island he had to navigate a precarious passage between the monster Charybdis and her companion Scylla ('th' other whirlpool', cf. 660n).

1044 *shrouds and tackle* ropes and pulleys supporting the mast of a sailing ship.

[Book III

God sitting on his throne sees Satan flying towards this world, then newly created; shows him to the Son who sat at his right hand; foretells the success of Satan in perverting mankind; clears his own justice and wisdom from all imputation, having created man free and able enough to have withstood his tempter, yet declares his purpose of grace towards him, in regard he fell not of his own malice, as did Satan, but by him seduced. The Son of God renders praise to his Father for the manifestation of his gracious purpose towards man, but God again declares that grace cannot be extended toward man without the satisfaction of divine justice: man hath offended the majesty of God by aspiring to godhead, and therefore with all progeny devoted to death must die unless someone can be found sufficient to answer for his offence and undergo his punishment. The Son of God freely offers himself a ransom for man. The Father accepts him, ordains his incarnation, pronounces his exaltation above all names in Heaven and Earth, commands all the angels to adore him. They obey, and hymning to their harps in full choir, celebrate the Father and the Son. Meanwhile Satan alights upon the bare convex of this world's outermost orb, where wandering he first finds a place called the Limbo of Vanity; what persons and things fly up thither; thence comes to the gate of Heaven, described ascending by stairs, and the waters above the firmament that flow about it. His passage thence to the orb of the sun. He finds there Uriel, the regent of that orb, but first changes himself into the shape of a meaner angel, and pretending a zealous desire to behold the new creation and man whom God had placed here, inquires of him the place of his habitation, and is directed. Alights first on Mount Niphates.]

Book IV

Satan now in prospect of Eden, and nigh the place where he must now attempt the bold enterprise which he undertook alone against God and man, falls into many doubts with himself, and many passions, fear, envy and despair; but at length confirms himself in evil, journeys on to Paradise, whose outward prospect and situation is described; overleaps the bounds, sits in the shape of a cormorant on the tree of life, as the highest in the garden, to look about him. The garden described. Satan's first sight of Adam and Eve, his wonder at their excellent form and happy state, but with resolution to work their fall. Overhears their discourse, thence gathers that the tree of knowledge was forbidden them to eat of under penalty of death, and thereon intends to found his temptation, by seducing them to transgress; then leaves them a while, to know further of their state by some other means. Meanwhile Uriel descending on a sunbeam warns Gabriel, who had in charge the gate of Paradise, that some evil spirit had escaped the deep and passed at noon by his sphere in the shape of a good angel down to Paradise, discovered after by his furious gestures in the mount. Gabriel promises to find him out ere morning. Night coming on, Adam and Eve discourse of going to their rest. Their bower described; their evening worship. Gabriel, drawing forth his bands of night watch to walk the round of Paradise, appoints two strong angels to Adam's bower, lest the evil spirit should be there doing some harm to Adam or Eve sleeping. There they find him at the ear of Eve, tempting her in a dream, and bring him, though unwilling, to Gabriel, by whom questioned he scornfully answers, prepares resistance, but hindered by a sign from Heaven, flies out of Paradise.

1 *that warning voice* in *Revelation* 12, after a second defeat by Michael and his angels, 'that old serpent, called the Devil, and Satan . . . was cast out into the earth', and a loud voice in heaven proclaimed 'Woe to the inhabiters of the earth and of the sea! for the

devil is come down unto you, having great wrath, because he knoweth that he hath but a short time'.

5 *now* the narrative gathers an apocalyptic urgency with the sevenfold repetition of the word 'now' in the first thirty lines of the book.

20 *The hell within him* cf. Marlowe's Mephostophilis: 'Hell hath no limits, nor is circumscribed/In one self place; but where we are is hell'. The counterpart to this existential concept of hell is the 'paradise within thee' of XII, 587.

31 *much revolving* considering, pondering.

32–113 Milton's nephew Edward Phillips reported that his uncle had shown him this soliloquy some years before beginning the poem, and that it had originally been intended as the opening scene of his projected tragedy on the fall (Darbishire 72).

87 *abide* suffer, bear the burden of.

115 *pale* used as a noun: pallor.

125 *Uriel once warn'd* in III, 621–735, Satan meets Uriel, the angel of the sun, and successfully disguising himself as a 'stripling cherub' curious to see what it is like, asks the way to Paradise. See 555ff.

126 *th'Assyrian mount* Mount Niphates (modern Aladag) in eastern Turkey, not far from the headwaters of the river Tigris.

134 *champaign head* open, grassy summit.

144 *our general sire* Adam, who can survey the whole of Eden from the wall of Paradise. But the phrase 'nether (lower) empire' lends an ominous suggestion of Satan, too.

151 *humid bow* rainbow. cf. the description of 'the gardens fair/ Of Hesperus and his daughters three/ That sing about the golden tree' in *Comus*, 981ff.: 'Iris there with humid bow/Waters the odorous banks that blow/Flowers of more mingled hue/Than her purfled scarf can show'. There are close mythological and iconographic connections between the two passages.

160 *Beyond the Cape of Hope* cf. II, 636n. Here the ships are on the return journey, sailing up the east coast

of Africa and held up ('slack their course') by a north-easterly headwind blowing from Arabia. 'Sabean odours' evoke the 'abundance of spices' given to Solomon by the Queen of Sheba or Saba (modern Yemen), *1 Kings* 10, 10.

168 *Asmodeus* a jealous demon in the apocryphal book of *Tobit*, who, infatuated with a young woman and having killed seven of her husbands, is driven away by the eighth, Tobias, with the smell of burning fish-offal, a trick suggested by the angel Raphael. Without implying exact parallels (though some editors have found them), the reference prepares for the erotic suggestiveness of Satan's relationship with Eve.

175 *continu'd brake* continuous undergrowth.

193 *lewd hirelings* the description of Satan's surreptitious entry into Paradise is loaded with political meanings. In *Lycidas* (1638), Milton had attacked the greed, worldliness and pastoral negligence of those Anglican clergy who 'for their bellies' sake/Creep and intrude and climb into the fold', leaving their 'hungry sheep' defenceless against the 'grim wolf' of Rome; the first of many passages drawing on the 'good shepherd' allegory of *John* 10: 'He that entereth not by the door into the sheepfold, but climbeth up some other way, the same is a thief and a robber . . . . But he that is an hireling, and not the shepherd, whose own the sheep are not, seeth the wolf coming, and leaveth the sheep, and fleeth; and the wolf catcheth them, and scattereth the sheep'. The interpretation of the wolf as the Roman church, and of 'hirelings' as beneficed Anglican clergy maintained by tithes, is common in Protestant polemic; but in his later writings, as here, Milton is less and less concerned to maintain the distinction between wolf and hireling, Catholic and Anglican, external threat and internal corruption, running them together into a single figure: 'Help us to save free conscience from the paw/Of hireling wolves whose gospel is their maw' (Sonnet to Cromwell, 1652). One of his last writings before the

Restoration was the *Considerations Touching the Likeliest Means to Remove Hirelings out of the Church* (1659).

196 *cormorant* traditionally greedy, and a comparison often made with clerical 'hirelings'. The 'middle tree' associates the tree of life with the cross on which Christ was crucified, a traditional association underlined by 'true life/Thereby regain'd'.

209 *in the east of Eden Genesis* 2,7. 'And the Lord God planted a garden eastward in Eden'. Auran (modern Harran in southeast Turkey) was the northeastern frontier of the land of the Israelites, established by divine ordinance in *Ezekiel* 47. 'Great Seleucia' was the capital of Alexander's Syrian empire. Thus Milton's Eden includes most of modern Syria, Iraq and eastern Turkey. The exact location of Paradise (a Greek word derived from the Persian for park or garden, not found in the Old Testament) was the subject of much debate.

219 *ambrosial fruit* ambrosia was the food of the Greek gods. The word means 'immortal'. cf. II, 245.

222 *Knowledge of good bought dear* the central paradox of the story, and a key theme of Milton's writings. cf. *Areopagitica* (1644):

> It was from out the rind of one apple tasted that the knowledge of good and evil, as two twins cleaving together, leapt forth into the world; and perhaps this is that doom which Adam fell into of knowing good and evil, that is to say of knowing good by evil.
>
> (*SSPP* 87)

226 *mould* soil.

237 *crisped* curled, wavy.

240 *nectar* the drink of the gods, as *ambrosia* (219n) was their food.

242 *boon* generous, congenial.

250 *Hesperian fables* the legendary garden of the Hesperides (the daughters of Hesperus) contained golden apples guarded by an unsleeping dragon. One of the

twelve labours of Hercules was to steal them, a story later allegorised into the triumph of Christ over Satan. cf. 151n.

257 *umbrageous grots* shady grottoes.

266 *Pan* the Greek shepherd-god is 'universal' in renaissance mythopoeia because his name was thought to derive from the word for 'everything'. From there it was a short step, for a neoplatonist, to identification with Christ (see the May eclogue of Spenser's *Shepheardes Calendar*, for example). The Graces and Hours (or Seasons), nature-goddesses closely associated with Aphrodite, were at the centre of much complex allegorical interpretation, as for example in Botticelli's *Primavera*, which depicts the metamorphosis of the nymph Chloris into Flora, 'the eternal spring'.

268 *Not that fair field* in a complex reverse simile, or comparison by negation, Paradise is compared in turn with the Vale of Enna in central Sicily, with the sacred grove of Daphne near Antioch, with the Libyan lake-island of Nysa, and with the royal palace-gardens on Mount Amara in equatorial ('under the Ethiop line') Abyssinia. Each of these places of legendary beauty is on or near a river, the Dittaino, the Orontes (modern Asi), the Triton and the Nile (cf. the four tributary rivers of Paradise itself). And in all but the last, a young woman is pursued by a god (in Miltonic terms, a devil): Proserpine (or Persephone), daughter by Zeus of the vegetation-goddess Ceres, carried off by Dis, the god of the underworld; the nymph Daphne, chased by Apollo and metamorphosed into a laurel-tree; and Amalthea, mother of Bacchus (Dionysus) by the Libyan king Ammon, often identified both with Zeus (Jove) and with the biblical Cham (Ham), son of Noah. Mount Amara, though it retains the connotations of protected vulnerability, is perhaps included as a popular candidate (here rejected in favour of an Assyrian location) for the site of 'true Paradise'.

334 *damask'd* intricately patterned, like Damascus silk.

344 *ounces, pards* panthers, leopards.

348 *Gordian twine* the Scythian king Gordus tied a knot so complicated that no-one was able to disentangle it, until Alexander the Great sliced through it with his sword.

354 *Ocean isles* the Azores (see 592). The 'ascending scale/ Of heaven' is the constellation of Libra (cf. 997-1001).

411 *Sole partner and sole part* Eve is at once his sharer in the pleasures of Paradise and herself all those pleasures in one.

474 *thence be call'd Mother* 'And Adam called his wife's name Eve; because she was the mother of all living'. The name (Hebrew *Havah*) means 'living'.

478 *platan* plane tree.

486 *individual* in its older sense: indivisible, inseparable.

541 *right aspect* either 'directly', or 'at right angles', or 'looking towards the right' (assuming a conventional north-south orientation; the Azores (354, 592) on latitude 36 north are just about due west of the 'Assyrian garden'. cf. 'right ascension', the equatorial succession of longitudes).

555 *gliding through the even* both 'evening' and (at sunset) 'level'.

557 *thwarts* crosses. Shooting stars were attributed to the ignition of gases ('vapours fir'd') rising from the earth's surface. They were thought to foretell storms.

590 *point now rais'd* cf. 555n. As the sun sets, it falls below the end of the beam on which Uriel slid down, so that he can now slide back again.

592 *whither the prime orb* most editors adopt the 18th-century emendation 'whether'; but 'whither' is an acceptable early spelling, and even in its modern sense (to where) retains the even-handed hesitation between two cosmologies, the Ptolemaic, in which the movement of the sun results from the day-long rotation of the first sphere ('prime orb'), and the Copernican, in which it is an effect of the slower ('less voluble') axial rotation of the earth.

605 *Hesperus* the evening star.

608 *apparent* appearing, evident.

628 *manuring* originally meant only 'tending', 'cultivating'.

630 *dropping gums* cf. the 'Groves whose rich trees wept odorous gums and balm' (248).

642 *charm of earliest birds charm* (originally = 'spell') is from the Latin *carmen*, song. As always with Milton's semantic latinisms, modern and intermediate meanings persist alongside the original one, bringing out the 'polysemy' (the multiple and mutable nature of meaning) and historicity of language.

698 *jessamine* jasmine.

707 *Pan, Silvanus, Faunus* Pan (see 266n) is the Greek, Sylvanus the Roman god of woodland and pasture (also found together at *Comus* 268). *Faunus* is generic, = 'fauns', goat-footed and priapic followers of Pan.

711 *hymenean* wedding song, after Hymen, Greek god of marriage. His function is here taken by the 'genial angel'.

714 *Pandora* the Greek Eve, a woman created from earth by Hephaistos and sent by Zeus, in revenge for the theft of fire by Prometheus, to be married to his brother Epimetheus. As dowry she brought a sealed casket, which when opened by her husband released evil and misfortune into the world. Prometheus ('foresight') and Epimetheus ('caution') were sons of the Titan Iapetus, here syncretically identified with Noah's son Japhet. Pandora means 'all gifts'. The story was often read as a pagan analogue of the fall, but Pandora herself was not generally held responsible for the disaster, and the claim that 'she ensnar'd Mankind with her fair looks' introduces a Miltonic misogyny not found in the original story.

746 *I ween* suppose, imagine: a tactful refusal to recount their lovemaking directly.

748 *Our maker bids increase* 'and God said unto them, Be fruitful, and multiply, and replenish the earth' (*Genesis* 1, 28).

751 *sole propriety* the only form of private property in an otherwise communistic Paradise.

763 *Love his golden shafts* the arrows of Cupid, often associated with the adulterous and extramarital 'court amours' of 767, but here firmly identified with marriage.

778 *port* gate.

785 *shield . . . spear* left and right: ancient Greek military terms.

804 *inspiring* breathing into her. 'Animal spirits' are spirits of the soul, envisaged as a vapour rising from the blood into the head.

816 *fit for the tun* ready to be loaded into barrels.

817 *smutty* sooty.

869 *regal port* royal bearing.

899 *durance* imprisonment.

945 *practis'd distances to cringe* to bow servilely.

962 *aread* warn.

967 *facile* easily opened; perhaps also recalling *Aeneid* vi, 126: 'facilis descensus averno' ('the way down to hell is easy'), cf. II, 81n.

971 *limitary* guarding the boundary.

980 *ported spears* carried in front of and diagonally across the body, in a manoeuvre resembling the swaying of ripe corn ('Ceres') in the wind.

986 *dilated* enlarged. For the comparison with 'Teneriffe or Atlas unremov'd (i.e. immovable)', cf. the description of Beelzebub, II, 306n.

989 *horror plum'd* a pun on two meanings of horror: bristling, like the plume of a helmet, and fear.

998 *Betwixt Astraea and the Scorpion* the constellation and zodiacal sign of Libra, the scales, comes between Virgo (here identified with the virgin goddess of Justice) and Scorpio.

1001 *ponders all events* weighs (literally) all possible outcomes.

1012 *shown how light* in fact it is not Satan who is the lighter in the scale, but the option of fighting as against separation.

[Book V

Morning approached, Eve relates to Adam her troublesome dream. He likes it not, yet comforts her. They come forth to their day labours; their morning hymn at the door of their bower. God, to render man inexcusable, sends Raphael to admonish him of his obedience, of his free estate, of his enemy near at hand: who he is, and why his enemy, and whatever else may avail Adam to know. Raphael comes down to Paradise; his appearance described; his coming discerned by Adam afar off sitting at the door of his bower. He goes out to meet him, brings him to his lodge, entertains him with the choicest fruits of Paradise got together by Eve. Their discourse at table: Raphael performs his message, minds Adam of his state and of his enemy, relates at Adam's request who that enemy is and how he came to be so, beginning from his first revolt in Heaven and the occasion thereof, how he drew his legions after him to the parts of the north, and there incited them to rebel with him, persuading all but only Abdiel a seraph, who in argument dissuades and opposes him, then forsakes him.]

[Book VI

Raphael continues to relate how Michael and Gabriel were sent forth to battle against Satan and his angels. The first fight described. Satan and his powers retire under night; he calls a council, invents devilish engines which in the second day's fight put Michael and his angels to some disorder; but they at length pulling up mountains overwhelm both the force and the machines of Satan. Yet the tumult not so ending, God on the third day sends Messiah his Son, for whom he had reserved the glory of that victory. He in the power of his father coming to that place and causing all his legions to stand still on either side, with his chariot and thunder driving into the midst of his enemies, pursues then unable to resist towards the wall of Heaven, which opening, they leap down with horror and confusion into the place of punishment prepared for them in the deep. Messiah returns with triumph to his Father.]

Book VII

Raphael at the request of Adam relates how and wherefore this world was first created; that God, after the expelling of Satan and his angels out of Heaven, declared his pleasure to create another world and other creatures to dwell therein; sends his Son with glory and attendance of angels to perform the work of creation in six days. The angels celebrate with hymns the performance thereof, and his reascension into Heaven.

1 *Urania* the name, meaning 'heavenly', of the classical muse of astronomy; but Milton distinguishes his christianised Urania, sister of sacred Wisdom (Sophia), from her classical namesake ('nor of the Muses nine'), just as he insists on the higher seriousness of Christian epic over its Greco-Roman predecessors ('above th' Olympian hill'). The winged horse Pegasus is a common figure for poetry, as is Bellerophon, who, attempting to ride him to heaven, fell and was blinded, for the over-ambitious poet. Having dealt with heavenly and infernal matters in the first six books of the poem, the poet asks to be led safely back to earth, the setting of the last six.

19 *Aleian field* the plain of Alea ('wandering') in *Iliad* vi, 201. Ancient geographers located it in Cilicia (southern Turkey).

27 *in darkness* blind. The 'dangers' probably refer to the risk to Milton's life during the hunting down of the regicides in 1660–1. See pp. 3–4.

29 *nightly* an anonymous early biography, probably by Cyriack Skinner, tells how Milton, 'waking early . . . had commonly a stock of good verses ready against his amanuensis came; which if it happened to be later than ordinary, he would complain, *saying he wanted to be milked*'. cf. III, 30–2: 'Thee Sion and the flowery brooks beneath . . . Nightly I visit.'

34 *that wild rout that tore the Thracian bard* the story of the murder and mutilation of the Thracian poet-singer Orpheus by the female followers of Dionysus

(Bacchus), and the helplessness of his mother Calliope, muse of poetry, is always charged with intensely personal connotations in Milton. cf. *Lycidas* 58-63: 'What could the Muse herself that Orpheus bore,/The Muse herself, for her enchanting son?/-Whom universal nature did lament,/When by the rout that made the hideous roar/His gory visage down the stream was sent,/Down the swift Hebrus to the Lesbian shore'. Here, the 'wild rout' of Bacchus and his revellers, like the insolent and drunken 'sons of Belial' (I, 500-2), may evoke the gangs of royalist toughs who terrorised dissenters and supporters of the Good Old Cause in the years after 1660.

52 *admiration and deep muse* wonder and bemusement.

61 *yet sinless* although the tree of knowledge let sin into the world, 'desire to know' is not itself sinful. In Milton's reading of the myth, it is not curiosity but disobedience that killed the cat.

66 *drouth* thirst.

90 *florid* flowery.

94 *absolv'd* completed.

99 *suspense in heaven* both 'suspended motionless' and 'held in suspense'.

107 *watch* stay awake.

116 *infer* render, prove.

131 *Lucifer* Satan's name before his rebellion, also used of the morning and evening star (the planet Venus), means 'light-bearer'.

154 *in a moment* this seems to contradict the *Genesis* narrative, followed by Milton, of a six-day creation. But 176-9 explain the hexameral narrative as a myth, a discursive convention ('process of speech') made necessary by the physiological and intellectual limitations of human language and understanding. This can be taken as Milton's answer to those fundamentalists, in his own time and since, who assert the literal truth of the *Genesis* account.

162 *inhabit lax* both 'relax' and 'take up the room vacated by the rebel angels'.

163 *my Word* the idea of the Messiah as the *Logos* or 'Word' of God comes from *John* 1, 14: 'And the Word was made flesh, and dwelt among us, (and we beheld his glory, the glory as of the only begotten of the Father,) full of grace and truth'.

168 *I am who fill* 'I am' is the name by which Jehovah identifies himself to Moses (*Exodus* 3, 14). The theology of these six lines has been taken as evidence both of Milton's extreme heterodoxy and of his true-blue orthodoxy.

192 *hierarchies* orders of angels (see I, 360n).

205 *heaven open'd wide* a structured parallel and contrast to the opening of the gates of hell, II, 879ff.

212 *dark, wasteful, wild* the description of the abyss of chaos as a sea underlines the structural and thematic parallelism with Satan's journey, II, 890ff.

217 *omnific* all-creating (a Miltonic coinage, from Latin).

224 *fervid* glowing hot.

238 *tartareous* infernal (Tartarus was the Greek hell); but 'purg'd' also suggests an allusion to 'cream of tartar', an acidic medicine used as an emetic and purgative.

239 *then founded, then conglob'd* laid the foundations and formed into a globe.

244 *quintessence* in ancient Greek philosophy, the quintessence (literally 'fifth substance') is the primary material ('first of things') of the universe, preceding and informing the four elements of matter.

252 *ev'n and morn* the formula of *Genesis*: 'And the evening and the morning were the first [etc] day'. Thus the day runs, in the Jewish tradition, from sunset to sunset.

261 *firmament* in the Authorised Version of *Genesis* 1, 6, the word is glossed 'expansion' (cf. 'expanse', 264). The idea seems to be that the primal waters were separated and divided by air, 'those above' being removed to the outer limits of the universe ('this great round'); so that the entire 'world' (i.e. cosmos) is surrounded by 'circumfluous waters', as the earth is within it.

279 *main ocean* the 'main' is the open sea.

280 *prolific* the original sense is 'producing offspring', fertile; cf 'genial' two lines later, which has a similar sense.

292 *conglobing* as at 239n, separating out into a globe.

296 *of armies thou hast heard* Raphael has already given an account, in Book VI, of the war in heaven.

302 *serpent error wandering* an ostensibly innocuous phrase meaning 'meandering' (*serpent* = crawling; *error* = wandering); but the context loads every word with ominous though as yet unrealised significance.

312 *Whose seed is in herself* this rather obscure phrase sticks closely, with a change of gender, to the Authorised Version: 'and the fruit tree yielding fruit after his kind, whose seed is in itself, upon the earth'. The New English Bible translates 'fruit-trees bearing fruit each with seed according to its kind'. The AV text suggests that the line should have a comma after 'herself'.

319 *scarce blown* hardly blossomed.

321 *swelling gourd* Richard Bentley's 1749 emendation of 'smelling' has been universally accepted.

322 *embattl'd* reversing the simile of IV, 980ff., where the spears of the warrior angels are compared to a cornfield.

323 *implicit* tangled.

325 *gemm'd* the word 'gem' derives from the Latin for 'bud'. Both senses may be operating here.

348 *altern* alternately, in turn.

351 *vicissitude* regular alternation.

357 *globose* spherical. 'Magnitude' is used technically, = degree of brightness.

366 *her horns* the second edition's interesting change from the 'his horns' of the first. The morning planet is Venus, also known as Lucifer, so either gender is possible. It is horned because, being closer to the sun, it can be seen as cusped at certain phases.

375 *sweet influence* the phrase comes from *Job* 38, 31: 'Canst thou bind the sweet influences of Pleiades.'

382 *dividual* divided, divisible. cf. *Areopagitica*: 'his religion is become a dividual moveable'.

403 *bank the mid sea* cause the surface of the sea to rise.

412 *leviathan* the sea-monster of *Job* 41, usually identified as a whale. cf. I, 200ff., where a similar scene is charged with Satanic menace.

419 *kindly rupture* in the same sense as 311: 'yielding fruit after her kind'.

420 *callow* unfeathered. Once 'fledge' (= fledged), the young birds 'sum' (complete) their 'pens' (feathers).

422 *clang* loud cry.

439 *mantling* covering, cloaking (with 'wings').

444 *th' other* the peacock.

457 *wons* an archaic word meaning 'lives'.

466 *ounce, libbard* panther, leopard (cf. IV, 344).

470 *Behemoth* the land-monster of *Job* 40, terrestrial equivalent of Leviathan; usually identified as an elephant.

474 *river-horse* literally translating the Greek *hippopotamus.*

482 *Minims* miniatures (Latin *minimus*, smallest).

485 *emmet* the ant, traditionally thrifty.

530 *race* offspring, family.

564 *pomp* procession.

579 *the galaxy, that milky way* 'galaxy' is from Greek *gala*, milk.

595 *had work and rested not* perhaps an ironic reference to the extreme sabbatarianism that prohibited all activity on the seventh day.

596 *organs* instruments, in the broadest sense.

605 *giant angels* Satan and his fellow-rebels are frequently compared to the Giants who attempted to overthrow the Olympian gods (e.g. I, 196ff., 576–7, 778).

619 *hyaline* glass. The whole passage, with its music, incense and 'glassy sea', recalls *Revelation* 15: 'And I saw as it were a sea of glass mingled with fire: and them that had gotten victory over the beast . . . stand on the sea of glass, having the harps of God. And they sing the song of Moses . . . saying, Great and marvellous are thy works, Lord God Almighty.'

624 *nether ocean* cf. 268, 'The waters underneath from those above', divided by the firmament. The 'nether (i.e. terrestrial) ocean' is 'circumfus'd' because the

sea, envisaged in Greek cosmography as a continuous river called Oceanus, was thought to completely surround the land.

634 *halleluiahs* Hebrew for 'praise God'.

[Book VII

Adam enquires concerning celestial motions, is doubtfully answered and exhorted to search rather things more worthy of knowledge. Adam assents, and still desirous to retain Raphael, relates to him what he remembered since his own creation: his placing in Paradise, his talk with God concerning solitude and fit society, his first meeting and nuptials with Eve. His discourse with the angel thereupon, who after admonitions repeated departs.]

Book IX

Satan, having compassed the earth, with meditated guile returns as a mist by night into Paradise, enters into the serpent sleeping. Adam and Eve in the morning go forth to their labours, which Eve proposes to divide in several places, each labouring apart. Adam consents not, alleging the danger, lest that enemy of whom they were forewarned should attempt her, found alone. Eve, loth to be thought not circumspect or firm enough, urges her going apart, the rather desirous to make trial of her strength. Adam at last yields. The serpent finds her alone: his subtle approach, first gazing, then speaking, with much flattery extolling Eve above all other creatures. Eve, wondering to hear the serpent speak, asks how he attained to human speech and such understanding not till now. The serpent answers that by tasting of a certain tree in the garden he attained both to speech and reason, till then void of both. Eve requires him to bring her to that tree, and finds it to be the tree of knowledge forbidden. The serpent now grown bolder with many wiles and arguments induces her at length to eat. She, pleased with the taste, deliberates a while whether to impart thereof to Adam or not; at last brings him of the fruit, relates what persuaded her to eat thereof. Adam, at first amazed, but perceiving her lost, resolves through vehemence of love to perish with her, and extenuating the trespass eats also of the fruit. The effects thereof in them both: they seek to cover their nakedness, then fall to variance and accusation of one another.

5 *Venial discourse* 'venial' can mean 'permissible', without any suggestion of fault; but as the Fall moves into view, reverberations of the other sense, 'wrong but forgivable', are strong, especially in its opposition to 'mortal [literally death-bringing] sin'.

15 *Achilles* his 'wrath' is the subject of the *Iliad*, in which he pursues the Trojan leader Hector around the walls of Troy before killing him. The *Aeneid* tells of the wanderings of 'Cytherea's (Venus') son' Aeneas, pursued by the jealous anger of the goddess Juno, and of his arrival in Italy, where his betrothal to the king's daughter Lavinia led to war with the local chieftain Turnus. The even more circuitous travels of 'the Greek' Odysseus, persecuted by the sea-god Poseidon (Neptune) on his way home from the Trojan war, provide the material for the *Odyssey*. Through these instances of epic anger, contrasted with the 'anger and just rebuke' of heaven, the subject-matter of *Paradise Lost* itself is compared with the three major exemplars of heroic narrative and found 'not less but more heroic'.

21 *celestial patroness* see VII, 1n.

30 *fabl'd knights* those found, for example, in chivalric epics like Ariosto's *Orlando Furioso* (The Madness of Roland), Boiardo's *Orlando Inamorato* (Roland in Love) and even the admired Spenser's *Faerie Queene*.

35 *impreses* heraldic devices. *Caparisons* are the elaborate armour of a horse.

38 *sewers and seneschals* butlers and stewards. As with impreses and caparisons, the mock-archaic terms underline the sarcasm.

44 *That name* the 'heroic name' of line 40. Of the three misgivings about his ability to do justice to the 'higher argument' of the last four books of the poem,

'an age too late' refers to the view that the universe was ageing, with each epoch feebler and more degenerate than the last (a view widely held in the seventeenth century, and perhaps reinforced by Milton's profound disenchantment with English history); 'cold climate' was often held responsible for the dullness of the British character (cf. Milton's own *Character of the Long Parliament*:

> For sun which we want [i.e. lack] ripens wits as well as fruits; and as wine and oil are imported to us from abroad, so must ripe understanding, and many civil virtues, be imported into our minds from foreign writings and examples of best ages, we shall else miscarry still, and come short in the attempts of any great enterprise.
>
> (*CPW* V, 450))

and Milton himself was fifty-nine in the year *Paradise Lost* first appeared.

49 *Hesperus* the evening star.

56 *maugre* despite (French *malgré*).

64 *equinoctial line* the equator. The 'colures' (66) are the two 'great circles' joining the poles to the equinoctial and solstitial points on the ecliptic (the apparent annual path followed by the sun through the stars); but only one colure is described at 77-9. The 'car of night' is a nocturnal counterpart to the classical chariot of the sun, and perhaps, underlining the parallels between the week-long creation and Satan's sevenfold girdling of the earth, to the Messiah's chariot (VII, 192ff.).

67 *coast averse* the side away from the eastern gate. According to IV, 223, the river of Paradise, here identified with the Tigris, flowed 'southward through Eden'; so Satan's entry must be on the north side.

77 *over Pontus* his circuits of the earth, starting at the western boundary of Paradise (IV, 862), take him northwards over the Black Sea (Pontus) and the adjacent Sea of Azov (the 'pool Maeotis') to eastern

Siberia (the river Ob) and the north pole, southwards to the opposite pole, and north again to the river Orontes in northern Syria; then westwards on a roughly equatorial route via Panama (Darien, where the Atlantic and Pacific Oceans are 'barr'd') to India, and so back to his starting-point.

89 *imp* a grafted shoot, and hence a demonic offspring or small devil.

92 *none would suspicious mark* cf. IV 349–50, where the newly-created serpent 'of his fatal guile/Gave proof unheeded'.

112 *gradual life* stages in the hierarchy of natural being, from the simple 'growth' of plants via the 'sense' (physical sensation) of animals to the 'reason' of humankind.

148 *our room* the space created by the departure of the rebel angels. (cf. VII, 162n).

166 *incarnate and imbrute* cf. *Comus* 466–7, where 'by lewd and lavish act of sin' the soul 'imbodies, and imbrutes, till she quite lose/The divine property of her first being'. The structural and thematic parallelism between Satan and Messiah here takes the form of a satanic incarnation. cf. the opposite process promised by Raphael at V, 497–9: 'Your bodies may at last turn all to spirit . . . and wing'd ascend Ethereal'.

170 *obnoxious* in the sense, now obsolete, of 'vulnerable'.

173 *reck* care (cf. 'reckless').

186 *nocent* harmful.

296 *asperses* spatters, casts *aspersions*.

301 *misdeem* misconstrue, misunderstand.

306 *contemn* despise (i.e. underestimate).

335 *And what is faith, love, virtue . . .* strongly recalling *Areopagitica* (1644): 'I cannot praise a fugitive and cloistered virtue, unexercised and unbreathed, that never sallies out and sees her adversary.' (See p. 260).

387 *Oread or dryad* oreads are mountain-nymphs, dryads wood-nymphs, both associated with 'Delia', the virgin goddess Diana (born on the Aegean island of

Delos). As a huntress, Diana was traditionally 'with bow and quiver arm'd'.

392 *Guiltless of fire* the association of fire (and hence of metal tools and weapons) with guilt alludes to the story of Prometheus, who stole the fire of the gods and gave it to humankind, and so recalls the earlier comparison of Eve with the ill-fated Pandora (IV, 714-19).

393 *Pales or Pomona* Roman goddesses of gardens and orchards. Pomona was pursued and seduced by the woodland god Vertumnus. For Ceres (395) see IV, 268n.

437 *arborets* ornamental tree-gardens.

438 *hand of Eve* i.e. her handiwork.

439 *gardens feign'd* the mythical gardens of Adonis (described in the third book of Spenser's *Faerie Queene*) and Alcinous, king of Phaeacia and host of 'old Laertes' son' Odysseus (the gardens are described in *Odyssey* vii, 78-132), contrasted with the 'not mystic' (i.e. non-mythical, because biblical) gardens of Solomon, described in the *Song of Songs*.

450 *tedded* spread and turned to dry.

472 *gratulating* rejoicing.

476 *for hell* instead of hell.

481 *opportune* exposed, available. The Latin *opportunus* originally referred to a favourable wind, blowing towards harbour, or to a port accessible in such a wind. Satan's great metaphorical sea-journey, begun at II, 927 and sustained by many satanic similes, is nearing its destination.

500 *carbuncle* red garnet or ruby; hence red.

506 *Hermione and Cadmus* Cadmus, legendary founder of Thebes, and his wife Harmonia (or Hermione) were changed to serpents at their death. The god of healing, Aesculapius, who had a shrine at Epidaurus in the northeastern Peloponnese, sometimes took the form of a snake. The Ammonian (Libyan) and Capitoline (Roman) forms of Jupiter, thought to have fathered Alexander the Great (by his mother Olym-

pias) and Scipio Africanus respectively, both had serpentine incarnations.

522 *Circean call* in *Odyssey* x, the enchantress Circe changes men into obsequious animals. cf. *Comus* 50ff.: 'Who knows not Circe,/The daughter of the Sun, whose charmed cup/Whoever tasted lost his upright shape/And downward fell into a grovelling swine?'

549 *gloz'd* flattered, spoke smoothly. The *proem* is the preamble to a speech or book.

581 *fennel* folklore connected snakes with fennel, and suspected them of taking milk from sheep and goats.

630 *conduct* leading, guidance.

634 *wandering fire* ignis fatuus ('fool's fire') or will o'the wisp.

640 *amaz'd* lost and confused, as in a maze.

667 *as* as if.

670 *some orator renown'd* the comparison of Satan to a classical orator is particularly apt, since many of the arguments that follow are close to those of Milton's own neoclassical *Areopagitica* (1644), whose title recalls the Athenian Isocrates. Satan begins 'in height', straight into the heart of the argument, without 'preface'; but his first five lines are in fact an epic invocation to the tree, recalling the invocations to books I, III, VII and IX of *Paradise Lost* itself, which also seeks to 'discern/Things in their causes' and 'trace the ways/Of highest agents'.

707 *yet are but dim* the immediate source is *Genesis* 3, 5: 'in the day ye eat thereof, then your eyes shall be opened, and ye shall be as gods, knowing good and evil'; but the Miltonic version of the metaphor also recalls *1 Corinthians* 13, 12: 'For now we see through a glass, darkly; but then face to face'.

737 *impregn'd* impregnated.

771 *author unsuspect* Eve sees the serpent as an innocent informant.

788 *whether true/Or fanci'd so* leaving open the question

of whether the fruit really does have a particularly delicious taste, as claimed by Satan (596–7).

793 *boon* cheerful (cf. 'boon companion').

807 *experience* with the older sense of 'experiment'.

845 *divine* prophetic, guessing.

854 *prologue . . . prompt* a theatrical metaphor, with 'excuse' as prologue and 'apology' as prompter to Eve's performance; a reminder that the action of Book IX would have been the 'catastrophe' or climax of the originally intended tragedy, *Adam Unparadiz'd.*

901 *deflower'd* beyond the close association of Eve with flowers, the word underlines the sexual overtones of Satan's temptation and recalls her similarity to other young women seduced or raped by a god, like Proserpine, who 'gathering flowers/Herself a fairer flower by gloomy Dis/Was gather'd' (IV, 269–71). 'Devote' means consecrated.

944 *loose* lose.

1001 *in pangs* in labour, as at IV, 454 the earth 'Opening her fertile womb teem'd at a birth/Innumerous living creatures'. These second 'pangs', however, are painful, recalling the curse on Eve: 'children thou shalt bring/In sorrow forth' (X, 194–5).

1017 *exact of taste* the motif of tasting, which runs through the poem, here produces a little cluster of self-explicating puns: sapience–savour–judicious. Latin *sapere*, to be wise, also means to taste.

1053 *eyes how open'd . . . minds/How darken'd* an ironic half-fulfilment of Satan's promise. See 707n.

1067 *Eve, in evil* the internal rhyme, echoed by 'give ear' and 'Even shame' (1079), makes Eve etymologically as well as morally responsible for evil. For the actual meaning of her name, see IV, 474n.

1102 *such as at this day* the banyan, also known as Indian fig.

1111 *Amazonian targe* the Amazons, a tribe of warrior women (hence the 'targe' or shield) who fought on the Trojan side in the Trojan war.

1128 *her lore* her (i.e. understanding's) lesson, teaching.

[Book X

Man's transgression known, the guardian angels forsake Paradise and return up to Heaven to approve their vigilance, and are approved, God declaring that the entrance of Satan could not be by them prevented. He sends his Son to judge the transgressors, who descends and gives sentence accordingly, then in pity clothes them both and reascends. Sin and Death, sitting till then at the gates of Hell, by wondrous sympathy feeling the success of Satan in this new world, and the sin by man there committed, resolve to sit no longer confined in Hell, but to follow Satan their sire up to the place of man. To make the way easier from Hell to this world to and fro, they pave a broad highway or bridge over Chaos, according to the track that Satan first made; then preparing for earth, they meet him proud of his success returning to Hell. Their mutual gratulation. Satan arrives at Pandaemonium, in full assembly relates with boasting his success against man; instead of applause is entertained with a general hiss by all his audience, transformed with himself also suddenly into serpents, according to his doom given in Paradise. Then, deluded with a show of the forbidden tree springing up before them, they greedily reaching to take of the fruit chew dust and bitter ashes. The proceedings of Sin and Death. God foretells the final victory of his Son over them, and the renewing of all things, but for the present commands his angels to make several alterations in the heavens and elements. Adam more and more perceiving his fallen condition heavily bewails, rejects the condolement of Eve. She persists, and at length appeases him, then to evade the curse likely to fall on their offspring proposes to Adam violent ways which he approves not, but conceiving better hope, puts her in mind of the late promise made them that her seed should be revenged on the serpent, and exhorts her with him to seek peace of the offended deity, by repentance and supplication.]

[Book XI

The Son of God presents to his Father the prayers of our first parents now repenting, and intercedes for them. God accepts them, but declares that they must no longer abide in Paradise; sends Michael with a band of cherubims to dispossess them, but first to reveal to Adam future things. Michael's coming down. Adam shows to Eve certain ominous signs. He discerns Michael's approach, goes out to meet him. The angel denounces their departure. Eve's lamentation. Adam pleads, but submits. The angel leads him up to a high hill, sets before him in vision what shall happen till the flood.]

Book XII

The angel Michael continues from the flood to relate what shall succeed; then, in the mention of Abraham, comes by degrees to explain who that seed of the woman shall be which was promised Adam and Eve in the Fall: his incarnation, death, resurrection and ascension. The state of the Church till his second coming. Adam, greatly satisfied and recomforted by these relations and promises, descends the hill with Michael; wakens Eve, who all the while had slept, but with gentle dreams composed to quietness of mind and submission. Michael in either hand leads them out of Paradise, the fiery sword waving behind them, and the cherubim taking their stations to guard the place.

1 *baits* stops for rest or refreshment. The first five lines of Book XII were added when the poem was extended from ten books to twelve, the original Book X being divided to make Books XI and XII.

24 *one shall rise* Nimrod, great-grandson of Noah in *Genesis* 10, 8–10: 'he began to be a mighty one in the earth. He was a mighty hunter before the Lord'. In *Genesis* he is the builder of Nineveh and a number of other Assyrian cities, but not of Babel (Babylon). Later traditions added that, and made him a prototype of monarchical tyranny.

36 *from rebellion shall derive his name* 'Nimrod' may be derived from the Hebrew for 'rebel'. There is no suggestion in *Genesis* that Nimrod accused others of rebellion (37), and the line may have a more contemporary point of reference. See p. 255.

41 *gurge* a Miltonic coinage, from Latin *gurges*, whirlpool (cf. 'regurgitate').

43 *cast* determine, resolve.

53 *a various spirit* a spirit of difference, variety. The story of the building of Babel, and of the sudden profusion of languages among its builders (often taken, literally or metaphorically, as the origin of all linguistic difference), comes from *Genesis* 11, 1-9.

62 *confusion nam'd Genesis* 11, 9: 'Therefore is the name of it called Babel; because the Lord did there confound the language of all the earth' (with the marginal note: 'Babel: that is, *Confusion*').

69 *man over men/He made not lord* the whole passage recalls *The Tenure of Kings and Magistrates* (1649):

> It being manifest that the power of kings and magistrates is nothing else but what is only derivative, transferred and committed to them in trust from the people to the common good of them all, in whom the power yet remains fundamentally and cannot be taken from them without a violation of their natural birthright . . . it follows from necessary causes that the titles of 'sovereign lord', 'natural lord' and the like are either arrogancies or flatteries.

77 *pine* starve.

85 *dividual* separate.

96 *no excuse* cf. IV, 393–4, where Satan 'with necessity,/ The tyrant's plea, excus'd his devilish deeds'.

101 *irreverent son* Ham saw his father Noah naked, for which his son Canaan was condemned to be 'a servant of servants' (*Genesis* 9, 25).

113 *one faithful man* Abraham (see *Genesis* 11, 27ff).

119 *wood or stone* cf. the description of (in that case, Catholic) idolatry in the sonnet 'On the late massacre in Piedmont': 'When all our fathers worshipped stocks and stones' (*SSPP* 137; an allusion to *Jeremiah* 2, 27; 3, 9).

132 *servitude* slaves.

152 *faithful Abraham* not named until this point because the name Abraham was given to him as a sign of the covenant with Jehovah. Until then he was known as Abram.

154 *A son* Isaac. The grandchild is Jacob, summoned to Egypt by his 'younger son' (160) Joseph. Jacob (also called Israel, see 267n) had twelve sons, founding patriarchs of the twelve tribes of Israel.

173 *lawless tyrant* the Pharoah identified as 'Busiris' at I, 307.

175 *signs and judgements dire* the plagues and other disasters inflicted on Egypt as a punishment for the Pharoah's refusal to allow the Israelites to leave (*Exodus* 7, 17ff.).

179 *murrain* an infectious disease of cattle.

191 *river-dragon* cf. *Ezekiel* 29, 3: 'Thus saith the Lord God; Behold, I am against thee, Pharoah king of Egypt, the great dragon that lieth in the midst of his rivers'.

192 *his sojourners* recalling the 'sojourners of Goshen' in an earlier allusion to this episode (I, 309).

202 *cloud and pillar of fire Exodus* 13, 21: 'And the Lord went before them by day in a pillar of cloud . . . and by night in a pillar of fire'.

217 *Lest entering on the Canaanite* in *Exodus* 13, 17, the Israelites detour southwards 'through the way of the wilderness of the Red Sea' to avoid an encounter with the Philistines.

221 *more sweet/Untrain'd in arms* contrast the essay *Of Education*, written in 1664, where training in the use of arms forms an important part of the curriculum.

225 *their great senate* the Sanhedrin of seventy elders, summoned by Moses to receive the Law at Sinai (*Exodus* 24). The same 'supreme council of seventy, called the Sanhedrim, founded by Moses' is recommended in the *Ready and Easy Way* (1660) as a model for a republican 'Grand Council' in England (*SSPP* 141).

242 *One greater* Christ, the 'one greater man' of I, 4. Moses and all the other prophets were regarded as prefigurative 'types' of the Messiah, whose coming is prophesied by Moses in *Deuteronomy* 18, 18.

247 *tabernacle* for the design and construction of the tabernacle, the tent or portable structure used as a shrine and sanctuary by the Israelites before the building of the temple (333–4), and housing the ark of the covenant (251-2), see *Exodus* 25ff.

256 *The heavenly fires* the menorah or seven-branched candlestick represents the planets.

265 *sun in Gibeon stand* during the battle against the Gibeonites, Joshua called on the sun and moon to stand still for a day 'until the people had avenged themselves upon their enemies' (*Joshua* 10, 13).

267 *Israel* 'prince of God', the name given to Jacob by Jehovah (*Genesis* 32, 28) and so collectively to all his descendants.

288 *pravity* depravity.

310 *Joshua* 'Jesus' is the New Testament (that is, Greek) form of the Hebrew Joshua, and biblical commentators drew out many parallels between the two figures.

321 *The second* David, promised through the prophet Nathan that God 'will stablish the throne of his kingdom for ever' (*2 Samuel* 7, 13).

332 *his next son* David's son Solomon. The building of the temple is described in *1 Kings* 5–8.

333 *clouded ark* when the building of the tabernacle was finished, 'a cloud covered the tent of the congregation . . . the cloud of the Lord was upon the tabernacle by day, and fire was on it by night . . . throughout all their journeys' (*Exodus* 40, 34–8).

350 *re-edify* rebuild.

353 *first among the priests* the apocryphal *2 Maccabees* recounts the clerical squabbles under the archpriest Onias in the second century BC, which led to Syrian intervention and the imposition of Greek worship on the Jews of Jerusalem.

358 *a stranger* Antipater, Syrian procurator (i.e. viceroy) of Judaea, under Pompey and Julius Caesar. He was the father of Herod the Great.

367 *squadron'd angels* recalling the chivalric imagery of the Nativity Ode: 'And all about the courtly stable/ Bright-harness'd Angels sit in order serviceable' (243-4; *SSPP* 113).

379 *The seed of woman* not of man, that is, because his mother was a virgin.

383 *capital bruise* the serpent's bruise will be on its head (*Genesis* 3, 15) and it will be lethal.

386 *Dream not of their fight* cf. the earlier repudiation of conventional epic heroism ('fabl'd knights/In battles feign'd') in favour of 'the better fortitude/Of patience and heroic martyrdom' (IX, 28–32).

396 *want* lack.

403 *love/Alone fulfil the law Romans* 13, 10: 'love is the fulfilling of the law', echoing *Leviticus* 19, 18: 'thou shalt love thy neighbour as thyself'.

416 *The law that is against thee Colossians* 2, 14, where Christ is described as 'blotting out the handwriting of ordinances that was against us', was an important text for dissenters, justifying conscientious disobedience to the civil magistrate.

467 *world's great period* the judgement, traditionally preceded by a 'pause'. cf. *Revelation* 8, 1: 'And when he had opened the seventh seal, there was silence in heaven about the space of half an hour'.

487 *comforter* the 'Comforter, which is the Holy Ghost, whom the Father will send in my name' (*John* 14, 26).

501 *speak all tongues* the Pentecostal glossolalia of the Apostles described in *Acts* 2, 4.

508 *Wolves* see IV, 193n.

513 *those written records pure* the central doctrine of Protestantism is the sufficiency of the 'pure' word of scripture (the origin of the term 'puritan', originally intended satirically), the understanding of which comes not through priestly or scholarly interpretation but 'by the spirit'.

530 *Infallible* a reference to the Catholic doctrine of papal infallibility.

584 *charity* the Authorised Version translation of the Greek word meaning 'love' in *1 Corinthians* 13: 'Though I speak with the tongues of men and of angels, and have not charity, I am become as sounding brass, or a tinkling cymbal.

588 *top/Of speculation* viewpoint. Michael and Adam have been surveying the future history of the world from the highest hilltop in Paradise.

591 *expect/Their motion* await their orders to move.

630 *marish* marsh. The cherubim 'gliding meteorous [= through the air] as evening mist' recall Satan 'like a black mist low crawling' (IX, 180).

635 *adust* scorched, parched.

640 *subjected* lying below them; but also subject, like them, to time, decay and death.

THE HISTORY OF BRITAIN

173 *barbarous inudations* barbarian invasions. *Of Reformation* (1641) has 'the impetuous rage of five bloody inundations', meaning the Roman, Pictish, Saxon, Danish and Norman invasions of Britain (*SSPP* 83).

our old philosophers the Druids Celtic priests, 'by whom this island was the cathedral of philosophy to France' (*Doctrine and Discipline of Divorce, CPW* II, 231). *Areopagitica* (1644) records the view that 'even the school of Pythagoras and the Persian wisdom took beginning from the old philosophy of this island' (*SSPP* 100); but later in the *History* they are described more sceptically as 'a sort of priests or magicians called Druids from the Greek name of an oak, which tree they had in great reverence, and the mistletoe especially growing thereon . . . , yet philosophers I cannot call them, reported men factious and ambitious, contending sometimes about the arch-priesthood not without civil war and slaughter' (*CPW* V, 60–1).

174 *first supposed author* many of the earliest legends about Celtic Britain were derived from the *Defloratio* of

'Berosus', supposedly a Chaldee historian of the fourth century BC, in fact probably a fifteenth-century forgery (Milton later calls him the 'forged Berosus').
approved story authenticated history.
as we read in poets cf. the many quasi-syncretic passages in *Paradise Lost* exploring the similarities between the 'feigned' narratives of Homer, Hesiod and other classical writers and the 'undoubted witnesses' of scripture (e.g. I, 507–21; I, 738–47; II, 577–628; IV, 264–79).
effectual words of God perhaps *Genesis* I, 28: 'Be fruitful, and multiply, and replenish the earth, and subdue it: and have dominion over the fish of the sea, and over the fowl of the air, and over every living thing that moveth upon the earth'. cf. *PL* VII, 531–4.

175 *Gomer the eldest son of Japhet* *Genesis* 10, 2–5 records that 'the isles of the Gentiles' (usually identified with mediterranean and north-western Europe) were settled after the flood by the descendents of Gomer and Javan, eldest and fourth sons respectively of Noah's son Japhet. 'Affinity of divers names' was invoked to argue the derivation of 'Cambria' or 'Cymru' (Celtic Britain) from *Gomer*, and 'Ionia' (Greece) from *Javan* (cf. *PL* I, 508 and *SA* 715–16)
forged Berosus see 174n.
seeming less impertinent less irrelevant, since unlike 'Berosus' this tradition does at least connect 'Samotheus' with Britain.
Mela Pomponius Mela, first century AD Roman geographer, records the tradition that the Crau, a stony coastal plain in Provence (Languedoc), was the scene of the battle between Hercules and the two giant sons of Neptune, Albion and Bergion, eventually defeated with the help of Hercules' father Jupiter, who rained stones onto them.

176 *Nennius* eighth-century Welsh historian, credited with the compilation called *Historia Britonum* (History of the Britons).
of one original with the Roman the Romans traced their

ancestry to Aeneas, legendary Trojan prince and hero of Virgil's *Aeneid*. The Brutus story attempts similarly to root the British in Homeric antiquity.

177 *Geoffrey of Monmouth* 1100–45, Welsh cleric, antiquarian and Bishop of St Asaph, compiler of the *Historia Regum Britanniae* (History of the Kings of Britain), primary source for the stories of Arthur, Lear, Cymbeline and other legendary British heroes. The authenticity of his work was widely disputed.

181 *Corineus* the manuscript of *Lycidas* shows that line 160 originally read 'Sleep'st by the fable of Corineus old', and that an afterthought substituted 'Bellerus old', a Miltonic invention derived from *Bellerium*, the Roman name for Land's End.

182 *Langoemagog* variously identified as Dover cliffs and Plymouth Hoe.

Eli Israelite high priest in *1 Samuel*.

Loegria . . . Cambria . . . Albania cf. modern Welsh *Lloegr* (England), *Cymru* (Wales) and *Yr Alban* (Scotland).

183 *Sabra* the Sabrina of Milton's masque *Comus* (1637), who 'flying the mad pursuit/Of her enraged stepdame Gwendolen/Commended her fair innocence to the flood,/That stay'd her flight with his cross-flowing course' (829-32). The *Comus* version of the story makes no mention of her mother Estrildis.

Sora modern Soar.

186 *his name to the place* i.e. Glamorgan, supposedly named after Morgan or Margan.

about the time when Rome was built the building of Rome by Romulus and Remus was traditionally dated 753 BC.

Gorbodugo the subject, with his contentious sons Ferrex and Porrex, of Sackville and Norton's tragedy *Gorboduc* (1579).

fond of the title of king. The Saxon chieftain Cerdic and his son Cynric invaded Britain in 495CE. Cerdic assumed the title of king after the battle of Cerdicsford (Chardford, in Hampshire) in 519CE.

187 *Huntingdon* Henry of Huntingdon, twelfth-century author of the *Historia Anglorum* (History of the English).

surcharged encumbered, overloaded.

Gildas sixth-century British historian, whose *De Excidio et Conquestu Britanniae* (The Decline and Conquest of Britain) contains contemporary and eye-witness accounts of the Saxon conquest.

conceited biased, partial.

Ambrose a semi-legendary figure, often identified with Merlin; supposedly the unacknowledged son of a Roman officer, and the first successful leader of the Britons against the Saxon invaders. In some accounts he is the brother of Uther Pendragon, father of Arthur (see below).

Badon hill medieval accounts vary widely as to the location, date and even combatants of the famous battle of *Mons Badonicus*, where Arthur was reputed to have killed nine hundred Saxons single-handed. Modern historians place it between 490CE and 516CE.

Nennius see 176n. Milton suggests that the eighth-century placenames he gives for Arthur's twelve battles did not exist two hundred years earlier; but modern historians tend to regard them as genuine, if unidentifiable.

monk of Malmesbury William of Malmesbury, author of *Gesta Regum Angliae* (Chronicles of the Kings of England).

he of Monmouth Geoffrey, see 177n.

188 *Sigebert* Sigebert of Gembloux, eleventh-century chronicler.

notist annotator, editor.

cruel son from Welsh *mab*, 'son', and *uthr*, 'terrible' or 'wonderful'. The name Arthur itself was sometimes derived from *arth*, 'a bear'.

Caradoc Caradoc of Llancarvan collaborated on Geoffrey's *Historia Regum* and wrote a life of Gildas.

Glaston modern Glastonbury.

answerable equal, proportionate.

189 *overcome at last with endless overcoming* a pun: 'defeating' and 'coming over' (from Germany).

Withgarburgh perhaps Carisbrooke.

190 *Saracens* the Muslim peoples of the middle east. Their appearance in the more fanciful Arthurian stories is an obvious anachronism.

chamber colony, dependant.

Buchanan George Buchanan, Scots historian, author of *Rerum Scoticarum Historia* (History of Scottish Affairs, 1643).

191 *blazing star* Halley's comet.

my author Milton is using William of Malmesbury here.

Lindsey on the Lincolnshire coast.

Malcolm son of the murdered Duncan in Shakespeare's *Macbeth.*

192 *his promise and oath* an earlier episode of the *History* tells how Harold, 'putting to sea one day for his pleasure in a fisher boat from his manor at Bosham in Sussex, caught with a tempest too far from land, was carried into Normandy, and by the Earl of Ponthieu, on whose coast he was driven, at his own request brought to Duke William, who entertaining him with great courtesy so far won him as to promise the Duke by oath of his own accord not only the castle of Dover then in his tenure, but the kingdom also after King Edward's death, to his utmost endeavour, thereupon betrothing the Duke's daughter, then too young for marriage' (*CPW* V, 389-90).

Matthew Paris twelfth-century author of *Historia Major* and *Chronica Majora*, from which this anecdote comes.

St-Valéry a port at the mouth of the Somme.

Harold Harvager more usually known as Harald Hardrader.

193 *won York* in fact York was captured by Tostig and the Norwegians after the battle of Fulford.

contemned scorned.

194 *things related of Alexander and Caesar* Alexander told his soldiers to respect the lands they conquered since they were their own; and Caesar, falling, said (according to Suetonius) 'Africa, I take possession of you'.
obnoxious vulnerable.

195 *hold it of him* hold it (the sceptre) as his viceroy or subordinate.
song of Roland the *Chanson de Roland* tells of the exploits of the medieval champion Roland, friend of Charlemagne, culminating in his defeat by the Saracens at the battle of Roncevalles (cf. *PL* I, 585–7).

196 *Florence of Worcester* eleventh-century author of the *Chronicon ex Chronicis* (Chronicle of Chronicles), a contemporary account of the conquest.
great church Westminster Abbey.

197 *stews* brothels.
security in its Latin sense, the feeling rather than the reality of safety; complacency.
revolution recurrence.

SAMSON AGONISTES

Of That Sort of Dramatic Poem which is Called Tragedy

gravest, moralest and most profitable the title-page of *Samson Agonistes* carries a quotation, in the original Greek and in a Latin translation, of part of the well-known passage from Chapter 6 of the *Poetics* where Aristotle defines the nature and purpose of tragedy, the 'most philosophical and most profitable of all kinds of poetry', as 'an imitation of a serious action' which 'by arousing feelings of pity and terror effects a purging ('catharsis') of such emotions'; and Milton's prefatory essay starts with a paraphrase of the same passage, which is echoed once more in the closing lines of the poem itself.

verse of Euripides the quotation from a fragment of a lost play by Euripides (see below), sometimes attributed also to the comic dramatist Menander, is 'evil communications corrupt good manners'.

Paraeus in *The reason of Church Government* (1642) Milton himself had claimed the authority of this German scholar's *On the Divine Apocalypse* (1618) in describing the Revelation as 'the majestic image of a high and stately tragedy'.

Dionysius fourth-century ruler of Syracuse, patron of the philosopher Plato, he wrote a number of tragedies. Other public figures who aspired to be tragic dramatists include the first Roman emperor Augustus, his younger compatriot Lucius Annaeus Seneca, and the early Byzantine churchman Gregory Nazianzen.

Martial Roman epigrammatist (AD 40–104).

the measure of verse in ancient Greek tragedy, the Chorus moved from one side of the stage to the other, singing or chanting its lines in alternating stanzas known as *strophes* ('turns') and *antistrophes* ('counter-turns'), and concluding with a final, stationary *epode.* Since *Samson* is without music, and since in any case the play is intended for reading rather than performance, these divisions are unnecessary, and the choric passages are *monostrophic* (in one unbroken stanza) and *apolelymenon* (metrically free); and where they are divided into stanzas, these are of irregular length and metrical structure (*alloeostropha*).

intricate or explicit Aristotle's classification (*Poetics* 6) of the two principal types of plot.

ancient rule actually, the 'unity of time' is not a 'rule' in the *Poetics*, merely the usual practice of the Athenian dramatists; but renaissance theory formulated it into a fixed precept, with its sister unities of place and action.

The Argument

equals here probably in the Latin sense, 'contemporaries'.

catastrophe Greek for 'overturning' or 'sudden conclusion', the technical term for the climax and denouement of a tragedy.

Samson Agonistes

11 *day-spring* daybreak. To *respire* is to breathe again, to refresh oneself. Both words have strong apocalyptic

associations, recalling Zacharias' prophecy of the 'dayspring from on high' that gives 'light to them that sit in darkness' (*Luke* 1, 78-9), and Michael's promise of a 'day . . . of respiration to the just' (*Paradise Lost* XII, 539–40), which translates the biblical notion of a 'time of refreshing' (cf. *Acts* 3, 19).

13 *Dagon* the 'sea monster, upward man/And downward fish' of *PL* I, 462–3. cf. 597n.

16 *popular noise* noise of the people.

23 *from heav'n foretold* in *Judges* 13, an angel twice prophesies Samson's birth, first to his mother and again to both his parents, before ascending 'in the flame of the altar'.

31 *separate to God* Samson was 'a Nazarite ['separate one'] to God from the womb' (*Judges* 13, 5). The dietary and other restrictions imposed on this ascetic military caste are detailed in *Numbers* 6.

38 *promise was Judges* 13, 5.

63 *bane* ruin.

83 *O first created beam* cf. the invocation to 'holy light, offspring of heav'n first-born' in *PL* III, 1, which also leads to an eloquent lament for lost sight. The 'great Word' is the primordial creative utterance of *Genesis* 1, 3, here identified with the Logos that was 'in the beginning' (*John* 1, 1).

87 *silent* in Latin the moon is 'silent' when in conjunction and so not shining. Such moonless times of the month were called the 'interlunar days'.

95 *obvious* exposed, vulnerable.

106 *obnoxious* not 'harmful' but 'liable to be hurt'.

110 *joint pace* the chorus move in step.

118 *diffus'd* stretched out.

131 *forgery* shaped or beaten metal. A *cuirass* is armour for the upper body, a breast and back plate hinged together. The Chalybes, a people on the southern shore of the Black Sea, were believed by the Greeks to have been the first to work iron. *Adamantean proof* means tempered to the greatest possible hardness.

135 *safest he who stood aloof* an example of the condensed

and idiomatic syntax characteristic of the poem: the safest Philistine was the one who stood aside when Samson's foot, advancing irresistibly in spite of their weapons, kicked them contemptuously aside and killed them in great numbers.

138 *bold Ascalonite PL* I, 464–6 records the worship of Dagon in the five principal Philistine cities (following *1 Samuel* 6, 17): 'in Azotus [Ashdod] . . . in Gath and Ascalon [Askelon]/And Accaron [Ekron] and Gaza's frontier bounds'.

139 *lion ramp* rearing like a rampant lion.

140 *plated* armoured.

143 *jaw of a dead ass* the story is in *Judges* 15, 14ff., where Samson names the place Ramath-le-hi (Jawbone Hill). The Philistines are 'foreskins' because, unlike the Israelites, they are uncircumcised.

147 *gates of Azza* in *Judges* 16, 1–3 Samson escapes the Philistines waiting to ambush him by picking up the city-gates of Gaza ('Azza') and carrying them 'up to the top of an hill that is before Hebron', described as a 'seat of giants old' because it was the birthplace of Arba, grandfather of the giant Anakim of *Numbers* 13. Hebron is about forty miles from Gaza, far more than the 2,000 ells (about three-quarters of a mile) permitted on the Sabbath by Jewish law. This feat of strength recalls Atlas, the Titan who carried the sky on his shoulders (see *PL* II, 306n). Milton does not mention that Samson had spent the previous night with a 'harlot' (see p.204).

161 *incorporate* combine.

165 *since man on earth* since the beginning of human history.

167 *by how much from the top* these lines restate the Aristotelean formulation of tragedy as the fall of a person of high estate, but redefine the 'high estate' of the hero in individual and meritocratic rather than social and hierarchical terms.

190 *superscription* the inscription on a coin, here applied

metaphorically to spurious or superficial claims to friendship.

208 *pair'd* matched, balanced.

209 *transverse* sideways, askew.

210 *tax* in the legal sense: examine, call to account.

230 *specious monster* beautiful but cruel and unnatural, Dalila was a trap ('snare') at once clever and successful ('accomplish'd'); but 'accomplished' is also a courtly term of address (cf. *PL* IV, 660: 'accomplish'd Eve'), used here with sarcastic effect.

235 *peal* both 'appeal' and 'ceremonial discharge of guns', the military metaphor sustained by 'fort of silence'.

240 *all his sons* the twelve tribes, descended from the twelve sons of Jacob, renamed 'Israel' (*Genesis* 35, 10).

245 *acknowledg'd not* the ingratitude, cowardice and treachery of the leading Israelites is not found in the *Judges* narrative, and 268-76 have a topical and personal significance more appropriate to 17th-century England than to biblical Palestine.

263 *trivial weapon* the ass's jawbone; see 143n.

280 *Gideon* like Samson, Gideon and Jephtha were Judges (tribal chieftains) of Israel (see *Judges* 8 and 11-12). 'Shibboleth' was the Hebrew word used by Jephtha to identify and put to death the forty-two thousand Ephraimites unable to pronounce it correctly.

294 *justifiable to men* cf. *PL* I, 26.

298 *the heart of the fool* Psalms 14 and 53 begin with the words 'The fool hath said in his heart, There is no God'; and in *Ecclesiastes* 2, 14 'the fool walketh in darkness' (cf. 'they walk obscure', 296).

300 *doubt* suspect.

302 *wand'ring thought* cf. the philosophical fallen angels of *PL* II, 555–61, whose theological speculations 'found no end, in wand'ring mazes lost'.

323 *though reason here aver* Carey (356) paraphrases 'even reason must confess that the woman . . . was, at the time, neither morally unclean nor unchaste', so providing a rational justification for God's 'unsearchable

dispose'; but it makes better sense to take 'aver' as subjunctive and read 'down reason then . . . *even though* it asserts that she was not unclean'. The point is that she *was* 'unclean, unchaste', but that God can dispense with his own laws if he chooses (307–14). The Chorus's complacent quietism and anti-rationalism need not be taken as Milton's own.

333 *uncouth* strange, unfamiliar.

352 *barrenness* before the visit from the angel (see 23n), Manoah's wife 'was barren, and bare not' (*Judges* 13, 2).

373 *appoint* arraign, blame.

382 *oft* adjectival: frequent.

388 *prime* height, climax (cf. 'prime of life').

390 *though offer'd only* in *Judges* 16, 5 the Philistine lords offer Delilah 'every one of us eleven hundred pieces of silver'.

394 *capital secret* both 'fatal' and 'on his head' (cf. *PL* XII, 383n).

402 *must'ring all her wiles* the military metaphor (cf. 235n) in 'must'ring' is sustained through 'blandish'd (flattering) parleys', 'assaults', 'tongue-batteries', 'storm' and 'overwatch'd'.

423 *infest* with the sense of Latin *infestare*, 'assail'.

433 *rigid score* inescapable debt.

446 *the most with shame* most shameful.

453 *idolists* idolaters. *Paradise Regained* IV, 234 speaks of the 'idolisms, traditions, paradoxes' of the gentiles.

454 *diffidence* disbelief.

455 *propense* liable.

463 *enter lists* challenge to single-handed combat.

471 *blank* make pale, appal.

500 *Gentiles in their parables* a reference to the story of Tantalus, punished for revealing his father Zeus's secrets. For his punishment see *PL* II, 614n.

518 *sacred house* the tabernacle (see *PL* XII, 247n), housed at Shiloh in this period (cf. 1674n).

528 *sons of Anak* giants (*Numbers* 13, 33).

533 *venereal trains* sexual allurements.

538 *wether* castrated ram.

545 *gods and men* discreetly correcting the Authorised Version translation of Jotham's parable (*Judges* 9, 13), 'Should I leave my wine, which cheereth God and man', where the Hebrew reads *elohim*, 'gods'.

548 *against* towards.

549 *fiery rod* ray, sunbeam. '*Clear milky* juice' looks like an oxymoron; but as with the 'milky stream,/Berry or grape' of *PL* V, 305–6, 'milky' probably refers to sweetness of taste rather than appearance or consistency, so there is no contradiction with the transparency of 'clear'. Carey (362–3) adds that 'the concept is of earth as mother'.

568 *redundant* a triple pun: copious (because they have now regrown), superfluous (because his strength is no longer any use to him) and wavy (from Latin *unda*, 'wave'). *Robustious* means strong.

571 *craze* weaken.

574 *draff* dregs, refuse. The prison food is 'servile' because fed to slaves.

581 *caus'd a fountain* the incident is in *Judges* 15, 18–19. The Authorised Version has the water springing, improbably, from the ass's jawbone, rather then the 'dry ground' of the hill named after it (see 143n).

597 *my race of glory* the whole passage reverberates with associations. The figure of Samson (*Shemesh-on* = sun-god, cf. *Dag-on*, 'fish-god') probably originates in Canaanite sun-worship. *Psalms* 19, 5 compares the rising sun to 'a bridegroom coming out of his chamber, and rejoicing as a strong man to run a race'; and that passage may in turn lie behind *Areopagitica*'s Samson-image of England 'rousing herself like a strong man after sleep, and shaking her invincible locks'.

600 *humours black* a literal translation of the Greek *melancholy*.

603 *prosecute* pursue.

609 *reins* loins.

612 *accidents* incidental effects, symptoms.

622 *black mortification* gangrene (itself used as a verb, 621: 'to become gangrenous').

639 *nerve* strength.

654 *patience as the truest fortitude* cf. *PL* IX, 31-2: 'the better fortitude/Of patience and heroic martyrdom'.

657 *consolatories* works of consolation.

659 *lenient* soothing, relieving.

674 *rout* crowd.

678 *but such as thou* the whole passage to 704 has been read as a commentary on the treatment of the regicides and leading commonwealth politicians after 1660. Milton himself was 'remit[ted]/To life obscur'd', while the bodies of Oliver Cromwell, his son-in-law Henry Ireton and John Bradshaw, the judge who condemned Charles I, were disinterred and hung from the public gallows at Tyburn, 'to dogs and fowls a prey' (the phrase echoes the fate of the Greek and Trojan dead, *Iliad* i, 4–5); and Milton's friend Henry Vane was condemned to death by 'th'unjust tribunals', under which many others were 'captiv'd'. See pp. 3–5.

700 *crude* here probably 'premature' (one of its Latin senses).

701 *disordinate* undisciplined, intemperate. The phrase is condensed: 'though not themselves disordinate, yet without cause suffering . . . '

715 *Tarsus* the biblical Tarshish (e.g. *Ezekiel* 27, 25), here identified with Tarsus in Cilicia (southern Turkey). The 'isles of Javan' (also mentioned in *Ezekiel* 27, 13) are the Ionian (= Greek) islands (cf. *PL* I, 508n), and Gadier is Cadiz, in southern Spain.

719 *hold them play* keep them playing.

728 *surcharg'd* weighed down.

737 *perverse event* the unexpected outcome of her action ('fact').

748 *hyena* believed to be capable of weeping and of imitating the human voice, so luring the unsuspecting to their death. Her '*wonted arts*' are her usual tricks.

751 *as* as if.

755 *urg'd* pushed, pressed.

763 *bosom snake* as in the proverbial 'nursing a viper in one's bosom'.

775 *importune* importunate, pressing.

785 *parle* parley, negotiate.

812 *fond* foolish.

840 *knowing* i.e. knowing myself (betrayed). cf. 'And knew not eating death', *PL* IX, 792.

841 *in vain thou striv'st* for the idea that shame cannot conceal itself, cf. *PL* IX, 1058-9: 'To guilty shame he cover'd, but his robe/Uncover'd more'. The same passage compares Adam and Eve directly to Samson and Dalila.

854 *press'd* insisted.

857 *the priest* the association of priests with political power and intrigue is a Miltonic addition to the *Judges* narrative. cf. 1653: 'Lords, ladies, captains, counsellors and priests'.

865 *grounded maxim* established principle. *Rife* means current, widespread.

890 *the law of nature, law of nations* that married women are the property of their husbands, and can have no higher allegiance; the 'universal law' spelt out uncompromisingly in lines 1053-7.

906 *peals* appeals; but cf. 235n.

932 *trains* tricks, snares (cf. 533). *Gins and toils* are traps and nets. The *fair enchanted cup* connects Dalila metaphorically with Circe, whose 'charmed cup/Whoever tasted lost his upright shape/And downward fell into a grovelling swine' (*Comus* 51-3), as her *warbling charms* associate her with another of Odysseus' near-fatal encounters, the Sirens.

936 *adder's wisdom* according to Psalm 58, the adder 'stoppeth her ears'. Odysseus blocked his companions' ears with wax to protect them from the enchanted song of the Sirens (*Odyssey* xii, 174-7; see previous note). A sermon of 1663, preached before Charles II on the anniversary of his father's death, denounced Milton 'who like a blind adder has spit so much

poison on the King's person and cause' (Parker, I, 582).

940 *forgo* abandon.

943 *contemn'd* despised.

945 *uxorious* under the influence of a wife.

948 *gloss* comment.

981 *Ecron, Gaza* see 138n.

989 *Jael* the wife of Heber (*Judges* 4) who, having invited the Philistine general Sisera to rest in her tent, murdered him in his sleep by driving a tent-peg through his head.

995 *repines* complains.

1016 *thy riddle* Samson gave his wedding-guests seven days to solve a riddle ('Out of the eater came forth meat, and out of the strong came forth sweetness'), and they persuaded his wife to reveal the answer. In anger at her betrayal, he killed thirty Philistines (*Judges* 14).

1020 *paranymph* after the incident described in the last note, Samson returned to his father's house, and his abandoned wife was 'given to his companion, whom he had used as his friend' (*Judges* 14, 20). Milton takes the 'companion' to be Samson's *paranymph* or best man.

1022 *disallied* dissolved.

1038 *intestine* internal, domestic.

1039 *cleaving* a strong pun, yoking two sharply opposed senses: 'clinging' and 'splitting apart'. Dalila clung to Samson to destroy him.

1057 *lour* scowl.

1062 *contracted* combined, drawn together.

1068 *Harapha* the encounter with Harapha (the name means 'giant', *2 Samuel* 21, 16) has no basis in the *Judges* story.

1069 *pile* here probably 'fortress'.

1073 *habit* dress. It 'carries peace' because he is unarmed.

1075 *fraught* cargo, sustaining the nautical metaphors applied to Dalila, 713–19 and 1044–5.

1076 *condole thy chance* commiserate your ill-fortune.

1080 *Og, Anak, the Emims* biblical giants.

1081 *thou knowst me now* cf. Satan's contemptuous reply to Ithuriel and Zephon, 'Not to know me argues yourself unknown' (*PL* IV, 830).

1087 *listed field* cf. 463n.

1088 *noise* reputation.

1092 *single* challenge.

1093 *gyves* fetters, manacles.

1109 *assassinated* here, treacherously wounded rather than murdered.

1116 *feign'd shifts* dishonest tricks.

1120 *brigantine* the catalogue of chivalric armour recalls the ironic recital of 'Impreses quaint, caparisons and steeds' at the beginning of *Paradise Lost* IX. A *brigantine* and a *habergeon* are kinds of body armour; *vantbrace* and *greaves* protect the arms and legs respectively. Goliath's spear is compared to 'a weaver's beam' in *1 Samuel* 17, 7; and the shield of Ajax is made of seven layers of bullhide (*Iliad* vii, 219–23).

1138 *chaf'd* angry.

1169 *from thine* from your people (the Philistines).

1181 *tongue-doughty* brave in words.

1186 *thirty men* see 1016n. Samson's description of the wedding-guests as 'spies' (1197) is without basis in *Judges*.

1223 *enforce* effort.

1228 *descant* hold forth.

1231 *Baalzebub* for this Philistine deity, described in *2 Kings* 1, 2 as 'the god of Ekron', see *PL* I, 81n.

1234 *van* vanguard, the advance guard of an army.

1237 *baffl'd* here means 'dishonoured', 'ridiculed'.

1242 *Astaroth* see *PL* I, 420n.

1245 *unconscionable* inordinate.

1246 *sultry chafe* hot temper.

1248 *five sons* four 'sons of the giant' are defeated by the Israelites in *2 Samuel* 21, 16–22, and one of them is described as 'the brother of Goliath' (killed earlier by David), so making five altogether.

1300 *behind* behind the last trouble, so still to come.

1307 *voluble* fluent, articulate.

1309 *remark him* mark him out, distinguish him.

1326 *tir'd* perhaps both 'weary' and 'attired'.

1346 *stoutness* stubbornness.

1369 *sentence* judgement, principle.

1377 *dispense* grant a special dispensation. cf. 307–14.

1382 *rousing motions* in devotional writing 'motions' denoted the promptings of conscience or inner workings of the spirit. Fowler, in a note on *PL* XI, 91, defines it as 'God's working in the soul', and cites Izaac Walton's description of Donne as having 'a blessing of obedience to the motions of his blessed spirit'. The 'rousing' of Samson is evoked in *Areopagitica* (1644) as an image of a triumphantly resurgent English people: 'Methinks I see in my mind a noble and puissant nation rousing herself like a strong man after sleep, and shaking her invincible locks' (*SSPP* 103).

1396 *engines* devices, means.

1404 *master's commands* the three lines have an ironic double meaning. For the Officer, they refer to the absolute power of the Philistine lords; for the Chorus and Sampson himself, to the power of God.

1410 *doff these links* take off these chains.

1415 *girt* surrounded.

1431 *angel of thy birth* see 23n.

1453 *give ye part* let you share.

1457 *attempted* courted, solicited.

1481 *fix'd* determined.

1484 *wanting* lacking.

1507 *next* that is, friends and relatives.

1529 *dealing dole dole* means both 'misery' and 'that which is dealt'. For similar 'etymological rhymes' cf. 1278, 'feats of war defeats', and *PL* I, 642, 'tempted our attempt'.

1538 *rides post . . . baits* to ride post is to travel continuously, using relays of horses; to bait is to break the journey for rest or refreshment (cf. *PL* XII, 1).

1554 *needs* is necessary.

1557 *tell us the sum* the *sum* is the broad outline or summary, the *circumstance* the details.

1596 *occasions* affairs, appointments.

1610 *banks* benches.

1611 *aloof* separate, apart (as at 135).

1617 *timbrels* tambourines. In the Nativity Ode Osiris is worshipped with 'timbrel'd anthems' (219).

1619 *cataphracts* suits of mail-armour, used here of the soldiers wearing them, as *spears* of those carrying them.

1622 *thrall* slave.

1646 *nerves* muscles, strength.

1647 *force of winds and waters* volcanoes and earthquakes were sometimes attributed to the action of subterranean wind and water; cf. *PL* VI, 195–7: 'as if on earth/Winds under ground or waters forcing way/ Sidelong had push'd a mountain from his seat'.

1659 *the vulgar* the common people, an exception not found in *Judges*. For the ethical problems raised by the Samson narrative, see p. 264.

1664 *self-kill'd/Not willingly* if indiscriminate genocidal slaughter is one of the problems of the Samson story (see last note), the other is suicide. Milton omits Samson's prayer 'let me die with the Philistines' (*Judges* 17, 30), noting only that he stood 'as one who pray'd' (1637). 'Dire necessity' is the Chorus's way of excusing him, but it can hardly be Milton's. See p. 264.

1674 *Shiloh* a mountain settlement (modern Seilun) some twenty miles north of Jerusalem. The tabernacle and ark of the covenant (*PL* I, 386n) were kept there until the Israelites brought them down into Canaan, where they were seized by the Philistines (*1 Samuel* 4, 3–11).

1680 *unweetingly importuned* unsuspectingly invited.

1685 *insensate left or to sense reprobate* driven out of their senses or into vicious senses.

1691 *into sudden flame* cf. *Lycidas* 74, 'And think to burst out into sudden blaze'; but the image of flame bursting from ashes looks forward too to the Phoenix of 1699–1707.

1692 *evening dragon* serpents were thought to prey on birds and their eggs, including domestic chickens ('tame villatic fowl').

1695 *as an eagle* the bird of Zeus, whose thunder issued from a clear sky.

1699 *self-begotten bird* the Phoenix, a single unique creature ('that no second knows nor third'), self-regenerating from its own ashes (a *holocaust* is the burnt offering of a whole animal), and living for a thousand years (*secular bird*), is a frequent symbol of self-regeneration.

1713 *sons of Caphtor* the Philistines, who came originally from 'Caphtor' (*Amos* 9, 7), variously identified as Crete, Phoenicia and the Nile delta.

1727 *lavers* basins, particularly those used for ceremonial washing. cf the 'nectar'd lavers strew'd with asphodel' in *Comus* 838.

1729 *in plight* in a condition.

1736 *acts enroll'd* deeds recorded, published (cf. 290, 653).

1745 *all is best Samson Agonistes* contains many echoes of the plays of Euripides, and the final chorus has been compared to the fatalistic closing lines of his *Medea* (also found, with minor changes, in the same playwright's *Alcestis, Andromache, Bacchae* and *Helen*): 'Zeus on Olympus is the dispenser of many things,/ Many things unhoped-for the gods accomplish;/And the expected things are not fulfilled,/While the god finds means to bring about the unexpected./ So ended this matter'. To this tragic resignation, in itself not far from the radical irony, scepticism and even open criticism of religion with which Euripides has often been associated, the text adds the passionless 'calm of mind' of an Aristotelian *catharsis*, the apocalyptic urgency and assurance of Psalm 104 ('Thou hidest thy face, they are troubled') and *Isaiah* 42 ('Behold my servant, whom I uphold'), and a hint, in one final turn from Old Testament Palestine to postrevolutionary England, of the ultimate defeat of all those who 'band them to resist' the working-out of a providence at once 'unsearchable' and 'uncontrollable', as unknowable as it is absolute.

1755 *acquist* acquisition, stock.